PENGUIN TRAVEL LIBRARY

BORDERLINES

Charles Nicholl was born in London in 1950. His most
recent book is *The Fruit Palace*, a highly acclaimed
account of life in the cocaine underworld of Colombia.
His articles and stories have appeared in *Rolling Stone,
Granta*, and other magazines and newspapers. He lives
with his wife and three children in Hereford, England.

Borderlines

A Journey in
Thailand and Burma

CHARLES NICHOLL

PENGUIN BOOKS

PENGUIN BOOKS
Published by the Penguin Group
Viking Penguin, a division of Penguin Books USA Inc.,
375 Hudson Street, New York, New York 10014, U.S.A.
Penguin Books Ltd, 27 Wrights Lane, London W8 5TZ, England
Penguin Books Australia Ltd, Ringwood, Victoria, Australia
Penguin Books Canada Ltd, 2801 John Street,
Markham, Ontario, Canada L3R 1B4
Penguin Books (N.Z.) Ltd, 182–190 Wairau Road,
Auckland 10, New Zealand

Penguin Books Ltd, Registered Offices:
Harmondsworth, Middlesex, England

First published in Great Britain by
Martin Secker & Warburg Limited, 1988
First published in the United States of America by
Viking Penguin, a division of Penguin Books USA Inc., 1989
Published in Penguin Books 1990

1   3   5   7   9   10   8   6   4   2

Copyright © Charles Nicholl, 1988
Map Copyright © Martin Secker & Warburg Limited, 1988
All rights reserved

LIBRARY OF CONGRESS CATALOGING IN PUBLICATION DATA
Nicholl, Charles.
Borderlines: a journey in Thailand and Burma/Charles Nicholl.
p.   cm.
Reprint. Originally published: New York: Viking, 1989.
ISBN 0 14 00.9590 X
1. Thailand—Description and travel—1976–   2. Burma—Description
and travel—1981–   3. Nicholl, Charles—Journeys—Thailand.
4. Nicholl, Charles—Journeys—Burma.   I. Title.
[DS566.2.N53   1990]
915.9104'5—dc20   89–78427

Printed in the United States of America

for my daughter
Georgia
and
for my friend
Nopporn

Author's Note

I spent three months travelling in and around Thailand in 1986. This book is a record of some of the people I met, and some of the places I passed through, and some of the feelings I felt. I make no other claims for it.

Many people gave me their help, or their knowledge, or simply – by no means least – their good company along the way. Of these I wish particularly to thank: Nopporn Wannato, Geoffrey Walton, Ajahn Pongsak Tejadhammo, Suk Soongswang, Mon Chanyaem, Tony Davies, John Everingham, David Love, David and Toi Parry, Francis Deron at AFP, Yves at Lek House, Tan and Ami in Ban Nam Rin, Rin in Mae Hong Son, Sayam Tipkhome and all at Wat Mau Komtuang, Dominic and Caroline Faulder, Ben Feldman, Juan Carlos Gonzales, Edwina Pascal, Khun Saw Lwin, David Irwin, Stew Taylor and Marie Balduc.

Many Thais, whose names I have forgotten or perhaps never knew, added some brief touch of warmth and charm to my time there. They call Thailand the 'Land of Smiles'. It sounds suspiciously like a promotional catch-phrase, but in my experience it is true.

Back home, for patience and other virtues, my thanks to David Godwin, Jacqueline Korn, Hilary Davies, and, of course, to Sally.

Those who know the language may find my presentation of Thai phrases and names a little haphazard. I have tended to follow the sound, rather than any systematic transliteration from the Thai alphabet. The name Katai, for instance, is more correctly written 'Kratai', but the Thai 'r' is hard to catch, and I heard the name as Katai, and that is how I've written it down. I suppose something similar is true of this book as a whole. It is not a book 'about' Thailand, and certainly not a book 'about' Buddhism. I am not qualified to write those. My only qualification is that I was there, and this is what I made of it all.

Contents

In the sky there is no east nor west.
We make these distinctions in the mind,
then believe them to be true.

Everything in the world comes from the
mind, like objects appearing from the
sleeve of a magician.

Buddha, *Lankavatara Sutra*

Night Train

DUSK WAS falling as the train pulled slowly into Lop Buri. A few minutes from the station there was an ambush of small boys, some of them jumping aboard with wares to sell – iced drinks in polythene bags, smoked fish strung on poles, corn cobs, green mangoes – and some of them just running and shouting alongside the train for the hell of it.

They woke the old man opposite me from his nap. He grumbled at them: '*ling ling*', little monkeys.

I leaned out the window. The air was warm and dusty, lilac-coloured. The station was lit with sodium lights and the fires of fry-stalls. The clatter of the train met the chatter of the platform, and further off I could hear a diffuse tinkling of temple bells.

Among the crowd I spotted a *farang*, probably an American. He was clearly visible because he stood a head taller than anyone else on the platform. He had sandy hair and wore a red singlet that showed a lot of muscle. There was a small circle of space around him, where the crowd had fallen back to make room for his fidgety movements. Thais give big *farang* a wide berth, as one might a large muddy dog.

The word *farang* is actually a Thai derivation from '*Français*', but it is used to describe any fair-skinned, round-eyed foreigner from Europe or the USA. According to Thai tradition, the *farang* inhabit a far-flung region called the *muang nauk*, the 'outside kingdom'. One chronicle, the *Thai Nya Phuum*, sums them up as follows: 'They are exceedingly tall, hairy and evil-smelling. They school their children long, and devote their lives to the amassing of riches. Their women, though large and round, are very beautiful. They do not grow rice.' When the Thai call you *farang* it is not pejorative. They disarm the word with a grin or a giggle. But they remain cautious. The *farang* does not have the great Thai virtue of *jai yen*, a 'cool heart'. His heart is liable to overheat.

The big guy swung a backpack onto his shoulder and made ready to board. He spoke a few words to another, older man. I saw that this man too was a *farang*, though not from the look of him American. He was thin and wiry, with a long nose. He had a moustache beneath a scrub of stubble. He was less conspicuous, partly because he was smaller, and partly because he wore the same kind of hat – a rattan hat, much in the shape of a trilby – as many other men on the platform. He was sitting on a packing case, smoking a cigarette. He threw it away as the train came to a halt, but he didn't seem to be hurrying.

As soon as the train stopped you could feel the heat again, but it was now the gentle, lifting warmth of evening, not the laden heat of daytime. This is an hour the Thais love, when the lights go on, and it's cool enough to promenade, and the all-importance of *sanuk* – having a good time – is beyond dispute.

I was beginning to feel a lot better myself. Bangkok was four hours away now. It wasn't enough but it was something.

I watched the big *farang* struggling in a couple of carriages down from me: third class, no air-con. There was a scrum round the door and even after he'd got himself in, it took another few heaves to get his backpack in. The man in the rattan hat was still on the platform, talking to one of the cooks at the fry-stalls, a woman in a scarlet and yellow *sarong*. In the harshness of the strip-light above the stall, the colours of her *sarong* were mesmeric. He seemed to be thanking her for something. His luggage was light – a cloth shoulder-bag of hill-tribe design, a battered leather satchel, a cotton sleeping-roll tied up with rope and fastened beneath the satchel. He slung the two bags crosswise, one from each shoulder. The big American was back on the platform now, minus his backpack. I guessed he had got them some seats. Their clothes were dusty. They looked like they had done some hard travelling. The American's shoulders gleamed from recent tanning. They talked for a bit: the American tense and rangy, chewing hard on some gum, the other more poised, seeming to keep an eye on everything.

The train hooted, lurched forward, stopped. There was a last-minute surge of people. A Chinese couple joined our carriage. They had passed everything in through the window – cartons done up with twine, baskets of food, finally a baby, sound asleep in a green blanket – and now they were collecting their belongings around them, nodding and smiling and saying, 'Kam sha, kam sha'. There were many Chinese on the train. It was early February, coming up to Chinese New Year. I had been down in Sampaeng – Bangkok's Chinatown – that morning. There were kites and lanterns in the shops, scrubbing and sluicing in the grille-fronted restaurants. Soapy water flowed down the gutters, lapped around the wheels of the sleek black Mercs. A time of purification.

The two *farang* made for their carriage, but still the one in the hat seemed to linger. He let the other passengers in before him, and only as the train began to pull out did he climb up onto the step. He scanned the platform for a moment. Then, seeing that all was apparently in order, he braced himself against the hand-rail and swung out of view.

The lights of Lop Buri soon fell away, but some of the young vendors stayed aboard a bit longer. It was good psychology: the passengers were nestling back into their seats, glad to be on the move again, feeling disposed after all to buy a snack before the long night's journey. One boy cleared his entire stock of corn-cobs in this last few minutes. The train slowed in the darkness. It was some kind of crossing. I could make out a thatched roof, some fencing, a pitted dirt road. Here the last of the kids jumped out. They set off back down the tracks to Lop Buri, clutching their few precious baht, and we set off north, the train soon settling into the leisurely pack-mule rhythm that had brought us up from Bangkok, and would take us on through the night to Chiang Mai.

A bit later, I went down to the compartment at the end of the carriage, to stretch my legs and have a cigarette. One of the railway police was there. He wore a gun, and he was drunk on rice whisky. We conversed in the lingua franca of these encounters: part pidgin

Thai, part GI English. The window was open wide and we had to shout above the din of the tracks.

He said, 'Do you know what Lop Buri is famous for?'

I recalled my guide book. The town, though now very modest, was once a royal Siamese capital. Did he mean the old summer palace? The fine Khmer-influenced temples?

He shook his head in tipsy pleasure. 'No, no,' he said. 'It is famous for its monkeys.'

The monkeys of Lop Buri, it transpired, are notorious thieves. A troupe of them lives around a ruined temple, the Sarn Phra Karn, and steals cameras and handbags from the tourists. They are skilled and cunning, he said. They are trained up by the locals, a regular troupe of Artful Dodgers. All the cameras they steal are raked in for resale on the black market.

He moved easily with the lurching of the train. He had worked on the railways for eighteen years. It was in the family: his father had been a guard on the train when the line was first opened, back in the 1920s. Before the railway came it took a week by boat and elephant to get from Bangkok to Chiang Mai.

I asked him if he had ever had to use his gun. He shook his head. 'In the old days there were many attacks on the train. Bandits, communists. But no more.' There was a tint of regret in his voice. Nowadays, he said, there are just a few sneak-thieves to deal with. He told me to beware of people offering me sweets or cigarettes, because they might be drugged, and then I would be robbed while I slept. I have heard this warning on buses and trains all over the world but I don't think I've ever met anyone who has been the victim of these Mickey Finns.

While we were talking, the big American I'd seen at Lop Buri came out to use the lavatory. He nodded at us. His face was reddened with sun, his eyes were a fierce pale blue. He was still chewing gum. When he came out of the lavatory he stopped a drinks boy who was walking through, and bought a can of Kloster beer. He felt the can, grimaced, and said to the boy, 'Sure you can't get it any warmer?' The boy laughed back uncomprehendingly. The American took a long slug of beer, let out a hiss of satisfaction, wiped his mouth with the back of his hand. There was reddish dirt under his fingernails. 'Needed that,' he said, 'Yes sir,' and tipped the can back again.

His name was Khris – 'with a K, like Kristofferson'. He was in his early thirties, I guessed. His hair was fine and frizzy and beginning to recede. His arms were wide and smooth. He had a small tattoo on his right forearm, a dagger with a snake twined round the blade.

I asked him if he'd spent time in Lop Buri. He shook his head. 'Just passing through.' He strummed on an imaginary guitar, sang in a gravelly voice: 'Busted flat in Lop Buri, waiting for a train.' He frowned. 'Weird place, man. These fucking monkeys.'

I glanced over at the policeman, but he was tipping the bottle of Mekong to his lips. 'I've heard about them,' I said. 'They're trained to steal.'

'Trained? You're kidding. Those are wild sons of bitches, man.'

He told me how they'd nearly pulled off this woman's arm getting her camera from her, how you get rabies if they bite you, how personally he'd shoot the whole bunch of them. I asked what they did with the camera once they got it.

'Carried it to the edge of the trees and tore it apart. You could see them beating it against a rock to get at the good bits.'

So much for the Artful Dodgers of Lop Buri.

I asked him where he was travelling from. He told me that he and his friend had been up in Kanchana Buri Province, in the far west of Thailand. 'We got right up to the Burmese border, a place called Three Pagodas Pass, but they wouldn't let us across.'

'Fighting?'

'Nah, just some border police who didn't like our faces.'

'Why did you want to get across the border?'

He shrugged. 'Harry wanted to. That's the guy I'm travelling with. Just to get a jump on things, I guess. You know how it is with borders.'

I nodded, wondering quite what he meant. He finished off his beer and crumpled the can in his big fist. I saw there were letters tattooed below his knuckles. His fist spelt 'Carol'. He made to throw the can out of the window, but the drunken policeman moved forward to block the window.

'No throw, danger, no throw,' he slurred.

'Oh yeah?' said Khris, his arm still raised with the can in his hand. I thought for a moment he was going to make something of it, but he checked himself and laughed. 'Guess you're right, sergeant,' he said, and turned the gesture into a mock salute. He turned to me, blue eyes flashing, sweat on his face. 'Guy with the gun buckled on is always right, ain't that the truth?' The policeman muttered something in Thai and moved away from the window.

Another drinks boy came through and we bought more beer. Khris offered to buy the policeman one. The policeman shook his head, but it eased things up a bit. 'Not while you're on duty, huh?' said Khris, and we all three laughed. The train whistled as we rolled through a village, tin roofs beneath big dark trees, a snatch of Thai dance music on some jukebox. The buildings threw back the sound of the train to us, then we were out again in the empty rice-fields.

'So what's in Kanchana Buri apart from the border?' I asked.

His blue eyes went wide. He said in a stage whisper, 'Stones.'

'Stones?'

'Gem-stones, man. Siamese sparkies. Sapphire, ruby, topaz. Harry's kind of a trader. He deals in stones.'

'I thought most of the sapphire and ruby came from the east of Thailand.'

'Sure, that's the main area, down along the Gulf, near Cambodia. But that's where everyone else is. It's all sewn up there. Harry's looking for new strikes. Get in with the local boys, cut out the middlemen. We were up at a place called Bo Ploi, a day north of Kanchana Buri Town. They've been mining the area for a while, but there's word going round that they've hit a new strike. Harry says they're panning out star sapphire somewhere up there. Man, did you ever see one of those little babies smiling up at you?'

I shook my head. 'Did you find any?'

Khris shrugged. 'We bought some stuff. You'll have to ask Harry. I was just along for the ride.'

When someone starts to rein in, that's when you start to feel there's a story. I liked the sound of star sapphires. I was about to ask what exactly they were, when the policeman blathered into view again. He had decided it was his turn to show there were no hard feelings after the beer-can incident. First he offered us some of his Mekong whisky. Thanks but no thanks. Then he pulled out a grubby piece of paper and thrust it in my hand. We peered at it in the dull yellow light. It was a mimeographed leaflet advertising some hotel in Chiang Mai.

'You go Noi Hotel,' he urged. 'Number one guest house.' He pronounced it, as Thais invariably do, 'guess how'.

Khris shook his head. 'I'm fixed. Harry's got friends in Chiang Mai.'

I said that I was fixed up too. It wasn't true, but I like to make my arrangements on the ground. Khris turned back to me. 'So what takes you to Chiang Mai?' he asked.

I said, 'I'm going to visit a forest temple.'

It had begun by chance, or so it seemed, one winter's night in England, looking for a late-night movie on the TV, and finding instead an Open University broadcast about Buddhism. And there on the screen was a famous Thai monk, Ajahn Cha, small and bald, with a beatific, frog-like face. He was describing the beauties of life in a forest temple. He said, 'Your mind will become still like a pool in the forest. Many strange and beautiful animals will come to drink at the pool. You will see wonderful things, but you will be still. This is the happiness of the Buddha.'

Who could resist a promise like that?

For a long while after, his words hung in the mind, serene and cool amid the small fevers of one's life. I was not entirely clear what a forest temple was, but the more I thought about it, the more I knew I wanted to visit one. I would learn all about Buddhism, take that spiritual rest-cure I had always promised myself. I would become a new man. And of course, this being my trade, I would write a book about it.

The rest followed, bit by bit. I had arrived in Thailand ten days ago, bound for a remote temple in the hills of the north: Wat Tham Tupu, the Temple of Tupu's Cave.

But first a little look around Bangkok. Not the best place to start your pilgrimage: stepping from an English winter into this fetid hothouse, the air as thick as broth, the streets paved with broken promises. Bangkok made it very plain that I could always change my mind if I wanted to. There were small, plausible men on the corners: 'You want something? I get you what you need.' They could get me girls. They could get me boys. They could scratch my itches any way I pleased. Their hands dangled by their sides, little canisters nestling in the palm: 'Ganja? Smack?'

In Bangkok there was Heinz, the connoisseur of cut-price sex, who insisted on showing me round the pleasure-dens of Patpong. And there was Sunny. She was a plump, buck-tooth Lao girl who offered to be my 'wife' for the duration of my stay. This meant she would travel with me, look after me, minister night and day to my sugar-daddy whims. There were good reasons for refusing: my actual wife, for one. My alleged quest, for another. Also the possibility that she had AIDS. She had been on the game since she was fifteen. For many years after, she had a trick to fool the customers: a sachet of catfish blood hidden up inside her. 'Men pay big money for virgins. Big money to see fish blood.' She also had a heroin habit. She mostly smoked it, but sometimes she used the needle, in her knuckle to leave no scars. Heroin smokers are called *moo* (pig), she explained, 'because they sound like a pig when they smoke'. Those who shoot are called *pei* (duck), 'because they live with dirty water'. All this was good reason to refuse her, but I knew there would be times when I would remember none of this, only her quick smile, her hurt eyes and her smooth brown skin. 'The law on Thai wives' – a *farang* later told me – 'is to take two. If you take one you'll fall in love with her.'

And then, coming from another tack, there was Dixon, a beer-bellied, denim-shirted Australian I met one night at Tiger's bar on Suriwong Road. 'Don't call me a journalist,' he snapped. 'I'm a reporter. That's when you write it *before* you go home.' Predictably, the forest temple didn't cut much ice with Dixon. 'Honky features stuff,' he said, when there was real hard news crying out all over the country. There was fighting on the Kampuchean border in the east, fighting on the Burmese border in the west. There was Vincent Arnoni, a MIA hunter mounting covert reconnaissance operations into Laos. There was AIDS, heroin, prostitution, boat people, and – perennially – there was the disappearance of the silk magnate, Jim Thompson.

'But I'm going north,' I said.

'Well, get your arse up to the Golden Triangle then. You'll find some *real* stories up there.'

Every weak card in my hand, the city knew it, the city played to it. But now I was on my way, sweat drying off in the cool night breeze, heading at last for Tupu's Cave.

Khris shook his head. 'Forest temple, huh? That's a new one on me.'

'And you?' I asked. 'What takes you to Chiang Mai?'

He flashed a grin and waggled his tongue. 'All the prettiest girls in Bangkok said they came from Chiang Mai.'

'And you believe them?' said a voice behind me. I turned round and there – suddenly there, it seemed, but that was surely an illusion, it was just that the noise of the train covered his arrival – was the other *farang*, Harry the gem-trader.

He spoke quietly, a seedy looking man with an air of formality. He was older than I'd taken him for. His black hair – he was no longer wearing the rattan hat – was thinning and swept straight back. There was dust in the lines of his face. His long nose, slightly bulbous at the end, had a thin but prominent scar running up from the left nostril. It made me think of the scene in *Chinatown* where Jack Nicholson has his nose slit.

Khris introduced us. Harry said, 'I'm very pleased to meet you.' I couldn't place the accent. It had an American overlay, certainly, but there was a twang of some other language underneath it. His handshake was hard. I felt the dust on his hand, the same red dirt.

He nodded a greeting to the policeman. We swayed in the smoky compartment. He was dressed like an out-of-luck card-sharp: faded blue waistcoat, big silver rings on his left hand.

'You are an Englishman,' he observed.

I said I was. He smiled and gave a faint shrug, as if to say that no one is perfect. I was beginning to get a suss on his accent now. The shrug gave him away. 'And you, I think, are French.'

The same sardonic smile, wrinkling his dark eyes out of view. 'Bravo!'

'But you speak excellent English.'

'A necessity these days.'

'This guy,' said Khris loudly, laying a hand on Harry's shoulder, 'speaks Thai, Lao, Vietnamese and Chinese, as well as fucking French and English. Have I left any out, captain?'

'I speak them all badly, especially the French.'

'What the hell,' said Khris. 'We're all goddamn mongrels out here.' He seemed suddenly moody. He drained his beer. The policeman was dozing against the lavatory door. Khris winked at me, and deliberately lobbed the empty can out of the window. 'Old Siamese proverb, right? Don't take shit from a sleeping cop.'

Khris was beginning to make me nervous. He was restless, and he brought his face up close when he spoke. But it's not every night you're stuck on a train with a couple of prospectors fresh in off the sapphire fields. I was intrigued by Harry. I wondered why he was called Harry, and was his real name Henri. I wanted to know how he came to speak all those local languages, and how he got that scar on his nose, and which animal the big yellow tooth hanging on a chain round his neck came from. And I wanted to hear all about star sapphires.

But it was not tonight, Josephine, for Khris was now leaning out of the window singing, 'Asia, Asia, just an old sweet song keeps Asia on my mind,' and Harry was pulling him in, saying, 'OK, Khris. Cool down and I'll tell you something. I've got one of the boys back there to fix us some chow. I've even told him to tell you it's called American Fried Rice, OK? So, we go and eat now. Then we get some shut-eye.'

'Sounds good to me, captain.'

Harry turned to me. 'I would invite you to dine with us, my friend, but we are in third class and a little crowded.'

They were going, leaving me with none for company but the snoring policeman. Harry shook my hand. Khris slapped me on the shoulder and said 'Good luck'.

'Perhaps we'll meet up in Chiang Mai,' I said.

Harry said, 'Where are you staying?'

'I don't know yet.'

'Try the Noi Guest House, near the old town walls. It is run by an old friend of mine, a compatriot. His name is Guy. Tell him you're a friend of Harry's. He'll fix you up.'

'That's funny. The policeman here told me to go there too.'

Harry looked at the policeman. 'But, of course. We must listen to what the locals tells us. Even when they're drunk and asleep they know more than we do.'

'Thanks for the advice,' I said. I heard a sour note in my voice. They headed off through the bucking concertina passageway that linked the carriages, Khris stumbling as he went, Harry moving neatly, like a fox through a hedge.

I went back to my carriage. It was quiet, and had the muggy smell of sleep in it. Men slept straight out, legs splayed, mouths open. Women nested, curled ingeniously into the narrow seats. A pair of young soldiers lay against one another, a crew-cut head on a khaki-green shoulder. Some people wore a cloth or *sarong* over their faces. Sleep is a private business: you go off across some borderline and leave your body alone and unguarded.

The old man opposite was awake, having slept all afternoon. He was smoking a cigarette, staring out at the blackness, or at his reflection, or at neither. He nodded and smiled when I sat down. That had been the extent of our communication through the journey. He didn't speak English and he didn't understand me when I spoke Thai. All I knew was that he was heading for Tak, a crossroads town a couple of hours before Chiang Mai, and that his only luggage seemed to be a gearbox for a Massey Ferguson tractor.

The train rolled on, a little arrow of light and purpose bisecting the dark plain. We were still in the flatlands of the Mae Nam basin, the 'rice bowl of Asia'. Stubble fires burned in the distance, flickerings of orange light like a message one couldn't understand.

I settled down to try and sleep. The old man reached out to touch the window-pane. I felt I knew what he meant: that the window must be strong to hold all that emptiness at bay.

Lan Na

I SLEPT a bit: inconsequential dreams into which the reality of the journey inserted itself from time to time. The old man disembarked at Tak. He wished me luck, '*Shoke dee na, kap.*' Dawn over the paddy fields, the shadowy blue promise of the hills on the horizon. Then suddenly it was morning, the carriage was awake, Chiang Mai was half an hour away.

Somewhere in the night we had crossed an invisible but not forgotten borderline. We were in Lan Na now, the Kingdom of a Million Rice Fields.

Lan Na, or Lannathai, is one of the old kingdoms that make up modern Thailand. Its early history is hazy. According to the chronicles, the founder of the Lan Na dynasty, King Lao Cankaraja, ruled in the eighth century AD. His capital, Ngoen Nyang, was on the south bank of the Mekong River, near present-day Chiang Saen. The early monarchs of Lan Na are semi-legendary, but they represent a historical reality – the southward migration of the Thai people from their ancestral home in southern China; their pacification of the aboriginal tribes of the region, mainly Mon and Khmer; and their establishing of small principalities or city states (*muang*). In the thirteenth century, under threat from the Mongol armies of Kublai Khan, the various *muang* buried their differences. King Mengrai, a descendant of Cankaraja, founded Chiang Mai in 1296, and ruled over the unified kingdom of Lan Na. To the east, in present-day Laos, was Lan Chang, the Kingdom of a Million Elephants (the name survives in Frenchified form as Vientiane, the modern capital of Laos). In the lowlands to the south was the kingdom of Sukhothai, 'Dawn of Happiness', the forerunner of Siam.

Lan Na flourished for a couple of centuries. Its art and literature

reached a peak in the mid fifteenth century, under King Tilokar-
aja. The eighth world synod of Theravada Buddhism was held at
Chiang Mai in 1477. But the incursions of the Burmese and the
growing political power of Siam combined to weaken it, and in
1796 – exactly five centuries after the founding of Chiang Mai –
Lan Na was annexed by Siam. It continued to have a measure of
autonomy, and it was less than fifty years ago that the office of *chao*
(prince) of Chiang Mai was formally abolished.

The people of northern Thailand still call themselves *khon
muang*, the people of the principalities. They consider themselves
Thai in as far as they are citizens of the nation-state of Thailand,
and Thai in the broader ethnic sense as well, but they are very
conscious of their difference from the Siamese Thai of the central
plains. The Siamese are their tribal cousins, no more, as are the
Lao of Laos and the Shan of Burma, and the various smaller tribes
of ethnic Thai origin: the Lue, the Phuan, the Black and White
Tai.

A young man I met in Chiang Mai pointed to a map of Thailand
on the wall and said, 'Our country is in the shape of a bird, like a
rooster.' The eastern bulge is his tail-feathers, the long narrow
isthmus of the south his legs. 'So you see, the land of the Muang is
the head of the rooster, and Bangkok is his arsehole.'

Travelling in northern Thailand one senses the hidden shapes
beneath the map. The modern nation is both a unifying of older
divisions and a dividing up of older unities. There are more Lao in
north-eastern Thailand than there are in Laos itself. The Shan of
Burma do not call themselves Shan at all, but Thai Yai, the 'great'
Thai, as opposed to the 'little' Thai of the lowlands. Some of the
cultural base of northern Thailand is Mon and Khmer, not Thai in
the ethnic sense at all. Other groups, like the Karen and the Haw
Chinese of the Yunnan, have been here for centuries, and the more
recent migration of Chinese hill-tribes into Thailand has further
clouded this complex nationality. The hill-tribes – Akha, Hmong,
Mien, Lahu, Lisu – belong to clans spread indiscriminately
through Thailand, Burma, Laos and southern China. They cross
and recross the frontiers as if they don't exist.

Early morning villages, misty banana groves, a bent figure fanning a small fire of brushwood, a tattered *sang khati* – the monk's orange robe – tied around the bole of an enormous jackfruit tree. Finally we were at the station on the eastern outskirts of Chiang Mai.

Everyone's got someone to meet them, it seems, and I'm in that blithery melancholy mood, alone after a night journey, a strange city to deal with before breakfast. It's best to arrive somewhere in late afternoon or evening, when there's *sanuk* in the air and the people are disposed to greet you. In the morning they have many chores, and the *farang* is just another one.

There were trishaws outside the station, and the pick-up trucks converted for passenger travel which they call *song taow*, 'two benches'. Various touts waved bits of paper on behalf of various guest houses. The early morning light was grey and flat, and the street leading off into town looked nondescript. As I negotiated with a trishaw boy, a pick-up passed, and in the back I saw Harry and Khris. Khris leaned forward to wave, called 'Hey!', but Harry had his rattan hat tipped low over his eyes and was apparently dozing.

Closer to town were signs of the Flower Festival: the policeman on the train had mentioned this. The trishaw boy said it would be opened by the Prime Minister himself, General Prem Tinsulanoinda. I asked when it would begin and received the typically Thai answer, 'When Prem comes.' The floats were parked in a long line leading up to the bridge over the Ping River. They were elaborate constructions, a brilliant topiary of statues and emblems: elephants and monkeys, *garuda* and *naga*, and one or two more Disneyesque creations. Each float looked like a solid, sculpted mass of flowers. In fact the flowerheads are tacked onto a frame of wood and polystyrene built over the chassis of a truck or car. The vehicle is invisible except for the wheels and a thin visor of windscreen for the driver.

By the time we drove over the grey sluggish waters of the Ping, the sun was beginning to break through. The light quivered amid the lush bankside greenery. There was something tonic about it: it revived me like a strong cup of coffee.

As recommended by Harry, I made my way to the Noi Guest

House. It was a two-storey building, L-shaped, tucked down a rickety side-street near the north-eastern corner of the town walls. Wicker tables and chairs were set out in a courtyard shaded by banana and palm trees. It looked cheap and amiable, and I was disappointed to see a carboard sign on the bar, saying 'Hotel Full' in several languages.

A tall, bespectacled man in well-pressed jeans was standing by the bar. It was Guy, the *patron*. I said, 'I'm a friend of Harry's. He told me to try here.'

He smiled cautiously. 'Harry Vincent?'

I realized I didn't know Harry's full name. I said, 'Frenchman, gem-trader, I met him on the train.'

'I didn't know he was back in town.' His eyes narrowed. 'I wonder what he's up here for?'

I shrugged. 'He didn't say much.'

'Well, of course, any friend of Harry's is welcome at the Noi. I think I can squeeze you in, but you must wait while the rooms are cleaned. Why don't you take some breakfast?'

He showed me a handwritten menu. For breakfast there was muesli, yoghurt, tropical fruit juices, eggs all ways. For dinner, buffalo steak *aux poivres*, shish kebab Noi, chicken *grand-mère*. 'One does what one can,' said Guy modestly. 'I am from Lille. It is a town not beautiful to look at, but beautiful to eat in.'

'And Harry?' I asked. 'Where's he from?'

'Ah!' He pouted sceptically. 'Not truly a Frenchman, of course. *Pied noir*. Born in Algiers, I believe, lived most of his life in Indo-China.'

He broke off to greet a pair of *farang* girls coming down the stairs. He had that busy, affable, hotelier's way, a little gobbet of small-talk for each of the guests. I sank into a wicker chair, and ordered scrambled eggs with all the trimmings.

Chiang Mai is a town to wander in. The old town walls form a square, with each side a kilometre long. They are honey-coloured, in parts decayed, in parts renovated, at the corners virtually resolved back to nature, not so much walls as small sandy tumps topped off with low, twisty, feather-leaved trees. They date from the late eighteenth century, when the Siamese took over the depleted city. Around them runs the town moat, about twenty yards wide, its opaque green water hopefully fished by small boys leaning over the edge of the footbridges. Five gates open into the old town, with picturesque names like the White Elephant Gate, the Flower Garden Gate, the Spice Garden Gate. Inside, the old town is quiet and leafy, mainly residential. The touristic parts of the city are outside the walls, particularly in the streets between the Tha Pae Gate and the river. Here are the handicraft shops and trekking companies, the discos and massage parlours, the famous night bazaar for hill-tribe crafts, the snack-bars where you may witness a fat *farang* enjoying a bottle of beer that cost him fifty baht while reproachfully shaking his head at an old beggar who'd be glad of just five. It is wonderful to hear the high-principled arguments people advance against the dispersing of their small change to the poor.

Nowhere in Thailand is the temple ethos more casual, more interwoven into daily life, than in Chiang Mai. There are over a hundred temples within the city limits. Some are ancient and full of legend – Wat Chedi Luang, with its giant eucalyptus tree which, the story has it, will stand for as long as the city's fortunes prosper; Wat Chiang Man, with its crystal Buddha, said to have been brought from Haripunjaya, the ancient Mon capital of the region, by King Mengrai himself; Wat Suan Dok, which houses the ashes of the kings of Lan Na. Others are just casually there. You can hardly walk a block in the old town without stumbling on some old patina-stained cluster of buildings – pagodas and cloisters, *vihan* and *bot* – with its shady, ancient sense of a space reserved for the cooling of the spirit.

One morning at Wat Mau Komtuang near the Elephant Gate – dogs basking in the sun, astrologers and herbalists at little desks in the cloisters – I met a temple boy called Sayam. The temple boys (*dek wat*) of Thailand are remnants of the days when monasteries were virtually the only source of education in the country. In the old days, said Sayam, a *dek wat* was attached to a particular monk. 'He was like his apprentice. The monks were very strict: they punished the *dek wat* with beatings, they made them stand on one leg for a long time.' Nowadays – since the time of Rama IV, who introduced compulsory education in the 1920s – the temple's role has become more one of assistance. Most *dek wat* are poorer children, or orphans, or clever country boys who live too far from the urban high schools. Some are sent to 'make merit' (*tham boon*) for their family, some are destined to become monks, but most are simply there to enable them to continue their schooling. They typically enter the monastery when they're ten and stay till fifteen or sixteen, up to Grade Three secondary.

In return for this monastic hospitality, they perform menial tasks, much like the sizar scholars of mediaeval Cambridge. The day begins at six, and soon after they assemble for the daily *bintha baht*: out through the dawn streets with their alms baskets, collecting the day's food for the monks. Back at the monastery, they cook the food, or fill up the washing jars, or sweep and clean the living quarters. They breakfast on what is left by the monks, then they go off to school. After school, they are mostly free – monks do not eat supper: they may not eat anything solid after midday – though sometimes they are called upon to massage one of the monks, or to read passages from the Pali scriptures. Wat Mau Komtuang is a modest-sized *wat*, housing seven monks (*bikkhu*), four novices (*nen*) and seven temple boys. The boys' accommodation is spartan, but as Sayam assured me, 'We learn to see things clearly here.'

The most famous of Chiang Mai's temples is Wat Phra Dhat, on the 3,000-foot summit of Suthep mountain overlooking the city. The mountain is named after a holy man, Sudeva, who lived there as a hermit. The temple dates from the fourteenth century. It was built to contain a relic of the Buddha, brought from Sukhothai to Chiang Mai by the Sri Lankan wise-man Sumanathera. (The Theravada Buddhism of Thailand has its origins in Sri Lanka.) The site of the temple was chosen, in the time-honoured way, by a white elephant set free at the city gate. It headed into the hills, stopped half-way up, at a place still known as Doi Chang Norn, the Hill of the Elephant's Rest, then carried on to the summit. There, we are told, it trumpeted three times, traced three circles anticlockwise, and knelt down. Where it knelt the relic was buried. The temple's central *chedi*, over fifty foot high, marks the spot.

Trucks leave from the White Elephant Gate to make the switch-back ascent. I shared this rocking, reeling ride with an old man smoking one of those king-size cheroots of local tobacco rolled up in a dried banana leaf. As we began the ascent, we passed a statue. The old man made a reverent *wai* – the traditional Thai greeting or sign of respect: palms pressed together like a child at prayer. I could see the statue was not a Buddha, so I asked who it was.

'It is the late Kruba Sri Vichai,' he told me. 'He was once the most revered monk of Lan Na. You think this ride is rough? Well, think what it was like before there was a road. It was a five-hour walk then. I know, because I did it many times when I was a child. So now, when we ride up to Doi Suthep, we *wai* to Kruba, to thank him that the road exists.'

The road had been built, half a century ago, under the aegis of Kruba Sri Vichai. It was constructed totally by voluntary labour. At first it was just the citizens of Chiang Mai who worked on it, but the project gained such fame that people came from miles around, from as far as Phitsanaluk and Autaradit, to contribute their labour. Even the *khon doi*, the heathen hill-tribes, joined in. On any one day, as many as 4,000 people might be seen working on the road. So Kruba Sri Vichai decreed that each village should contri-bute a certain length of road. At first the figure was set at fifty feet per village, but as more people came this had to be reduced. Eventually each village contributed ten feet of the road. After just six months, with little more than hoes and axes, the road was completed. It covered seven miles from the base of the mountain at Houai Keo to the temple at the summit. It was opened in 1935, and the first to ride to the temple by car was the revered Kruba.

This story catches something of the Buddhist way in Thailand. Belief touches the people in a way that is deep, but pre-eminently practical. The schooling of the *dek wat* is another aspect of this. So is the early morning *bintha baht*, where the monks progress through their parish collecting gifts of food. All Thai temples survive by the wish of the people, concretely expressed day after day by this filling of the monks' empty bowls.

For those who had walked from Chiang Mai the final ascent to Wat Phra Dhat – a 290-step staircase, flanked by the traditional *naga* balustrades – must have been gruelling. It is tiring enough when you've come up by *song taow*. The place was crowded with holiday-makers, much as a famous cathedral would be in England. It was stately and beautiful, but oddly unmoving. In my notebook now I find images of the place – the golden parasols surrounding the *chedi*, the huge bells which the noisy children jangled, the Buddhas strangely plump and complacent, the sumptuous murals, the jumble of footwear left outside the *vihan*, the candle-lighting ceremony, the splashes of red and gold paint in the gutter, the giant durian tree outside the compound, the flitting of red and yellow minivers, the aromatic pinewoods on the slopes, the glimpses of Chiang Mai stretched out in the hazed valley below – but only images, because I couldn't feel what they added up to. Whatever I thought I might find just wasn't there. However tranquil the attractions of Buddhism, its more formal manifestations can seem unattractive: gilded, garish, trinkety.

To compound this feeling, or lack of it, I shared the downward truck with another old man, a peasant as bald as an egg, wearing denim work-clothes and straw hat. He was in a kind of trance. He sat in the back of the truck, staring back up at the temple, mumbling to himself. Long after the temple was out of view, he kept on muttering his mantric undertone. I tried to talk to him, but he wasn't listening. He wasn't focussing on anything outside him. It was like he was trying to keep it all in his head, and the further we got from the temple, the harder he had to concentrate on it. I could only guess at what it all meant to him, and perhaps I felt a bit of envy, and a sense of having so far to go – so many questions to ask and so many wrong questions not to ask – before I even started to understand what made this country tick.

Returning from Suthep mountain, I walked into the hotel court-yard and there, sitting at the table next to the bar, chatting in French with Guy, was Harry the gem-trader. He was looking cleaner and smarter than when I'd last seen him a few days ago. A thin black moustache had been salvaged from the stubble, his loose white shirt was freshly laundered, his thinning black hair was wetted and combed straight back. He looked less like a prospector, more like a tout of some sort.

He greeted me with that same slightly stilted manner as before. 'Very pleased to see you again,' he said. 'Guy told me you were here.' He motioned me to a chair. 'Won't you join me in a drink?'

There was a half-finished bottle of Mekong whisky on the table. Rice whisky is Thailand's favourite tipple. It is blander, browner and sweeter than grain whisky, and has a vague caramel savour like Fundador brandy. Drunk neat it will give you a hangover that starts in your throat at the end of the first glass, but taken long with soda and ice it is palatable enough.

He waved the bottle at me. 'This is very special stuff, my friend. You know why? Because it is free. Tonight, regrettably, I have no money, *je suis fauché comme les blés*, and so I must ask my good friend Guy for credit. I'm sure you appreciate. Credit from a Lillois. Very special.'

He turned to Guy, rattled off some quip. His *pied noir* French was fast, rough and flat, with hard consonants where Guy's were classically fluid.

Guy laughed indulgently. He was drinking beer, so I assumed the inroads into the whisky were all Harry's. The waitress, a sweet girl called Nid, brought me a glass. Harry poured me a generous slug, and pushed the soda and the ice-bucket over.

A half-drunk prospector in financial difficulties might not seem the best companion for the evening, but something about Harry fascinated me. He was an old Asia hand, a serious traveller, a man with a hundred stories to tell. Of course, I wasn't really here for *stories*. I was here to visit a forest temple, to get my head together, to write about the deep things in life. But in writing, as in much else, it's not what you go looking for that counts, it's what you find. And right now, what I'd found was Harry.

A pair of backpackers came in to the courtyard, looking for a room. Guy rose suavely to greet them.

I asked Harry how long he was planning to stay in Chiang Mai. He said, 'That's it. I have to leave very soon.'

'Where are you headed?'

'Further north.'

'Chiang Rai?'

'Further. Business, my friend. I go where business takes me.'
He pronounced the word with an untrustworthy leer: *beez-ness*.

'What business is that?'

He took a draught of Mekong, narrowing his mouth and his eyes
as he drank. I noticed again the big silver rings on his long fingers.
He said, with a rather chilly smile, 'Precious stones. I thought
Khris told you on the train. I deal in stones.'

I felt caught out. 'Where is Khris?' I asked.

Harry frowned. 'He split off. He met some girl he used to know.
They're going to walk to Pai, some damn thing.' He scratched his
chin reflectively. 'He said they met up by chance. I told him: don't
tell me about chance. No such thing. It's the code of road, my
friend. You come to a crossroads and you got to choose.' He
shrugged. 'He chose the girl. She was Quebecoise. She was OK.
Trouble is, he was a useful guy to have around.'

I wondered quite what he meant by that last remark, but now he
was leaning back in his chair, calling out, '*Noo! Noo!*' The word
means 'mouse', but it's a common mode of addressing young girls
and particularly waitresses. Nid appeared from the murky little
kitchen out behind the bar. Harry bantered and flirted a bit, soft
voice, crow's-foot wrinkles at his eyes. He didn't speak particularly
good Thai, I could tell that, but it was quick enough, and she
seemed to understand what he was saying. Once or twice she
laughed, and at the end she said, '*Ka*', and hurried off. She came
back with two more bottles of soda, a pack of Gold City cigarettes,
and a couple of sweetmeats done up in squares of banana leaf.

'Whisky, cigarettes and sticky rice,' said Harry, smiling. 'A man
could live for a hundred years on this.' It was the first time I'd seen
him properly smile. A tooth at the edge of his mouth glinted gold.

'So what's your line, my friend?' he asked, replenishing our
glasses.

I told him I was a writer. He laughed. I could see that this hadn't
impressed him. 'Sniffer, eh?'

'Well, sort of.' I was surprised to hear this Fleet Street term from him – 'sniffer and snorter' is rhyming slang for 'reporter'. I asked him where he had learned rhyming slang.

'I knew some Australians, out in Saigon. Journos . . . Sniffers . . .'

'Were you in Saigon during the Vietnam War?'

'During and before. I first came to Saigon in 1960. I guess I'm what you would call an old hand. As we say: *je connais la musique Indochinoise*. Saigon, Hue, Vientiane, Luang Prabang: I knew them all before . . .'

He trailed off. There was a silence. 'Long time ago,' I said.

He lit a cigarette. 'Sure,' he said, drawling the word out a little jokily, as if to dispel this troublesome moment of nostalgia. 'Plenty of blood under the bridge since then.'

'Have you been back there since?'

'You interviewing me for your paper?'

One thing I'll say for Harry: he was always very honest about what he thought about things. He let you know where you stood. At heart he was a secret man. He loved to play parts, to weave mysteries around himself. Some of them I penetrated in the weeks to come, others are still mysteries to me now. But in the business of life, in the commerce of travelling together, he was as straight as anyone I've ever met.

So when he said he was going to a club called My Place, a few minutes' walk away, would I care to come along, I knew the invitation for what it was. I was English, and he didn't much care for the English. I was a 'sniffer' – or so he insisted – which meant I asked too many questions. I was not ostensibly a 'useful guy to have around' like Khris. But I was someone with a few baht in his pocket, so I'd be OK for a couple of drinks at My Place, and – who knows? – perhaps there was some way in which I too could be 'useful' to him.

My Place was full of *farang* and bar-girls. There were coloured lights flashing and country music on the jukebox. A contingent of Americans sat at the bar, light shirts, Lee jeans, big bellies. They looked like they were drinking in some down-town bar in

Oklahoma City, except that each of them had a lissom young Oriental wrapped around him, and one of them had three.

Harry chose a table with care. It had a view of the door, and a wall behind it. I ordered Mekong: after drinking rice whisky the only viable option is more rice whisky. A couple of bar-girls came over, but Harry rose silkily to his feet, spoke something quietly to them. They giggled and shrugged, and went off.

I asked him what he had said to them. 'I told them we were waiting for someone. I told them they were too beautiful for tramps like us.'

'Thanks.'

'You want a girl?' His eyes fell to my wedding-ring.

I said, 'So are we meeting someone?'

'Hold on here a moment. I'll find out.'

He slid out with that slightly sinuous way he had, moved among the crowd of Americans, spoke to a big, grizzled man wearing a baseball cap. The man seemed to know him, but didn't look all that pleased to see him. Harry was asking him something. The man was shaking his head, mouth downturned. He was either saying, No, he didn't know something; or perhaps, No, he couldn't do something.

Harry came back. He said, 'Everyone's out of town when you need them.'

'Who are you looking for?'

'See those guys over there? They're pilots, aerial reconnaissance boys. They're working for a Canadian outfit. I've got a friend, very useful man. He gives me a ride in his chopper sometimes, takes me where the roads don't go.'

'Sounds like fun.'

'That depends how strong your stomach is. You're flying down at four hundred foot, going with all the contours. You can leave yourself behind doing that.' He leaned forward and said, 'And sometimes he gives me something else.'

'Oh?'

I turned over the possibilities in my mind. Drugs? Guns?

'You know why these boys are up here?' he asked. I shook my head. 'They're making a map, that's why. One to fifty thousand, hundred foot contours, tight stuff across the whole of the country. And do you know who it's for? It's for the Department of Mineral Resources.' He leant back rhetorically, studied my face. He was waiting for some penny to drop. 'OK, I'll spell it out for you. These guys are putting together a map of all the precious metal and gem-stone resources of Thailand. Well, I'm sure you appreciate. This kind of survey can be pretty interesting to an . . . independent like myself.'

'You mean your friend tips you the wink about new areas to look in?'

'Bravo.'

'And you get there before anyone else?'

'In this business being there first is the only way to make the big one. Down on the Gulf' – he meant in Chanta Buri Province on the eastern coast, Thailand's major gem-producing area – 'it's all sewn up. The Chinese have got the business by the balls. I don't mess with Chinese. It's a rule I have from way back. On the Gulf you mostly don't see a stone before it's polished up. OK, I've got my man down there, a Vietnamese, I've known him for years. He's got a small concession. He sells me stuff wholesale, unpolished, but it's getting tighter all the time. Too much hassle, too little money. So a few months ago I decided to get the hell out, take a look around. I'm getting too old for picking up *sous* off the sidewalk. I want to get my hands on the big one. It's waiting there. That's all it ever does. Just waits for a million years until someone finds it.'

This sounded like prospector's talk. I remembered what Khris had told me, and said, 'So you went up to Kanchana Buri looking for sapphires.'

The tight smile again. 'I like Americans but they got big fucking mouths.'

'Well, did you find any?' I persisted.

'I found shit. I paid . . . well, I put out a good few dollars US. I just had the merchandise assayed.' He ground out his cigarette. He spoke half to himself, mouth twisted: *'On a salopé le boulot.'*

I didn't understand the expression. He translated: 'I fucked up.'

'Fakes?'

'Hey look. I'm not an amateur. I don't have anyone putting fake sapphires over on me. But the quality, that's different. That's the gamble when you're buying at the farmgate. It's hard to tell before the stone's polished up. You back your instinct. I thought they were good and I was wrong.' He reminisced, as of some girl he had met too briefly. 'They sure were pretty, though. Pale but strong. We call it *bleu barbeau*, in English I think it is "cornflower". They were different. Most Thai stones are dark: Siamese indigo. But they were flawed inside, flawed the wrong way. Just like the rest of us, you know?' He shrugged. 'It's OK, I'll come out on top, but the man won't buy them off me. He's just fencing them for a commission. That's why I'm short right now.'

His voice trailed off. The way his rap came round to this point, and stayed there, made me think that any minute now he was going to start importuning me for money. I quickly prepared my alibis. Whatever my interests in Harry from a story point of view – 'A Day in the Life of a Siamese Sapphire Trader' – I was not in a position to start seriously bailing him out.

He had a way of pulling at his ear-lobe, staring off into space, absenting himself for a moment. It looked like he was day-dreaming, but soon enough you learned that these were his times of hardest thinking.

When he spoke, it was not to ask me for some money, but for the time. I told him it was eleven o'clock. He seemed to come to a decision. 'OK. It looks like I've got a problem,' he said. 'My friend's out of town, and the only other guy who might possibly help me isn't here either.'

'So no chopper ride.'

'Right. And no chopper ride means, my friend, I am going to have to ask you a little favour.'

'It does?'

He nodded, whisky-red eyes on my face. Springsteen was singing about Spanish Johnny on the jukebox, and I was wondering what the hell French Harry wanted from me. Would it be dangerous? And if so, would it be worth it? He refilled our glasses, and said, 'Really just a *little* favour, man.'

He was the soul of plausibility as he explained. He had to leave for the north tomorrow. Something had 'come up'. He *had* to be where he was going on Thursday, two days from now, and two days was what the journey took overland. That was why he needed his friend the helicopter pilot. You can do the same journey in three hours in a chopper.

I thought now he was going to ask me to drive him up there for some reason. I have known one or two perennial travellers who couldn't actually drive. I asked him where he was going exactly, but he shook his head. 'I told you. Up north.'

So what was the little favour?

'I need you to meet a friend for me, here in Chiang Mai.'

'What kind of friend?'

'A very special friend,' he said. 'Her name is Katai. She is coming from Bangkok especially.'

Relief and disappointment. All he wanted me to do was to meet his girl off the train. I listened blandly to the details. Katai would arrive with the night train on Thursday morning, the day after tomorrow. She was a room-maid in a big Bangkok hotel. This was her holiday: they were going to spend it together. He was damned if he was going to put her off just because he had to be out of town for a few days. Anyway he didn't 'believe in' telephones. So he needed someone to meet and greet her, to explain what had happened, and to look after her for a few days while he concluded his unspecified 'beez-ness' up north.

'So when will you get back?' I wasn't sounding very enthusiastic, I suppose. Harry hastened to answer – I was obscurely pleased to have made him hasty – 'No, no, my friend. I am not suggesting you stay in town with her. No, you will travel together up to Chiang Saen. This is a day and a half if you're not hurrying. It's a nice town, right on the banks of the Mekong River. I will be able to meet you there on . . . Saturday night.'

'But Chiang Saen's straight north from here. I told you, Harry, I'm going to a temple. The temple's west of here, another direction entirely.'

Harry was unperturbed. 'After,' he said. 'You go to the temple after, man. It'll still be there.' He waited for my reaction, got very little. 'OK,' he said. 'You're asking yourself what's in it for you. That's no problem. I'm a trader, my father was a trader. Something for something: code of the road, right?'

'Well, right.'

He drained the last of the Mekong into my glass, sat back with his fingertips pressed pedantically together. 'Well, I'll tell you this. She's a charming girl. Her English is good. She'll tell you all you want to know about Thailand.'

I nodded, but said nothing.

'And then, of course' – a faint air of moustache-twirling – 'there's the Triangle.'

'The Triangle?'

'Sure. Any sniffer worth his salt would want to get into the Golden Triangle. I mean . . . *right* in there. Know what I mean?'

Again I nodded. I did indeed know what he meant. The Australian, Dixon – a genuine 'sniffer' – had bent my ear on the subject in Bangkok. Drugs and guns, bandit armies and tribal rebels: all apparently more story-like, more *real*, than forest temples.

Harry went on, casual and persuasive. 'I know some people. I know how it works up there. OK, it's a while since I've been, but I know some places where *nobody* goes unless someone shows them. From Chiang Saen it is not far. We can go on up, take a look-see, the three of us: you, me and Katai. She'd like that. I can take you up to the poppy fields. The harvest is beginning soon: very beautiful.' He leaned forward. 'I can take you across the border, man.'

'You mean into Burma?'

'Sure.' He sighed, seemed suddenly tired. 'I don't know,' he said. 'Maybe you're not ready for it. Maybe I'll find someone else.'

It was a ticket to ride, and they are hard to turn down. I told him I'd do it. We raised our glasses, but they were both empty.

Out on the quiet night street by the old town walls, Harry was brusque again. He had an early morning departure: his mind was already on the road. He would sleep badly that night, he said.

After all these years, he always slept badly the night before a journey.

We ran through the logistics – how to recognize Katai at the station, the best routes to Chiang Saen, the guest house we should meet up at on Saturday evening, and so on – then he said he had two things he wanted to say about this 'deal', as he called it. 'The first thing: no goddamn sniffer questions about this business of mine. You might think I'm up to something funny, but you don't ask. What I'll tell you right away, because I know how people like you think, is that this business has *nothing* to do with drugs. That's not my style.'

'And the second thing?'

'Katai,' he said. I grinned, but he looked at me hard and I stopped grinning. 'There's no funny stuff. She's special to me, you understand? You look after her real good, and I'll look after you in the Triangle.'

There was a nail-paring of moon reflected in the moat, mist in the crenellations of the wall. I think we both noticed how the word 'triangle' had sneaked its way into the sentence.

'Sure, Harry. I understand.'

We shook hands. I wished him *bon voyage*. He said, 'See you on the Mekong,' and walked off across the bridge into the old town.

The next morning, a leisurely breakfast easing away my whisky head, Nid brought me an envelope. Inside was nothing but another envelope with 'KATAI' written neatly in capitals. This envelope was sealed at the back with candlewax and a pair of black hairs across the join. Harry must have dropped it in at the Noi while I slept.

Guy was doing his rounds – a *bon mot* for each of the guests, a list of chores and reprimands for the Thai maids, some check-outs to fatten the wedge of baht in his bill-fold. He settled himself with the *Bangkok Post* and a large black coffee.

After a bit of chat I asked him, 'Have you known Harry long?'

'I've known him off and on for a few years. He's never around for long. He doesn't stay here. He's got friends, up in the old town, I think.'

'Did you find out what he's doing up here?'

Guy shook his head. 'Harry's a dark horse.'

'Gem trade, I expect.'

Guy laughed. 'Who knows? Harry trades anything he can get his hands on. Last year he was up here, he bought a whole lot of carved teak eaves from a *wat* out near Sam Kampaeng. He said they fetch five thousand francs apiece in Paris. People hang them up in their apartments. He's full of ideas is Harry, but – I don't know – there's something wrong with him. He makes very big money sometimes, but he's always broke. He's like the gambler: he doesn't do it for the money.

'One time, he'd been across to Laos – this was a while ago – and he came back with some Kian Lung porcelain he'd bought off some China trader in Luang Prabang. It was a little teapot with four cups: I mean, this was beautiful stuff' – he kissed his fingers – 'maybe worth a thousand US in Bangkok. Well, you know what happened? Harry met a Lao girl here in Chiang Mai, working the streets. She lived with her mother out on the edge of town. They came from Luang Prabang, where he'd got the set from. So he goes and gives it to them. Said he'd rather they drank tea from it than some Yankee *farang* put it on his mantelpiece.

'He's a good man, Harry. You have to be careful with him, because *au fond* he's crazy, but a good man.'

'Crazy?'

Guy shrugged. '*Pied noir*. You can never be sure with them. They are mongrels.'

He went about his business, leaving me with more questions than answers. How much could I trust Harry? Was he setting me up in some way? Was he the kind of man it was wise to go travelling into the Golden Triangle with, a place where – by all accounts – it was best to keep your nose extremely clean if you didn't want it sliced off by some opium bandit's machete?

I just didn't know. As Harry had said last night, in philosophic vein, 'Life on the road is like the poker game they call One Up. It's all about how little you know. You're betting on just one card. Hell, you don't even know what's in your own hand.'

And then there was the Thai girl, Katai: another unknown quantity, awakening in me now certain *frissons* of anticipation, certain connections between beauty and danger, certain queasy memories of my first night in Bangkok . . .

Angels

THAI GIRLS, Thai girls: the words trip off the tongue in a way you just *know* they shouldn't. In Krung Thep, the City of Angels – known to the rest of the world as Bangkok – it begins before you've even had time to draw breath, begins as the taxi driver eases the car onto the freeway, rests his arm on the open window, and turns back to ask pleasantly, 'You want lay-dee?'

We stare back, sweating and jet-lagged. We have been in Bangkok about ten minutes. We can still smell the high-octane fuel from the runways. No, at this point in time, we do not want lady. We do not want to see pussy show, nor go to massage parlour. Nor – a couple of minutes later – do we want to tour the Grand Palace and a judicious sample of the city's three hundred temples.

We just want to go hotel, get shut-eye.

The driver shrugs happily, a skinny, pleasant man, with a wisp of moustache and a fake Lacoste T-shirt. He isn't really hustling: even in Bangkok the Thais never seem to hustle. It's just that we're *farang*, and he knows what the *farang* come to Bangkok for. They come for the angels, which the city duly provides.

My fellow passenger is a big blond German with gold-rimmed spectacles. His name is Heinz. I know nothing else about him. We are two pieces of human freight randomly stacked together. We are heading for different hotels, but thought we'd save money and time by taking the same taxi from the airport. Heinz has a reservation at the Royal Orchid, one of the high-rise hotels on the riverfront. I am bound for a mid-market, faintly notorious hotel called the Malaysia.

We come off the freeway into a lunch hour traffic-jam. The air is grey but painfully bright. *Tuk tuk* – little three-wheeled motor-scooter taxis – dart and buzz like wasps. At the intersections small boys sell garlands of white hyacinth and lotus: one kind for the Buddha, another for the spirit house, another to hang around the neck of your girl. The driver takes a short cut. We nose into narrow streets: cook-stalls and cloth shops, fruit-vendors and flower-sellers, people packed tight on the sidewalks, and seemingly packed down from above by the tangle of signboards and cables, and the heavy black haze of monoxide hanging over them. Then a sudden rise takes us up over a small canal, and for a moment the mayhem is gone. Stilted wooden houses straggle down along the banks. An old women squeezes out washing into the dirty green water.

Pulling up at the Royal Orchid hotel, we get our first glimpse of the Chao Phrya, Thailand's great arterial river. It rises in the Himalayas, flows down through the rice plains, and is now a half-mile swathe of turbid grey water dotted with ferryboats and barges and tiny bobbing *sampan*. Its traditional name, Mae Nam, simply means The River. It is called Chao Phrya in honour of Rama I, known before his coronation as Chao Phrya Chakri. He founded the royal capital here in 1782, after the sacking of Ayutthaya by the Burmese. Before that Bangkok was just a modest little river-port. The name means 'village of the *kok* trees', *kok* being a species of small wild plum.

Heinz says, 'Why don't we meet up for a drink tonight? Perhaps we go out for a little fun, yes?'

We arrange to meet at the Oriental, just downriver. Slender immaculate doormen spirit him up the steps of the hotel, his hand plucking clumsily at the back of his shirt, easing the sweat-soaked material off his skin.

The driver wants to show me a silk shop he knows. I say, a bit snappishly – a touch of *jai ron*, the hot heart – 'Just take me to the Malaysia.'

He frowns. 'So why you want to go Malaysia?'

'A friend told me it was a good hotel.'

'Good for the lay-dees,' he says with a grin. 'Malaysia coffee shop. Number one girls, very cheap, *na*?'

We are on Silom Road now, glossy haired office-girls eating noodles, boys riding raked-up Honda 125s, silk and antique shops,

Rita's Beauty Parlour, Saigon Bakery and Restaurant, Happy Saloon Barber Room. I see a small boy preening a rooster. Maybe it's a fighting cock. He's holding it in front of a plate glass door, showing it its reflection, ruffling its neck-hackle to get its dander up. In Bangkok, perhaps, your worst adversary turns out to be yourself.

At last we're speeding down a narrow *soi* and pulling up outside the gates of the Malaysia. It looks unpromising: a big dowdy building like a block of council flats, the walls stained beneath the squat boxes of the air-conditioning outlets.

Outside the taxi the heat is intense, that strange smell in the air like chicken broth left too long in the pot. *Tuk tuk* boys sit in the shade, playing draughts with bottle-tops. I head fast for the cool of the lobby. A girl lounges by the doorway, fanning herself with a magazine. She has long painted nails and looks about fifteen. There's a photo of Johnny Chan, the *kung fu* movie star, on the cover of the magazine. She smiles at me as I pass. That all-purpose smile, sweet and available. Perhaps just a touch of mockery at the edge of it, as another grey-faced *farang* strides purposefully into the swamps of Bangkok.

I woke at dusk, the din of the air-conditioning in my ears and its fluffy taste in my mouth. Outside the window I could hear birdsong and motorcycles. I didn't much feel like meeting up with Heinz, but on your first night any company is better than none. I showered and made my way downtown.

He was sitting in the lobby at the Oriental, under one of the giant wooden lanterns that hang from the ceiling. A bored-looking Thai string quartet was playing something classical. He stood up and shook my hand. 'Greetings.' He looked bigger and fresher and more freckled than before. A leather handbag hung from his ursine shoulder.

'They are playing Haydn,' he said.

'Do you like Haydn?'

'Not greatly.'

We strolled out onto the terrace. Candlelight, white tuxes,

cocktails topped off with esoteric salads and small paper parasols. A ferry docked at the jetty. A chafing-dish flared. The aromas of the terrace restaurant mingled with the archetypal fetor of the river: the *farang* dream of Asia.

Heinz ordered Singapore Slings at 100 baht a shot. 'Your first time in Bangkok?' he asked. I said it was. 'Well, you are starting at the top, yes?'

The Oriental is sometimes called the Raffles of Bangkok. Modernization has made some inroads, but it is still the most stylish of the riverfront hotels. The original hotel, a two-storey trader's house built in the nineteenth century, is now known as the Author's Wing, its lobby hushed with tall palms and sepia-tint photos, its suites named after the famous writers who once stayed here: Conrad and Coward, Maugham and Michener. This building is now dwarfed by the hotel's new high-rise extension, more or less indistinguishable from the towers of the Royal Orchid and the Shangri-La either side.

We raised our glasses to the City of Angels. If I was starting at the top, I reflected, the only way to go from here was down.

Heinz gave me his card. He was Sales Executive (Far East & Australia) for an auto-parts manufacturer in Düsseldorf. He did a swing through his territory twice a year, and always made sure his longest stay was in Bangkok. Ahead lay Manila, Djakarta, Taipei, Seoul and Tokyo, followed by a five-city tour of Australia. But Bangkok was the special one for Heinz. His 'little private holiday', he called it.

'I am like a Mercedes,' he said amiably. 'Every six months I need a good service.' He laughed, with his cheeks and his shoulders but not with his eyes, 'ho ho ho', like some outsize dwarf in a bad production of *Das Rheingold*.

He outlined his plans for the evening. He was a methodical man: he liked to know where he was going. We would have a couple of slings here by the river, and then stroll on up to Patpong. We would take something light to eat on the way: a soup, perhaps, or a shellfish omelette. On Patpong we would have a few beers, a few cuddles, 'get in the mood'. Then – unless we'd found someone special on Patpong, which frankly he thought unlikely, you have to watch these Patpong girls – we would remove by taxi or *tuk tuk* to a 'little place' he knew down on the Phetcha Buri Road.

I said I wasn't sure about all this. I didn't think I wanted to visit his 'little place'. He shrugged his big shoulders and said, 'Well at least you must see Patpong. You don't go to Pisa without seeing the Leaning Tower, do you?'

The night was hot and moist as we headed uptown. In the narrow streets around the Oriental they were hawking fake Rolex and Cartier watches, five on each arm. With a bit of bargaining you can get one for twenty-five dollars. Charoen Krung was clogged with people and cars. The cook-stalls were frying, the cloth shops were doing brisk business under the strip-lights. I wondered where all these people went when the city closed up for the night. Perhaps it never did. In a restaurant on the Suriwong Road we ate *tom yam kung*, a Thai favourite, spicy prawn soup flavoured with lemon grass, kaffir lime, bay leaves and lashings of red chilli. By the third bowl down it was at its fiercest.

Heinz talked on about the pleasures and the perils that awaited us in the sex-dens of Bangkok. My nose was streaming from the chilli, and I was beginning to feel uneasy: things moving too fast, the city prowling like a night beast outside the open-fronted restaurant. I had made a lot of big promises before I came here.

Heinz seemed to read my mind. Perhaps I was fingering my wedding-ring, perhaps it was just his own conscience. 'I am faithful to my wife,' he said. 'But in Bangkok what can I do? A faithful husband in Bangkok is like, is like – '

'A diabetic in a sweet shop?'

'Oh yes! Ho ho ho! A diabetic in a sweet shop!'

As he noisily drained the last dregs of soup, his front tooth – proving, like so much else that night, to be false – fell with a dull clatter into the bottom of the bowl.

Patpong, known to *farang* as The Strip, is Bangkok's main red light district. It lies on the edge of the banking and business quarter, Silom and Suriwong: the classic location, pleasure on the fringes of money. It consists of three streets, known simply as

Patpong One, Two and Three, the first two for straights, the third for gays. It is as well to know this basic topography. The Thais are noted for their androgyny, and there is large population of *katoy* – transvestites – in Bangkok. The tales are many of punters who have discovered the difference too late.

Bangkok was always a seamy city, but today's industrial-sized skin trade is an American legacy. It was essentially R & R – Rest and Recreation leave – that created Patpong. Throughout the Vietnam War, thousands of desperate young soldiers – 'fragged' in the Nam slang, as if the war had hit them with the force of a fragmentation grenade – were flown in from Vietnam, or trucked down the Friendship Highway from Laos, to be serviced with a few weeks' pleasure and oblivion, commodities that Bangkok took readily to supplying. The virulent strain of syphilis known as Saigon Rose – still doing the rounds here – is another legacy of the war.

Patpong is a brief neon hymn to desire, a cacophony of come-ons. The Pink Panther, the Playmate, the Fire Cat, the Starship ('Second Floor, Nightly Special Shows'), the La Costa Turkish Bath & Massage, the Lucky Strike Disco, the Gaslight Cocktail Lounge: the signs flash and jostle, peek out behind and above one another, competing for attention as jungle foliage competes for light. There's jazz and Country & Western, sausages and seafood, dice and roulette, anything to make the *farang* feel at home, and rest his butt long enough for the girls to get their hooks in. Patpong, said Heinz, is the showpiece of the Bangkok sex industry. There are other red light districts – more businesslike up on the Phetcha Buri Road, more upmarket in the well-appointed alleys off Sukhumvit, more raunchy down in the docklands of Klong Toey – but none of them are quite like Patpong.

We dipped into a place called the King's Castle. It was dark and crowded. A song by Paul Young – currently big in Bangkok – shuddered out of the speakers. Heinz shouldered confidently in.

The King's Castle is what they call a 'go-go bar'. These provide about the tamest of Patpong's entertainments. A long wooden bar divided the place, doing a brisk trade in cold Singha beer. Within the ellipse of the bar was a raised stage, no wider than a shelf. Here half a dozen girls in cut-away bikinis gyrated to the tune of 'I'm Going To Tear Your Playhouse Down'. At the far end of the bar was another strip of stage, with more girls dancing. Here Heinz set up camp. Our faces were a few feet away from the go-go girls' ankles. I could almost feel the static from their cheap lurex costumes. The girls looked very young. It is axiomatic that you cannot guess the age of an Oriental woman, but few looked over eighteen, and some – like the one Heinz had selected for attention – much younger. She was heavily made up. Caught in the glare of the spotlight her face looked flat, a carnival mask: white maquillage, mauve eyes, liverish red lips. Her face and her hips mimed excitement, but her eyes were somewhere else, staring off into the middle distance like someone growing old and absent-minded.

The girls did alternate shifts. Those not onstage were working the clientele. They were perched on laps, smooch-dancing on the floor, snuggling up close at dark corner-tables. A girl in a rose-pink miniskirt slid her arm into mine, and asked me to buy her a Coke. She spoke the usual bar-girl English and I was trying out my faltering Thai. The loudness of the music made our formalities intimate: it was hard to talk except by pressing my mouth to her ear, my nose into her scented hair. We found out each other's names. Hers was Lah. We asked each other's age. I told the truth but she didn't believe me; I believed her but she probably lied. She kept on pouring out my beer and holding the glass for me to drink, and I kept on thanking her, though I knew it was just business. The hostess's primary purpose, of course, is to get you to buy more drinks, for her and for yourself, and as the evening wears on the little dice-shaker in front of you fills up with pink chits. For every two dollar beer you buy, your hostess gets fifty cents.

She asked if I was from USA. I told her England. She seemed to like the sound of England. 'Ning,' she said, with a little flick of her fingers, a term of approval. 'Duran Duran, Paul Young, Sting.'

She was from Bangkok. 'I never go somewhere else,' she said, fluttering her eyelashes.

Her fingers ran lightly over mine, found my ring finger. She laughed, blew out menthol cigarette smoke at the ceiling. 'Oh,' she said. 'Wedding-ring.' She stroked my arm and asked about my children.

I got up to go to the lavatory. At reading height above the urinals was a wipe-clean board with the latest exchange-rates written up – presumably an aid, in this moment of respite, for clients negotiating with one of the girls. All the major currencies were there, including Saudi riyals and Hong Kong dollars. Patpong is nothing if not cosmopolitan.

Heinz had told me over the soup how it is with the bar-girls on Patpong. Dancers, strippers, waitresses, hostesses: they were all available for you to 'take away' (that was the phrase he used, like they were a fried snack of some sort). 'If you're in a hurry you have to pay twice,' he explained, 'once to the girl for her services, and once to the bar for taking her away. After the bar closes, about midnight, you just have to negotiate with the girl. Either way, Patpong is an expensive place to buy a girl. They're asking twenty-five dollars for a fuck, plus a couple of hundred baht on top to thank the barman.'

'That doesn't sound an awful lot,' I said.

'In Europe that would be cheap, of course. But here things are different. This is a buyer's market.'

I was sure he was right. I had seen figures claiming that 200,000 people in Bangkok – one out of every twenty-five citizens – were on the game or involved in it. Bangkok is filled up to here, Heinz said, thrusting a chubby hand under his chin, with available women, pros and casuals alike. You don't have to go to Patpong, or any of the other pleasure quarters. You can find them in the hotel coffee shops, 'like your Malaysia', in the night-markets and noodle-streets, under the bridges and outside the bus stations. 'And if you can't find them,' beamed Heinz, 'for sure they will find you!'

He said the proper price for a night with a girl was 300 to 400 baht, say around fifteen dollars. They won't start at that price, but after a bit of haggling they'll take it. 'And they like repeat customers, so they aim to please.'

When I got back to the bar, Lah was gone and Heinz was looking unhappy. His hostess was pawing at him, half angry, half laughing. 'You butterfly, you no good, you butterfly!' she said.

She was unhappy because he had bought another bar-girl a drink. This meant he was a faithless 'butterfly'.

'Well really, this is ridiculous,' said Heinz, reddening. He turned to the girl. She folded her arms defiantly. 'And what about you?' he said. 'You go with all the men. You're a butterfly too.'

The girl thought for a moment. 'Me no butterfly, me helicopter,' she said. She gave a toss of her head and walked off, clearly feeling she had won her point.

Heinz shook his head. '*Ach!* These girls. They always try to take advantage, yes?'

'Let's get out of here, shall we?'

We emptied our chits onto the bar. The bill came to several hundred baht. I was sweating as we pushed out of the saloon-style doors into the street. I waited for the relief of being outside, but the street was only a different bit of the same hot night, and the night – as Heinz was observing, steering us down towards a fry-stall on the corner – was still young.

We got some *satay* sticks from the cook-stall, and adjourned to a place called Bob's Pub. Ever mindful of the *farang*'s needs, Patpong has one or two spots where working girls are actively discouraged and the chaps can hole up for a while before returning to the fray. Bob's Pub was one of these, though who Bob was, and what he modelled his 'pub' on, I am not sure.

Heinz waxed lyrical about his 'little place' on the Phetcha Buri Road, with its 'little girls', so young, so pretty, so inventive.

Perhaps unfairly, I asked, 'Aren't you worried about AIDS at all?'

'*Ach!* We shut these AIDS people up in Germany. No, I don't worry about the AIDS.' He leaned closer in confidence. 'Look. Who needs to fuck? I get my fucking for free in Düsseldorf. In Thailand I get my kicks above the waistline, yes?' He was quoting the song 'One Night in Bangkok'.

'I think you can get it that way too.'

'From the mouth?'

'Gingival blood.'

'What is this gingival blood?'

I told him the unhappy story. 'If a girl has AIDS, and her gums bleed – not uncommon in cases of protein deficiency – she can transmit the virus during oral sex.'

He stirred his drink moodily. His safari shirt had stains down it: his gear was smart-casual, but beginning to look less so. 'I don't believe it,' he said. 'It is like a plot. They want to close up all the avenues with this AIDS. They want to make us stay at home with our TVs on, yes? I don't believe it.' He became avuncular. 'If you are worried about this AIDS, let me tell you, these Thai girls are very clever with their hands. They are very artistic, ho ho. They call it *shak wao*, which means pulling on the kite-string.' He mimed with his hand and a beer-bottle just to make it clear.

I was beginning to think about leaving. Patpong was palling, and so was Heinz. There was something about his big swollen schoolboy's face, his *Bierkeller* chortle, his eagerness to believe that Bangkok was founded solely for his sexual convenience. But it wasn't me who was leaving, it was Heinz, suddenly pushing back his chair, his beer glass still half full. 'I'm sorry,' he said, 'we must go.' He nodded furtively at a couple of *farang* women who had just walked in. There was nothing unusual in that: it isn't just male tourists who take a look around Patpong. I asked what was up, but he just said, 'You settle up, will you?' and shambled out. Out on the street I said, 'Did you know those women?'

'Know them? No. But I know what they were. They had these things sticking out their handbags.'

'Things? What things?'

'I think in English you call them clipboards. For the underneath holding documents and the note taking, yes?' He was upset and his syntax was suffering.

'So what does that mean?'

'It means that I bet you ten marks to a rotten *Wurst* they are these German sociologists.' He spoke the word with loathing. 'I have heard about them. They come round Patpong to catch out the men. They ask you why you want to go with the little girls. They say it is because you are not trained properly at the toilet, yes?

They say you are inadequate. Ha! Inadequate! I saw the clipboard in their bag. They are doing one of their surveys.'

It was the only cloud on his horizon. None of the usual worries – the dangers of sexually transmitted disease, the emotions of infidelity, the ethics of buying a girl to scratch your genital itches – seemed to touch him. Only the threat of sociology.

A man moved into step alongside us. He was small and swarthy, perhaps southern Thai, a touch of the strain they call *negrito*. He thrust a small sheet of laminated paper into Heinz's hand. In rickety capitals was written 'Pussy Show', underlined three times. Below this was the word 'Menu', then a list: Pussy Chopsticks, Pussy Coca-Cola, Pussy Smoking, Pussy Bananas, Pussy Razorblades. At the bottom, in vague imitation of the scrolly writing of old-fashioned advertisements, was a slogan: 'Enjoy with us!! No Extras!! No Cover charge!!'

'So, do we go and see a show?' Heinz enquired.

'What kind of show?' I asked, but we were already heading briskly off, down an alley-way towards Patpong Two, and anyway I had a pretty shrewd idea what kind of show it was.

We came to a doorway painted bright pink, with the name GIPSEE ROSE in neon above. A flight of linoleum steps led straight up from the door. The tout skipped up ahead of us. He spoke a few words with the doorman, a broad, Chinese-looking boy in a tux two sizes too small for him. His bow tie was pink, his teeth full of gold. We were ushered into a thin smoky room, with a bar in the corner, a few tables, and a small stage. There was a gaggle of middle-aged Americans at one table, loudly bandying names about – 'Say, Cy', 'Right again, Al' – but only a few of the other tables were taken.

In a backroom someone punched a button, and the thud of daddy-cool disco music filled the room. A girl walked onto the stage, pushing a small trolley, on which were plates, bottles and some other items I couldn't properly see. She wore nothing but heavy make-up and a small frilly apron.

'Oh *Liebchen*,' breathed Heinz. 'Just like a maid.'

The girl danced a bit, was quickly naked. Thai sexuality has room for many things, but a concept of strip-tease is not one of them. Her breasts were small, her pubic hair plucked clean away. She hit the floor and went into an athletic writhing routine. She ended up in something like the yoga position called the 'crab', her body arched, her head hanging down to the floor, her bare crotch staring out at us. The Americans guffawed and slapped each other on the back. 'Will you look at that, Cy!'

When she reached the chopsticks off the trolley I decided I'd had enough. I had already forgotten what her face looked like. There was just her body awkwardly splayed there, like a plucked chicken in a market-stall.

I said, 'I'm off, Heinz.'

His gaze didn't waver from the girl on the stage. 'Off?'

'I'm going.'

'No wait, look, she is –'

'Yes, I can see what she's doing.' She had inserted the chopsticks up herself and she was moving them about in a saucerful of rice. Dr Johnson compared a woman preaching to a dog standing on its hind legs – 'It is not well done, but it is remarkable that it is done at all' – and I suppose you could say the same of a woman eating rice with her fanny.

The act finished, the music stopped, the Americans whooped, and an implausible, Chinese-sounding voice said over the speakers, 'Thank you sensational Linda.' I stood up and put some money on the table.

'But you are not staying for the Pussy Coca-Cola?'

'I'm going back to the hotel. Thanks for an interesting evening.'

I made for the door. The sensational Linda was pushing her trolley back through the pink velvet curtain that led backstage. Another girl held the curtain open for her. In the passageway behind them I saw a little household shrine – Buddha statuette, wilted garlands, spent joss-sticks – and I had the feeling that whatever distinctions I was struggling to maintain right now had long ago been dispensed with here.

At the top of the stairs the Chinese boy stopped me with a hand on my chest. I flinched, thinking there was a misunderstanding about whether I'd paid up, but he was only peeling off a paper sticker and pressing it onto my shirt. It was pink, like everything here. It said 'Gipsee Rose', and underneath was the legend 'Have a Nice Night!'

Going down the stairs I heard Heinz's voice behind me. 'No, wait. We shall go to the little place up on Phetcha Buri. You'll like it there.'

He caught up with me outside the pink door. He was also wearing a Gipsee Rose sticker.

'I'm going back to the Malaysia, Heinz.'

'But it is not even midnight yet.'

I told him I didn't care what time it was. Right now I didn't even know what day it was.

'OK,' he said, cleaning his spectacles, working smoothly through the problem in hand. 'We will go back to the Malaysia. And before you go to rest, we will take a quiet night-hat together, at this coffee shop we hear so much about.'

He hailed a *tuk tuk*, and soon we were gunning up the Suriwong Road, sidewalk faces blurring, wind in our hair, through a red light and onto Rama IV.

They said they were sisters, but they didn't look much alike. May was tall with wavy black hair and a coy way of moving her head when she spoke. She wore a pair of scarlet-framed sunglasses perched on her head. She spoke good English. Her little sister, Fon – the name means 'rain' – didn't speak a word of English. 'Baby, you don't need to,' said Heinz, drinking her in with his eyes. She had the classic Thai beauty: almond eyes, black glossy hair cut page-boy style, a small rounded body in a red blouse and tight shiny slacks.

The coffee shop was jam-packed, and no one seemed to be drinking coffee. There were many foreigners, some *farang*, some Asian – Singaporeans, Malaysians, Hong Kongers: these are still the majority of Thailand's tourists. There were many Thai girls, some of them waitresses, most of them not. Down at the end was a quiet, dark area, where a few couples were cuddling. There was a

Kojak movie up on the screen, blown up to almost indecipherable vagueness. This was the coffee shop's 'Twenty Four Hour VDO Show', as promised at the entrance of the hotel. Heinz had hoped this meant some porno extravaganza, but visual pornography, like strip-tease, is not a Thai speciality.

'Anyway,' he said, 'when you've got the real thing climbing all over you, who needs to make believe?'

Heinz ordered whisky, the girls drank lemonade. He put his arm around Fon's shoulder. She giggled. I saw her eyes meet her sister's, but I couldn't understand the look that passed between them. I asked May where they were from.

'We come from Chiang Mai, rose of the north.' She waggled her head like a doll.

'How long have you lived in Bangkok?'

'Two years. We are students.'

'Students?'

'We study politics at Thammasat University.'

I assumed she was lying. If she wasn't, why was her hand now coming to rest on my knee like that?'

'Do you know Chiang Mai?' she asked. I said I didn't but I hoped I soon would. May relayed this to her sister in rapid sing-song Thai, and they dissolved into giggles. Fon hunched her shoulders and held her hand in front of her mouth when she laughed. Heinz said, '*Gott*, she is like a schoolgirl, this pretty little one.' He winked at me. 'Just my type!'

I asked them why they were laughing. May said, 'In Chiang Mai, when we ask "Do you know Chiang Mai?", we mean "Have you been with a girl from Chiang Mai?" So we laugh when you say you hope to soon.' She moved closer and slid her hand between my thighs. 'Do you want to know Chiang Mai tonight?'

Heinz said, 'We want to know *all* about Chiang Mai tonight, my little honey.' He hugged Fon close to him. She said 'Oh, Hize,' and fluttered her eyelashes at him.

I could see the way things were going. There was no good reason for being here, no good reason for May's long pale fingers to be fidgeting around my tropical lightweights. It was time, in the honoured hack's tradition, to make my excuses and leave.

But Heinz had other ideas, or rather the same idea from a different angle. He leaned over, shiny with anticipated pleasure. 'Shall we buy a bottle at the bar and go upstairs?'

'Upstairs?'

'These little girls are hot stuff, yes? We go up to your room, get down to some business.'

I shook my head. 'No way. I'm going to bed. Alone.' He looked disappointed. 'Take them back to your hotel if you want.'

'It is difficult at the Royal Orchid,' he said. 'They have rules about bringing the girls in off the street. Here, of course, it is OK.' He was half whispering across the table. The girls were talking, but I had the feeling that May was keeping an ear on us. 'Listen,' he went on, 'I know you did not like the pussy show. You do not like it shaved, yes? You like, ho ho, the secrets of the forest. In Germany too, we —'

'That's not the point, Heinz.'

Little Fon started nuzzling up to Heinz. She brushed her mouth up the side of his face. I could hear her lips rasp on his golden stubble. She whispered something in his ear. Heinz chortled. He asked May, 'What is your little sister saying?'

The girls conferred, fluttering, giggling, impish, predictable. May explained, 'My sister say she like you very much. She say you like Number One movie star.'

Heinz smirked. 'These girls. They know how to make you feel like a man, yes?'

'Jesus, Heinz! Don't let those sociologists hear you say that.'

May, proving herself thoroughly abreast of the situation, said to Heinz, 'You take room here at Malaysia? My sister want to go with you now. Come on.' They went out together, through the net-curtained doorway towards the lobby. He had the sweats on his back again, and a desire to pull down the tight safari shirt over his big bottom. Fon and I sat alone, either side of the table. Whisky and fatigue were clouding my brain. I could think of nothing to say. There was nothing between us, not even the *frisson* of penny-a-squeeze flirting, because she was obviously Heinz's 'take-away' not mine. She was unbelievably beautiful. I thought how appropriate her name was, Fon the rain girl, because behind the sexy gloss of her smile there was indeed something indistinct and somehow rainy.

We smiled and nodded at one another a couple of times, and then I got up and wished her goodnight.

There was quite a crowd at the reception desk. It was getting on for two in the morning, and the hotel's vacant rooms were in sudden demand. I tried to stay apart from Heinz and May, but she spotted me, and soon we were standing at the desk, arm in arm, a cosy threesome. I asked for my room key, prized myself from May's clasp, and once more said goodnight to Heinz. 'You must be crazy,' he said. 'Girls like these.' May was talking to the room clerk, jabbing a long red fingernail on the grubby page of the register. I made for the lift, but it closed just before I got to it. I was still waiting when they joined me. Fon carried the bottle of whisky, a walking tableau of innocence and experience. Heinz swung a door key jauntily in his hand, just as he would with his car-keys back home. May put her arm through mine once more, long body, cheap scent, lemonade breath.

'We got Room 527,' she said softly. 'It is just along from yours. We party all together, *na*? Then we go your room and we do it how you like.'

I felt myself sagging. She just wasn't going to give up. Well, obviously: from her point of view, two johns were better than one any day. It was imperative to get out now, to remove myself from her fluttering fingers, to avoid any fleshing out in the mind of 'doing it how I liked' with her. The stairs were just next to the lift. Stumbling through the knot of temporary lovers waiting for the lift, hearing an Australian voice say 'Hey, watch it, pal', I took the back stairs three at a time, and I was at my door, fumbling with the key, as I heard the lift arrive and disgorge its jovial cargo. I slammed the door shut behind me, fastened every lock and bolt provided, and sagged back against the door. Maybe this is what it's like to be sexually harrassed, I thought. Their footsteps passed, Heinz laughing like Father Christmas in the echoing corridor.

A voice was summoning me. I had to go up onto the stage. There was a beautiful girl up there, naked. She was banging in nails with a hammer that stuck out from between her legs. I said, 'No, I don't think I can do that,' and then I was awake. It took me a moment to work out where I was, and that it was Heinz calling my name and banging at the door. I looked at my watch. It was nearly four-thirty.

I called into the darkness, 'What do you want, for Christ's sake?'

A stream of German issued from the corridor. He did not sound happy. I stumbled across the room, threw back the bolts, and opened the door a crack. Heinz stood there, wild-eyed, in his ill-fitting safari shirt, a pair of white boxer shorts, and one sock. He was holding his leather handbag in one hand, and saying, 'Those little fucking bitches!'

No word of explanation was needed. The crumpled face, the loose dangling of the handbag like a wounded limb, told the story. He had fallen victim to the oldest trick of the oldest profession. In Thai, I later learned, they call it *lawk krap*, 'skinning the gecko'.

Reluctantly I ushered him in. I switched on the overhead light but he winced, and pawed unhappily at the brightness, so I turned it off again. The night sky was just beginning to pale. A lone motorcycle sped up the *soi* below. Heinz sat down heavily on the bed.

'So they ripped you off?'

He nodded. 'My head hurts,' he said. 'I think they put something in the whisky, after we . . . after I . . . *Ach*!'

'How much did you lose?'

'I don't know. My credit cards, some travellers' cheques, some dollars.' I tried not to show surprise that he'd been carrying so much around with him. I hadn't been complaining when he was picking up the tabs earlier. 'I don't exactly know how much,' he went on. 'The bitches took my glasses too.'

Part of me felt bad for him, part of me felt it was a touch of poetic justice, and part of me – the biggest part – wished to hell it wasn't my room he was in, my shoulder he was crying on, my obscure duty to lead him like some blinded bear through the ruins of his 'little private holiday' in Bangkok.

He had his elbows on his knees, his head in his hands. I thought for a moment he was going to vomit, but instead he sighed out a hollow kind of laugh and said, 'I think it is the most expensive blow-job in history, yes?'

With that, his torso sank slowly sideways onto my bed. He curled his great white legs beneath him, muttered softly to himself in German, and promptly fell asleep. I watched the dawn come up. There was unknown birdsong coming up from the vacant lot below. I tried to sleep in the chair, but it wasn't even comfortable to sit in. Eventually I relented, and so it was that I ended my first night in Bangkok, curled up beside a two hundred pound auto-parts salesman from Düsseldorf. I had been through many scenarios in my mind before I left on this trip, but frankly this hadn't been one of them.

Katai

I RECOGNIZED Katai straightaway at the station. Harry had told me she was tall for a Thai girl, and that she'd be carrying a big kind of carpet-bag. (He also told me to persuade her to leave most of the contents of her bag at the Noi: we'd be doing some foot-work up in the Triangle, and he didn't want anyone travelling heavy.) She was already there when I arrived. I hadn't been able to find a *tuk tuk*, and came slowly by trishaw instead. She was looking around expectantly, a still figure in the moving crowd, waiting to see Harry. She had black wavy hair fashionably cut: full on top, short at the ears and neck, a couple of rat's tails left long. She wore loose black trousers and a grey sweat-shirt with the words 'Hurts So Good' – the title of a song – printed above her left breast. Her tallness was boyish, willowy, small-breasted. Harry had called her, at one point, his *gamine*. I took this for a throwaway phrase meaning she was his girl, but it described well enough her urchin prettiness, her rangy look.

So here was a Thai girl waiting for her lover, and here was I, the hired gooseberry, hurrying in a little late, bearing the lover's letter in my already sweating hand.

'Katai?'

She focussed on the unexpected figure, proffering the envelope. 'I'm a friend of Harry's,' I said.

She smiled in her surprise. 'Oh, OK.' Then quickly, 'What happen to Harry? Harry OK?'

'Harry's fine,' I told her. 'He had to leave town. On business. He wants us to meet up with him.'

She was opening the letter. It was on lined yellow 'legal pad' paper. I could see it was a short message, in small sloping script. She went into a moment of privacy, listening to the words of the message. A fine, pale sheen was on her face: sleeplessness makes some faces grey and old, but others it makes shine. She folded the letter and put it in her pocket. A smile lit her face, she placed her hands together in a *wai*, and said, 'Thank you very much, sir!'

I picked up the carpet-bag. It was threadbare but had once been fine. The tortoise-shell handles were still warm from her hand. Just as Harry had predicted, the bag was heavy, and as we moved off its contents clanked against my leg.

We took a trishaw back into town, over the green Ping. *Sampan* glided beneath the bridge, watched by a group of Mien tribesmen, very Chinese in their pill-box hats and sashed black gowns. Katai smiled a lot. She was riding high on no sleep. It was the first time she had been in Chiang Mai.

'I never come to Lan Na before,' she said. 'I think it is very interesting.'

There was a snarl-up on the Tha Pae Road. The trishaw boy moved effortfully around a truck piled with sugar-cane. A traffic-cop was in the road making everything worse, and we came to a standstill.

'So we go to Chiang Saen together to find Harry,' she said. 'Shall we go there today?'

'I think it takes more than a day to get there.'

'Yes, but we *go* today. I don't want to stop now.' She thumped the side of the trishaw restlessly.

'Suits me,' I said, and a pang of adrenaline announced that my journey was properly beginning.

We were next to a couple of teenagers on Suzuki motorbikes. One of them – slicked hair, tight jeans, aviator sunglasses – kept grinning at Katai. He now leaned over and said something to her, doubtless suggestive. The other biker laughed. Katai didn't even look at him, just rattled out a reply, loud and nasal and very Bangkok. The boy looked surprised, his companion gave a whoop and a laugh, the trishaw driver turned round and stared at her.

We got underway again. I asked her what she had said.

'I am sorry, you will think me very bad. The boy say hello me. He call me *khai long*, little lost chicken. This is what we call the streetgirl, the girl who's lets a man take her home with him. Well, I don't like no one to call me *khai long*.'

'So what did you say to him?'

'I say *sakha bue din*. It means: your cock is on the ground, I tread it like a snake.'

We breakfasted on scrambled eggs and coffee at the Noi. She usually ate soup and rice for breakfast, she said, but now she was on holiday she would eat like the *farang*, who were always on holiday. She poked at one of the crusty white rolls that Guy was so proud of. They served rolls like this at the hotel where she worked: she called them 'dog's head bread'.

She was a room-maid at the Shangri-la, one of the high-rise hotels on the waterfront in Bangkok. She worked six days a week, sharing the entire fourteenth floor with one other maid. 'Twenty-eight rooms each, twenty-eight toilets to clean every day.' Her fine long-fingered hands were chapped and calloused. She earned 2,500 baht per month, and about the same again on service-charge and tips: in all some $200 a month. Being a secretary was a better job, and had a higher salary, but the tips made all the difference. She liked nationalities according to how they tipped. Americans, French and Italians were generous, Germans, British and Arabs were not. Best of all, she liked the Japanese. When the Japanese leaves a tip for the room-maid he puts it under the pillow. 'It is like a little secret between you, like getting a present when you're a kid.'

She was twenty-two years old. She had studied art for a year at Silpakorn University, but had to quit because of money problems. She wanted to be an artist, but there was no time for that now. Her father was dead. The family had some money, but she was the only real bread-winner. She had done a Hotel and Tourism course at the TAT college in Bang Saen. One day, perhaps, she would get into hotel management, get posted to hotels all over the world: Shanghai, Paris, New York. Harry was teaching her French already. '*Je t'aime*,' she said.

Her real name was Nopporn. She nearly died when she was born, so her father gave her a boy's name to give her strength.

Katai was just her nickname, but in Thailand your nickname is often used more than your proper forename: some are just diminutives, like Lek or Noi or Nid; others are taken from plants, colours, fruits, animals, etc, so for girls you have Nok (bird), Maw (cat), Tang (melon), Awi (sugar-cane), and for boys Mee (bear), Mo (piglet), Diang (red). One pretty girl I met was called Tum – rhyming with the last syllable of 'ee-bah-gum' – which was described to me as meaning 'a light swinging and tinkling, as of a pendant earring', perfect for the flighty girl who bore the name.

Katai means 'hare' or 'rabbit'. Why was she called that? 'Because I was born in the Year of the Hare' – in the West we know it as the Year of the Cat – 'and because I was born on the day of the full moon.'

I didn't understand the connection between the full moon and the hare. She couldn't believe it. 'You mean you have never seen the moon hare?'

'No, I don't think I have.'

She grinned. '*Farang* know nothing,' she said in her mock-tough way. 'I tell you about the moon hare sometime, and then you will know something more about Katai. But not now, because we must go to Chiang Saen, *na*?'

We finished our breakfast. Guy hadn't spoken to us yet. He'd zipped past several times, seeming distant and prissy. I guessed what he was assuming. He didn't mind a girl coming back for the night, but he didn't like them breakfasting here afterwards. They were supposed to slip off at daybreak, tiptoe down the balcony steps, clicking-clacking of the high-heeled shoes.

At a moment when he couldn't ignore me, I said, 'Guy, this is Katai. She's a friend of Harry's.'

She made a *wai*. Guy, charmed and a bit confused, said 'Oh, Katai from Bangkok? I did not know you were . . .'

He trailed off and looked at me uncertainly. 'Harry asked me to look after her,' I explained. 'We're all going to meet up at Chiang Saen.'

He was suave again. 'Harry has told me much about you.'

'Nothing good, I hope,' she replied. I guessed she was quoting Harry.

'Nothing but good, *mademoiselle*. I assure you.'

She lowered her head and said, *'Ka.'*

I told Guy I would be checking out shortly, and arranged to store some things here against our return. I went with Katai to my room, me to pack, she to unpack. She had meekly accepted Harry's orders to trim her baggage down. As I closed the door I saw Guy's quizzical eye on us.

Her bag was full of clothes and sandals and hair-brushes and sketch-pads, higgledy-piggledy; an electric water-heater, a can of Milo, tinned sweets to give to children, *The Teachings of Buddha* to give to Harry: 'he's so bad, he say he want to come back as a dog next time'. She tumbled it out on the bed, and selected the essentials. Among the things that went back in was a large, ornate, very business-like dagger, wrapped in a *sarong*. She called it a 'wedding knife'.

She went to take a shower. Like most Thais, she washed a lot and managed to look spruce in the hottest and dustiest circumstances. In matters of personal hygiene *farang* are secretly considered to be savages.

While she was in there, water running, I couldn't resist flipping over the little bit of lined yellow paper she had carelessly left lying on the bed. There I read, seeming to hear the stilted tones of the gem-dealer:

My Sweet Katai,

I have gone north. Come to Chiang Saen with my friend who brings this. I will meet you there Saturday at Tang Guest House.

Be careful. Always remember what we say: Eyes open, mouth shut.

And that I love you.

It was signed, 'Your mad dog.'

I drank it in for a moment: the rapid, sharp-angled script, the hardness and the softness of the words, the intimacy. I felt bad about looking, the sniffer at the keyhole. I heard Katai turn the tap off. I replaced the letter exactly where it had lain.

At the bar Guy shook hands with Katai. 'I hope to see you here again. Remember me to Harry, won't you.'

To me he said, as I settled up the bill, 'Take it easy up north. You'll have a good trip. Harry's a good man, but . . .'

'Crazy?'

'Crazy like a pirate if you cross him.'

We took a trishaw to the Arcade, where the buses go from, and by midday we were aboard the bus for Chiang Rai, seated near the back, windows wide open, fixtures rattling like maracas as we gathered speed, through the dusty outskirts, out past the lumber yards, the repair shops, the roadside stalls, the suppliers of spirit-houses, the shady temples, the stanchioned mango trees, the matted *klong*, the corrugated shacks, the scruffy edge-of-town allotments of rice and maize, and at last, at a point imperceptible to the eye but noted by the heart, into open country.

There are two routes between Chiang Mai and Chiang Rai, where we intended to break our journey. One is shorter in distance but the roads are bad, the other loops down through Muang Lamphun before joining the main north–south highway, Route One, on its last leg to Chiang Rai. Mainly by chance we were on the latter.

A few miles out of Chiang Mai we passed a sign to the right which said 'McKean Leprosarium'. Katai said, 'It does not tell you in the brochures that we still have lepers in Thailand.' The landscape broadened: paddy fields, metal-grey buffalo, orchards of longan and lychee. A glimpse of spires and golden *chedi* as we drove into Muang Lamphun, on the banks of the Kuang River. Lamphun was formerly the Mon city, Haripunjaya, which flourished in the days before the southward migration of the Thai. The city was subjugated by King Mengrai during his unification of Lan Na in the late thirteenth century. The Mons dispersed west and south to their present home on the Thai–Burmese border. They are one of the rebel tribes currently in conflict with the Burmese government. Three Pagodas Pass, where Harry and Khris had been when they boarded the train at Lop Buri, is controlled by Mon guerillas.

We picked up Route One, strung like a thread between the old towns of Lan Na: Lampang, Ngao, Phayao, Phan, each bearing the prefix 'Muang' in memory of its former state as the seat of some mediaeval Thai princeling. No time for historical rubber-necking now, the bus snorting impatiently as we purchase our pit-stop snacks, but the sights one sees along the road – the crocodile of orange-robed monks, the buffalo turning the rice-thresher, the palm-thatch huts, the bent figures in conical straw hats – are probably much the same as they were in the days of Lan Na.

The driver was a smooth little man in shades and a short-sleeved shirt with epaulettes. He had a Chinese-looking woman with him, very talkative: I was beginning to hear the broader tones of the local dialect, Kham Muang, now we were out in the sticks. The driver was in a hurry all through the journey. Once in alarm I grabbed at the seat in front, and Katai said sleepily, '*Farang* always fear to die. Thai people never fear to die. If it's time, it's time, no sense in worrying.'

'Ripeness is all,' I grunted, grabbing again as we side-stepped an oncoming convoy of army trucks. My hands left grimes of sweat on the plastic antimacassar.

At Ngao, Katai left the bus to take a pee, and we nearly left without her. The driver revved and hooted, and edged at the clutch. The bus strained like a dog on a leash. The vendors prepared for their last pitch, on the run. We began to pull out. I lurched down the aisle shouting in my best schoolboy Thai, '*Yout! Phuen young mai ma! Yout!*' ('Stop, my friend hasn't come, stop!'). There was kindly laughter such as an agitated *farang* usually engenders, and then Katai was there, loping aboard, grinning, playing to the crowd. She made a *wai* to me in the aisle. 'Thank you very much, sir,' she said. Everyone laughed, and I thought how beautiful she was.

At Phayao, she handed me a bagful of sliced fruit. I thought it was crisp green mango, a great roadside favourite. There was a little twist of polythene in the bag: salt, sugar and chilli to sprinkle over the fruit. But this wasn't mango. Katai said, 'This fruit is called *farang*, so I make you a present of it.' The taste was familiar, but elusive. I realized it was guava, but very different from the small, red-fleshed guava of South America. It was three times the size, its flesh paler, the taste less mealy and sugary. (Perhaps it is known as *farang* because it was introduced by French traders: they could have brought it from their colonies in the Caribbean, where it is native.)

The taste was different because the fruit had been picked so early. The Thai palate seems uneasy with ripeness. Mangoes are considered inferior in their fleshy orange ripeness: they are either eaten green, or just as they ripen. Then, delicate and peachy, they are whisked like Beaujolais Nouveau to the snack vendors, to be served with sweet, sticky rice, a consummate delicacy. The ripening of the mangoes in late March or early April signals the end of the long dry season. The first spittings of rain that come at this time are called the 'mango showers'.

We speared the slices out on little wooden picks. 'You like?' she asked.

'Very much.'

'So. What does the *farang* fear?

'Death?'

She cackled with laughter. 'No. *Farang* fear salt, sugar and chilli. It is Thai riddle, *na?*'

'Do you really not fear death?' I asked.

She shrugged. 'I am Buddhist. All Buddhists know that life goes on, that death is only a changing of forms. *Farang* always worries about what he has. Buddhist knows he has nothing. *Farang* is what we call *kio*. The *kio* is . . . I don't know . . . the man who drinks bloods?'

I didn't understand her. She said, 'I'm sorry, I must show you,' and made to bite my neck. It was unexpected. I moved. Her lips brushed my cheek.

'Oh, you mean vampire?'

'Ah yes, vampire. The *farang* is a vampire. He got to suck the blood out of everything. Harry, he's *kio*.'

'In what way?'

'He's always looking for something, always talking about the *big one* round the corner. I say: what is this big one, Harry? He says: I won't know until I find it.'

'Is he looking for the big one now?'

'Always.'

'Where's he gone, do you know?'

She smiled. 'I'm the same as you, Charlie. He don't tell me nothing.' I wondered if she was telling the truth, or if this was a case of 'Eyes open, mouth shut'.

At Phan we got a new driver, a bald man with an unlit cheroot permanently clamped between his teeth. He sat at the wheel like a Chinese Buddha. The ride changed its mood, became slower and more philosophical. The landscape grew wilder. We laboured up steep inclines, with sweeping views of the hills ahead. The paddies gave way to teak forest, broad savannah, moody outcrops of granite. We were in the foothills of the Shan mountains now. North and west the mountains stretched clear and unbroken to the Himalayas and the high plateaux of Tibet and Szechwan.

The light was opaque, faintly desolate, a dull haze drumming over the trees. The forest was just beginning to thin and desiccate at the outset of the hot season – early this year, and greeted with some fatalism by the locals. I wondered where Harry was, and what he was doing, and how this was all going to shape up.

Katai slept, her head on my shoulder, the smell of Tiger Balm where she had rubbed it on her forehead. I kicked my sandals off. The wind was warm in my hair. The bus rattled on up Route One, votive trinkets tinkling, little sticker on the sun-visor saying FOR GET ME NOT.

If we were in the foothills of the Shan mountains, we were also entering the southern stretches of the Golden Triangle, and though I was feeling good, feeling better all the time, there was this vague sub-text at the back of my mind, largely consisting of what Dixon had told me about 'the Triangle' that night at Tiger's.

What everyone knows is that the Golden Triangle means drugs, specifically raw opium and refined heroin. The whole Triangle area – about 150,000 square miles of hot rugged terrain spread through Thailand, Burma and Laos – produces something like 600 tons of opium a year. This is enough to supply forty per cent of the world's heroin market. Almost all of it is now produced on the Burmese side of the border, where the poppy is prolific and the forces of law and order non-existent.

But it wasn't the tons of drugs and the millions of dollars that Dixon was interested in. It was the fighting that inevitably goes with them. Dixon was an 'insurgency specialist', a regular contributor to *Soldier of Fortune*. He *liked* fighting, or anyway liked being around it.

Up in the Triangle, Dixon had said, there's not one but two quite distinct wars going on. 'I mean proper wars, sport: intermittent but pretty bloody nasty.'

The first is being fought for control of the Triangle drug-trade. This is a complex, four-cornered war. The most powerful faction is the Shan United Army, a fighting force of 20,000, run by the notorious Khun Sa. Khun Sa, whose real name is Chang Chi-Fu, is a half-Shan, half-Chinese in his early fifties. He processed his first morphine brick in northern Burma about twenty-five years ago, and has since risen to be the undisputed 'King of the Golden Triangle'. From their headquarters just across the Burmese border, his Shan bandits control the opium caravans, run the jungle refineries, and wholesale the heroin out through Thailand – which itself has half a million addicts – to Hong Kong, Singapore and points west. The second corner in the opium wars is occupied by the Kuomintang, or KMT. They are the remnants of Chiang Kai-Shek's defeated army, swept out of mainland China by the communists in the late 1940s. They set up in northern Thailand and Burma, and were armed by the Americans as anti-communist mercenaries: the 'watchdogs at the northern gate', as one old KMT general put it. They ruled the opium trade until the advent of Khun Sa in the mid 1960s. There are still about 10,000 KMT in Thailand, but as an army they are much depleted and curtailed, their old generals dead or senile. In the third corner – ideologically opposite to the KMT, but aligned with them against Khun Sa – is the Burmese Communist Party, which once looked to Peking for funds but now looks to opium. And in the fourth corner are the various anti-drug forces. The Thai 3rd Army is the spearhead, with the black-clad mercenaries called the Thai Rangers to do the dirtier work, and the US Embassy boys from the Narcotics Assistance Bureau in the background. They have succeeded in cleaning up the Thai end of the Triangle, and persuaded at least some of the hill-tribes to grow cabbages and strawberries instead of opium, but the main effect of this has been fatten Khun Sa's share of the market.

The other war in and around the Triangle, distinct but deeply intertwined with the drug wars, is the long-running conflict in Burma, between the tribal rebels and government troops. At least a third of the country – virtually all the high land north and east of the Irawaddy delta – is controlled by the rebels. The main guerrilla forces are the Karen and the Kachin, but there are in all eleven ethnic armies, with a total force of 20,000, banded together under the banner of the National Democratic Front. The Burmese civil war, said Dixon, is one of the most under-reported wars in the world. It has been rumbling on for the best part of forty years (ever since 1948, when the British granted the Burmese independence, but forgot the non-Burmese tribes) and claims many thousands of lives every year.

Both these wars belong geographically in Burma, but Dixon assured me that the fighting flared up frequently in parts of Thailand close to the border. 'You just have to be in the right place at the right time, and you've got a story.' He jabbed my chest with his beer-can. 'I mean, fighting just *is* a story, right?'

I can tell you now, so you won't be disappointed. I don't like fighting, and I didn't see any. I met some soldiers, and once or twice I heard gunfire, and that was about it. But right then, in the bus rolling north, I didn't know what kind of ticket I was carrying. A ticket to war in the Golden Triangle, a ticket to peace in the forest temple, or the usual aimless gadding in the plainer country between. I just didn't know.

It was late afternoon when we got to Chiang Rai. A trishaw took us through the scruffy, long-shadowed streets. We passed the long blank wall of the provincial jailhouse. We found a guest house down a side-street: it was really just a small wooden town-house with a couple of rooms to rent. One was taken by a Dutch couple, the other was free: twin beds, mosquito nets, no accoutrements.

We strolled out in the soft light. The new moon hung in the sky as the sun set. There was the scent of buddleia in the air. (I have heard this shrub's name derived from the Buddha, but it is in fact named after a botanist called Buddle.) We walked down the main street, Ban Pa Prakarn Road, dull concrete frontages, general stores, repair shops, eating-houses.

As we walked a black dog ran across the sidewalk in front of us. For me this was a homely sight, but something else for Katai. Dogs are not well thought of in Thailand: they are not taboo as in Arabia, nor are they eaten as in China, but they are low in the pecking-order of creation. It was odd that Harry had signed himself the 'mad dog'. It would be very rude to call a Thai that.

Katai said, 'The black dog is a bad sign. It is the spirit of someone coming to warn you, to make you take care.'

We dined on soup and rice in an eating-house off the main street, little tin tables, each with its fly-blown set of condiments: *nam pla* (literally 'fish water'), soy sauce, brown flakes of dried chilli, a plastic beaker filled with paper napkins so fine that on the first contact with greasy fingers they shrivel up to nothing. The people who ran the place were charming: easy and open in what I came to find was the Muang way, less subtle, less strategic than the plain-dwelling Siamese. The little boy brought his schoolbook to the table to show us, and a drawing, which I thought was of a circus, but turned out to be water-buffalo standing in a field.

There was the customary royal portrait on the wall: King Bhumibol Adulyadej – or Rama IX: he is a direct descendant of Rama I, Chao Phrya Chakri, the founder of the City of Angels – and Queen Sirikit. The picture showed them in their younger days. They have been on the throne since 1950, and King Bhumibol was now in his sixtieth year.

I asked Katai what she thought of the king. She put down her chopsticks and pushed her hand into her mouth.

I thought she had misunderstood the question, so I repeated it in beginner's English. She said, 'This means I would put my king's foot in my mouth to wash it.'

This was only typical. Most Thais are fanatical royalists, and you risk offence if you speak of the king without due deference. Centuries of absolute monarchy ended with the revolution of 1932, but the ethos remains strong. Unlike some of his predecessors, who blithely murdered their way to the throne – the traditional mode of execution for those of royal blood was to be placed inside a velvet sack and bludgeoned to death with sandalwood clubs – King Bhumibol seems to deserve the adulation. He is an attractive, high-profile figure, who spends a lot of time helicoptering around the remoter regions of the kingdom, setting up the Royal Projects one encounters everywhere: irrigation projects, hydro-electric schemes, schoolhouses, medical centres, immunization programmes, temple restoration, road construction, etc. The hill-tribes are devoted to him for championing their cause. Historians say he has revived the 'open monarchy' ideal of Sukhothai, when the famous King Ram Khamkaeng was said to be accessible to the meanest of his subjects. He is a cosmopolitan man: he was born in America, grew up in Switzerland, and speaks fluent English and French. He is a typical Thai blend of tradition and modernity, and the people love him.

Tonight Katai didn't want to talk about the king, though on other occasions she vouchsafed gobbets of royal gossip: that Queen Sirikit was the daughter of Thailand's ambassador to France, and they had met at Fontainebleau; that she, Katai, had heard the king on the radio playing saxophone, and that he had written a tune called 'Blue Day' which featured in a Broadway musical; that he was an accomplished sailor, and had won a gold medal at the Peninsular Games. She knew it all, just like our royal-watchers back home.

She wanted to talk about the black dog. It was worrying her. She was certain it was the spirit of her grandfather. He had died recently. She had travelled to Issan for the funeral. Issan is the old name for the vast poor flatlands of north-eastern Thailand: her father's family came from a village near Ubon Ratchathani, not far from the border with Laos.

'I tell you a story,' she said. 'One night I had a dream. I dreamed of a fish. It was swimming out of its fish-bowl, returning to the sea.

And in my dream I knew that the fish didn't want to go into the sea, even though it would be free there. It was trying to swim back into the bowl. In the morning my mama come in to tell me that grandfather has died. So you see, the fish was my grandfather's spirit, swimming out of this life. He didn't want to leave.

'And then there was something strange at the funeral, too. When we burned him, the fire wouldn't . . . wouldn't take the body properly. We had to cut down banana wood to make a fresh fire. Again it is like he was not wishing to leave. And now the dog.'

She snapped out of the mood and grinned. 'So, OK, even Thai fear death just a little . . . *Nid noi, na?*' She waggled her little finger. *Nid noi*, 'a little bit', always with this same gesture, was one of her catch-phrases. She used it particularly when she didn't like to say 'No', made it express a positive so doubtful, so infinitesimal, as to be really a negative. Harry once asked her whether she liked his friend Khris. 'Yes,' she said. *'Nid noi.'*

Though her father's family was from the north-east, her mother was from the south. You could see the mix in her. The tallness and the wavy, slightly negroid hair suggested the *negrito*, Malayo-Polynesian strain of the south. The wide face, the broad 'lion nose' (her phrase) and the sunny temper showed the Lao blood of the north-east. Her father had been a minor official in the national railway company. The family travelled. Katai was born at Nakhon Si Thammarat, a fishing town on the South China Sea. 'I'm what they call *Nakhon pio*,' she said, 'the sharp girl from Nakhon.'

When she was little, the family moved to Yala in the extreme south, close to the border with Malaysia. This was the late sixties: there was a lot of insurgent activity in the south: part Muslim, part communist. She talked of the south as a place of danger: many thieves, many Muslims, many bandits. She had no love for the Muslim, 'very bad people, always angry, always bad to their women'. To the rapacious south she contrasted Issan, her father's homeland, and Lan Na, where we were now travelling.

Her father was often absent. He was a distant father, and stern too: 'he pull my hair to make me learn the alphabet'. Her sister was mean, and wouldn't give her two baht to go to the movie-show that played in Yala once a week. So Katai, *Nakhon pio*, went to the market, and got work with a stall-holder, cutting the stalks off a heap of little red onions. The old woman paid her fifty satang an hour, so after an afternoon's work she could afford the movie after all. Her sister was surprised to see her there, and thought she had stolen the money. There was trouble. When her father found out the truth he was even angrier – that he, the important *fonctionnaire* of the national railways, should find his daughter hustling like an urchin in Yala market.

'But from that day on I knew I could do it. I knew I could make it for *myself*. In Thailand it is often the women who are the strong ones in the family. Chinese men work hard, but Thai men very lazy, too much *sanuk*.'

When daddy was away, she worked in the marketplace most afternoons after school. She collected left-over scraps of fish, and sold them by the kilo at the end of the day. In the durian season, she worked pulping the fruit for the ladies who make durian jam. For this she earned ten satang a kilo. She always chose the ripest durian to work with, softer and easier to pulp.

Her father died in a road accident when she was twelve. 'All the time he complain me, and then he go and leave me without saying goodbye.'

The family moved to Bangkok. They were well-enough off to begin with. They had a small rubber plantation in the south, property here and there. Katai finished high school: more strictness: 'they beat your fingers if your nails grew'. She lived on her wits in Bangkok. She teamed up with a young artist studying at Silpakorn, a Muang boy called Ti Am. They hung out around the Royal Palace. She used her charm and her good English to reel in the *farang*, and Ti Am painted their portraits.

'Teamwork, *na*?' Another of her catch-phrases.

She had three brothers and a sister – a fourth brother had died in infancy – but at the moment she was the family's only bread-winner. Her mother was not well, and sat at home chewing betel all day. Her sister was married. Her eldest brother lived down in Kantang, a small fishing and smuggling port on the west coast, where he had squandered family money on an ill-fated fish farm. Her other two brothers lived with her in Bangkok. The younger was a student, the other bone-idle. 'He lay at home all day. He change the TV station like this' – and she stretched out her bare foot, as if to flick a switch with her toe.

There was something touching and plucky about this girl. She was bright, capable, sceptical, artistic. She deserved more than she had got so far: maid's work in a hotel, heavy family responsibilities, ambitions faltering. She knew the easy way out: go on the game, use her maid's work to sell her body. There was no shortage of potential customers up on the fourteenth floor. But that wasn't her style: 'I sell my time to the hotel, but I don't sell myself to anyone. In Thailand we say, *Mai hai phet kae ling*: you don't give a diamond to a monkey.'

In some respects she was lucky, she knew that. Thailand is a poor country and she was relatively favoured. But for her too, poverty, or at least the ever-present threat of it, was a weight she had to carry. You saw this in her eyes, melancholy behind her big smile, and in the cracked, coarsened skin on her darting hands.

'All my life I run fast and get nowhere. I never stay still. All the bad things are waiting to catch you if you don't keep running. So you see, I am like the *katai* in that too. I keep moving to stay alive. This girl isn't very strong to fight, but this girl, she's quick. You better believe it.'

I asked her how long she had known Harry. She had met him a few months ago, she said. She was walking near the Yaowarat Road in Chinatown when a man she knew called out to her. He was drinking with a *farang* at a sidewalk noodle-shop. The *farang* was Harry.

'At first I don't like him. He smiles at me, he's very charming, but the things he says are . . . I don't know, not sweet. He seems like the hard man. Really he's not, but that's how he seems. Then when I get up to go he asks me to meet him again, and I don't want to. I really don't. I say: You don't want to meet me, you got plenty ladies. He says: Why you say that? I say: You must have got plenty ladies because you're so old.

'You see, I want to show him that I can be the tough girl too, and say the hard things.

'So, OK, I tell him: meet me under the Taksin Bridge on Saturday night. I wait there long time and he don't come, and when he comes he's so angry with me because he couldn't find which part of the Taksin Bridge I had meant. So really that was nearly it. We nearly never saw each other again.

'But, well, Charlie, you know how it is. You can't help who you fall in love with.

'I'm sorry, you are *farang*, but you will understand me when I say this: Harry is not like the other *farang*. He's not big, he's not rich, but he's very strong man. He knows how to be quiet, to listen. He says I have many things to teach him. It is not like the *farang* to say that.'

The waitress took our plates away, broke the mood. Katai was for a moment bashful, conscious of my inquisitiveness. I ordered another beer. She said, in her Bangkok drawl, '*Farang* always drink too much. Harry too. Sometimes he's so bad to me.'

She asked about my family, my home. I showed her a photo of my wife. 'Oh, she is very beautiful,' she said.

'Of course.'

She looked up at me with that satirical gaze. 'Of course!' she mimicked. 'Of course the *farang* gotta have pleetty wife. He have big house, fast car, pleetty wife.' She was putting on that tinkly kind of Thai voice which she called '*farang*-speak'. I didn't like it. It reminded me of May, the light-fingered tart at the Malaysia.

She asked to see a picture of my children. 'They are lovely. The boy so strong, the girls so pretty.' I nodded. She laughed. 'Now you *can* say "Of course". The daddy always think the best of his children, *na*?'

'Would you like to have children?'

'Some day. I gotta to find the good man first, though. I don't think Harry . . .' She laughed. 'He don't stay anywhere long enough to hang his hat.'

Her eyes met mine for a moment. She said, reflectively, 'I never go with a man who is married. I never want to be what you call the mistress. We have a saying in Thailand about the mistress. We say, *kin nam tai sawk*. This means to drink the water that runs down the elbow. You see, the husband gives the bowl of water to his wife. She drinks from it. And all the mistress gets is the little bit of water she spills, the water that runs down her arm as she drinks.'

That night I couldn't sleep. The mosquitoes seemed to know a way into my net. They grazed on their favourite pastures, the knobbly bits where the blood is closest to the skin: feet, ankles, hips, wrists. Lashings of Autan failed to deter them. Katai was long gone, making up for her lost night on the train. Once she started to mutter something, grating her face against her pillow. I tried to make out what she was saying, but I couldn't. She fell silent again in her cocoon of white netting. It was odd: I had met her only that morning, yet I felt I knew her well, felt I wanted to know her better.

I must have drifted off, because the next thing I knew it was morning, and Katai was standing over me, flushed and dewy from a walk by the river, holding a red flower like a lily out to me. She opened the shutters. The sun poured in, lighting up the dust of our lives.

Later, when we set out for breakfast, she got her purse out from under the pillow, and I noticed she had the big knife under there as well, wrapped up in its *sarong*. She saw me looking at it.

'Just in case,' she grinned.

'In case of what?'

But she was already out the door, two at a time down the steps to the street.

Morning had brought no noticeable activity to the scruffy, pot-holed streets of Chiang Rai, chalky concrete around the centre, wood and tin roofs elsewhere. There really isn't much to the place. It has had its glories – it was briefly a capital of Lan Na, founded by

Mengrai twenty-five years before Chiang Mai; and it was the place where the revered *Phra Keo*, the Emerald Buddha, was discovered in 1477 – but they are long gone. Even its more recent infamy is past. A few years ago, it was a major centre for the Golden Triangle drug trade. It is the nearest town of any size to the southern reaches of the Triangle, ideally placed as a wholesaling and trading post. Both the main actors in the Triangle heroin racket, Khun Sa and the KMT, made Chiang Rai their marketplace. In each case their actual headquarters were a few hours away – Khun Sa's at Hin Taek, the KMT's at Mae Salong and Tham Ngop – but Chiang Rai was where the deals were done, where the mustard got cut. There were frequent street shoot-outs between these two rival factions. In the early 1980s, the Thai 3rd Army moved in to clear up the area: the KMT's influence was waning anyway, and Khun Sa was chased back across into Burma in 1982.

It was a fresh morning: the town stands at a little under 2,000 feet, just enough to spice the air a little. We strolled down to the wharf. A long-tail boat was leaving for Ta Thon, a forty mile journey up the Kok River. A pleasant residential road led along the riverfront, shaded by tall mango and tamarind trees. We came to a hill called Doi Chom Thong, and climbed up the long staircase, fifty-two steps, to the temple at the top. The stairs were flanked by the traditional *naga*, as at Wat Phra Dhat above Chiang Mai, their dragon heads guarding the entrance, their undulant bodies forming a kind of stone bannister.

The *naga* is a complex, ambiguous figure in Eastern mythology. In essence it is a serpent-god associated with water. It represents both the dangerous powers of the great rivers, and the life-giving benison of water. In the lore surrounding *songkran* – the Thai New Year, celebrated in early April – the *naga* is the great rain-maker, a serpent-god who sucks up water from the oceans and spouts it over the paddy fields. At the firework festivals, *bun bung fai*, also rain-making ceremonies, the rockets are traditionally fired from launchers in the shape of a *naga*. When someone dies in the river they are said to have been devoured by the *naga*.

According to Thai lore, the *naga* is one of four supernatural beings – the others are the *garuda* (a kind of gryphon), the *kumbhanda* (a giant) and the *gandhabba* ('celestial sirens') – that weigh our life's accounts when we die.

In the north-east, Katai said, there was a *naga* story about the great swamp of Nong Harn in Sakhon Nakhon Province. Many centuries ago, when the land was ruled by the Khmer, the king ordained that there should be a firework festival to celebrate the birthday of his daughter. A *naga* came to watch the festival disguised as a white squirrel. The princess spied a beautiful jewel worn round the neck of the squirrel, and asked her huntsmen to kill it. When their arrows pierced the squirrel's body it turned back into the form of a *naga*. The king ordered the *naga*'s body to be cut up and eaten by all the people. When the *naga*'s father heard about this, he sent flood and devastation to the kingdom, which remains today an uninhabited swampland.

'This,' said Katai in a matter-of-fact way, 'shows how dangerous the *naga* can be if he is not treated right.'

So why, I asked, were the temples guarded by *naga*?

'Let me tell you about the *naga* and the Buddha. The Buddha was loved by all the animals of the forest. When he meditated alone in the forest, the monkey brought him honey from the trees, and the elephant brought him water in her trunk. So too the great serpent-god, the *naga*. It coiled its body into a seat for the Buddha to sit on. This shows how the Buddha was in control of the wild forces of the world. When the Buddah died at Kusinagara, the serpent turned its body into a flight of steps for the Buddha to climb up to the heaven. So today we have *naga* stairs to lead us up to the temple.'

At the top was a scattering of temple buildings and pagodas. We walked into a small side-temple. Katai seemed to know what she was doing. I just followed. An elderly couple was in the temple, busy and silent, preparing flowers for an offering. There was a small gilded Buddha surrounded by the customary votive bric-a-brac: joss, *puang malai* garlands, little rice sweetmeats in banana-leaf cups.

On another altar was a boiled chicken sitting in a silver-gilt dish. This was an offering to a spirit, Katai said. There are many spirit-cults in Thailand, and especially here in the north. They seem to co-exist happily with the more formal doctrines of

Theravada Buddhism. In India the Hindu *brahman* and the Buddhist *bikku* belong to opposed, exclusive traditions, but here the old animist lore mingles in with the Buddhist mainstream. The Thai have this genius for tempering, for accommodation and adaptability. Their 'cool heart' is a product of this, and their stability in a region of political extremes, and their easy-going Buddhism, so attractive to *farang* that some call it 'Coca-Cola Buddhism'.

Katai showed me the special *wai* that is reserved for the Buddha. You make the usual prayer-hands, palms together, fingers up, then bow your head till your forehead touches your fingertips. For full obeisance to the Buddha, she went on, you must touch the ground at five points: your knees, your forearms, your forehead. This is called *pen chang kapradit*, the five-fold worship. She did it so gracefully. I followed suit so clumsily. I got it wrong, my palms up, instead of flat to the floor. 'Not like that,' she said, laughing. 'That's like the Muslim.'

'So,' she said briskly, 'shall we see what our fortune is?'

As in most temples there was a *seeam see*, a canister of 'fortune sticks'. The canister was a section of bamboo stopped at one end. The fortune sticks were thin, yellowed lengths of wood like spillikins. She knelt before the Buddha, and shook the canister up and down until one of sticks popped out and fell to the floor. It was Number Eighteen. She went to the little chest-of-drawers on the side, about two foot square, doll's house furniture. She opened the drawer marked '18' to take out the relevant fortune paper. Typically this is a small page, with Thai script on one side and Chinese characters on the other. It gives both a seven-day fortune and a more general prognosis.

The drawer was empty.

Katai was put out by this. She went over to the old couple. They were still quietly working, threading flower heads. They listened to her complaint. They shook their heads, looked at one another, shook their heads some more. There didn't seem much they could do about it.

'To have the bad luck coming, that's OK,' she said as we walked back down the serpent steps. 'You know you got to have the bad luck sometime. But to have no luck, no fortune, *nothing* – well, Charlie, that's bad.'

It was another sign. It was like the black dog, like the oddities of her grandfather's death. Something was amiss in an unseen part of her world, something she couldn't quite make out. I was learning how important these things were – the Buddha and the King, serpent-gods and fortune sticks – and how urgently they spoke to her.

Mekong Days

CHIANG SAEN: a 'one elephant town', as Harry put it. It's little more than a large riverside village now, snug in an elbow of the Mekong where its southward flow out of China begins to bend east. The population is two thousand or so, farmers and fishermen, teak-loggers and workers at the government tobacco-kilns on the edge of town. In Chiang Saen, more than anywhere else in northern Thailand, you feel the presence of old Lan Na. The town is full of temples and scattered ancient *chedi*, looming among the trees, lop-sided and dilapidated, plinths with small trees growing out of them, grey plaster crumbling back to reveal red brick, the brick itself decomposing back into the tawny local soil from which it was first baked. In and around these forlorn mementoes, present-day Chiang Saen goes about its quiet business: a main street, a bus park, a market, a brief grid of wood and tin houses leading right up to the edge of the river, the edge of Thailand. The river forms the border here. Across the other side is Laos.

We checked in at Tang Guest House, where we had arranged to meet Harry. It was a small wooden house on the riverside road, up on the northern fringes of the town. You wouldn't have known it was a 'guess how'. There was no sign outside, and there seemed to be no other guests. It was run by a diminutive Muang girl called Suree. Sure, she knew 'Mister Harry'. No, she had heard nothing from him since he had last been here, a few months ago, in the rains. It was Friday afternoon now, twenty-four hours before he was due to meet us.

There were small cell-like rooms off a verandah. The windows of the rooms looked back onto the dusty yard – chickens, clothes lines, washing places – but the verandah looked out across a high tangle of bankside greenery to the hazy grey waters of the Mekong.

I lay on my bed smoking a cigarette, spellbound by the rectangle of brightness at my open door. I could hear Katai a couple of doors down. She was moving around, unpacking her bag, folding stuff, being neat and domestic. She had done the same the night before in Chiang Rai, and I had done the same too, lain on my bed smoking, feeling hot and indolent and obscurely happy.

The empty room between us was, I supposed, for Harry.

We strolled up Main Street, full of noodle-shops and general stores, and past Wat Pa Sak, the Temple of the Teak Trees. A thin old monk in spectacles was at the gate of the temple, spearing up fallen teak leaves and putting them in a sack. He hailed us as we passed. He spoke English. He said, 'I have no work to do, so I do this. There are always leaves.' He asked us to come and visit him tomorrow.

The light was softening and we walked around the edge of town. The streets shaded off into ragged, fertile plots of maize, tomato and tobacco. We skirted round, moving west and north by the sun, expecting to be coming back along the riverfront at sunset, but as the gloom gathered we found ourselves further from town than we thought. We were walking down a sandy, scrub-bordered track. We could hear the sounds of the town, vivid in the still evening air: the gunning of a motorbike, the barking of dogs, the calling of the boatmen. We couldn't see the river, but could sense it where the sky seemed open and spacious above it.

Katai was quiet. She walked so slowly I had to keep checking myself. It was dark now. We were coming back into the outskirts: a few scattered houses, knotty acacia-wood fencing.

She said, 'Why you hurry? You got a train to catch?'

I said, 'I'm not sure where we are.'

She laughed. 'What does the *farang* fear?'

'Salt, sugar and chilli.'

'Right. You tell me how you want to see the Golden Triangle. Well, here we are. Shall we go and meet someone?'

'Meet someone?'

'Yes, of course. You must meet the people, *na*?' We were standing by the gate of a house, apparently unlit. She walked in the gate, leant against the wooden ladder that led up to the verandah, and called out in the Muang idiom she was busy picking up: *'Sawadee, chow!'*

I heard movements in the house. 'Do you really think we should just barge in like this?' I whispered.

'We will do the interview,' she said firmly. 'I will translate for you.'

A man appeared on the dark verandah above us. I couldn't see his face. Katai asked him if we could stop and rest here. He answered softly. She turned to me and said, 'He invites us to take water here.'

To 'take water' at a house is meant literally. Wherever you go in northern Thailand you will find a pitcher of water, the *han nam*, outside the entrance of a house. Often there are two: one for drinking, the other for washing your feet. It is basic Muang hospitality to offer water to someone, friend or stranger.

The pitcher stands at the bottom of the steps, with its own little leaf-thatch awning. The invitation to take water may or may not be followed with an invitation to ascend the ladder, onto the verandah or entrance platform, called the *jaan*. In this case it was.

'So shall we go up?'

'Why not?'

We kicked off our sandals and climbed the wooden steps. The man who greeted us was a man of about thirty, a farmer, with a quiet graceful wife, and three children. His name was Boul. We sat on the floor of the *jaan*. He lit a small wick-lamp. It became the centre of our grouping. Katai asked him all sorts of questions for my benefit. She seemed to have no inhibitions. He answered politely, *'kap'* at the end of every phrase, deferent but apparently unsurprised by this sudden visitation in the dusk.

He farmed a smallholding which he shared with a couple of neighbours. They bought the land for 40,000 baht per *rai*. (The *rai* is the traditional Thai unit of land: about two fifths of an acre.) He mainly grew tobacco. The harvest, which lasted from September to January, had recently finished. All of his crop was bought up by the state tobacco monopoly, and processed at the factory on the edge of town, a ramshackle structure of corrugated tin, with tall stacks belching smoke like some Stygian furnace. He had a stash of his own home-dried tobacco in an earthenware jar. He rolled me a generous cheroot, using a section of dried banana leaf for a cigarette paper. He sprinkled in a handful of wood shavings. The wood is called *kio*, and gives a pleasant aromatic taste to the smoke. This type of cheroot is called a *burri kio*.

Katai complimented him on the house. He had built it himself, of course. He explained to us that all the houses of the Muang are built according to the compass. The purlins (*pae*) run north–south, and the cross-beams (*khue*) run east–west. The reception part of the house where we were now sitting, the *huean noi*, or 'little home', is at the southern end. The private part, the *huean yai* or 'big home', is to the north. The family altar and the spirit house stand by the eastern wall. The east is auspicious. The west is the direction of death.

Not only are the houses laid out like this, he said, but so too are the old Muang towns like Chiang Saen. Its long main street runs north–south, and the cross streets east–west. He said, speaking simple Thai for me, 'The house and the village are the same. House like a small village, village like a big house.' His point was backed up by the fact that the standard Thai word for 'village' and 'house' is the same: *ban*.

Also, when a Muang describes directions in a town he uses terms that belong to house-building. The town's north–south axis is called *luang pae*, the 'direction of the purlins', and its east–west axis is called *luang khue*, the 'direction of the cross-beams'. Most Muang towns are built alongside a river, and most of the big rivers in northern Thailand flow south. The Muang words for 'north' and 'south' are the same as the words for 'upstream' and 'downstream'.

Boul told his son, who was ten, to show me his English books. Most of these were Thai productions, based on the pictorial work-books used in our own primary schools, but one book caught my eye. This was a seasoned old campaigner, mottled with ink and finger-smudges, with a dull green cover reminiscent of *Kennedy's Latin* – or, as it was invariably altered, *Eating – Primer*. The book was called *Many Lands*, *One Flag*, being 'A Brief History of the British Empire, Written in Basic English Suitable for Native

Students'. It was by one P. B. L. Frobisher, MA, FILC, Dip Ed, &c, Asst Vice-Comm, Punjab. It was printed at Delhi in 1923. On the fly-leaf, among later rubber-stampings in Burmese and Thai script, was the name of the original owner, in spidery blue-black ink: K. Ranjit Singh. And beneath it, 'Maymyo, 1926'.

For a moment I thought I had stumbled upon a real bibliophilic curio: a schoolbook owned by the legendary cricketer, Prince Ranjit Sinhji (or 'Ranji'). Sadly the dates were wrong: Ranji was stroking them through the covers at the turn of the century. It was none the less curious to find this book, with its fly-spotted pages, its Kiplingesque line-drawings, its grey, stingy type-face, its smell riffling up at me a redolence of old class-rooms, a quintessence of chalk dust, disinfectant soap, pencil shavings and the school-dinner farts we called 'eggies'.

Maymyo is a former British hill-station in Upper Burma, an outpost of the Raj. As the crow flies, and as the smuggler travels, it is a couple of hundred miles north-west of where we were now sitting. The book must have come along the old caravan trails through the Shan hills, a bit of flotsam in the giant flow of contraband between Burma and Thailand, a two-way traffic that covers everything from Double Globe heroin to Pepsi Cola (which fetches up to two dollars a can in Mandalay).

It was strange to come to the Golden Triangle and find an old British school book as my first instance of cross-border traffic. This wasn't what I'd expected: to be sitting in the hot Mekong night, thinking about my schooldays, feeling that they'd happened to someone else.

We met the old monk the next day, in the big open-sided *sala* of Wat Pa Sak. We sat beneath a large gilded Buddha in the sleek, etiolated, Burmese-influenced style of Lan Na. His name was Moonsong. He was a thin, knotty, myopic man. He said he was seventy but he looked younger. He was unshaven, his orange robe creased and tattered, his heavy spectacles sellotaped at the hinges. He had once been a *tuk tuk* driver in Bangkok. He showed us an old photo: a tough bare-chested man leaning against the door of a repair shop. It's odd how the monk's robe seems to partition the wearer off from 'normal' life, so one is surprised at this secular past. He had gone into the monkhood twelve years ago, seven of those spent as a novice.

Did he prefer being a monk?

'Of course.' Then, with a little laugh, 'Most of the time.'

He was keen to practise his English. He taught English to the temple boys of the locality. There were certain rather specialist points he wanted me to explain to him. On the blackboard in the *sala* I defined as best I could the distinction between angels and fairies. I corrected his impression that Martin Luther was a 'famous English monk', and that Henry VIII had murdered him. I said he was thinking of Thomas à Becket and Henry II. Luther is a well-known figure in Thai religious circles, because he opposed a corrupt and mercenary clergy, and because, as Moonsong now put it, 'he taught that God was inside us, not' – he gestured to the raftered roof of the *sala* – 'up there. So it is with Buddhism. It is just following the good inside you, and putting aside' – an effortful pushing-away gesture – 'the bad.'

I said, 'It is difficult to put aside the bad.'

'Of course,' he said quickly, a touch of irritation in the reedy voice. 'Of course. The spirit of Mara is always ready to make trouble. But look.' He gestured up at the bronzed Buddha above us. 'You see our Buddha here. He is seated on Mara. Mara is all that you wish for, all you desire. The Buddha has risen above this, and now he may sit in meditation on top of Mara.'

Mara was in the form of a serpent coiled up like a cushion beneath the Buddha. I remembered Katai talking of the *naga* performing this office for the Buddha, and asked if they were the same.

'Mara is much greater,' said Moonsong. 'The evils of water brought by the *naga* are perhaps a part of Mara's work, but the *naga* brings the good things of water too. No, Mara is *phanyaa mahn*, the Prince of Demons. If you do not know it, I will tell you the story of Buddha and Mara.'

We settled at his feet, which were dusty and crooked.

'When our Buddha attained to truth beneath the *bodhi* tree,

Mara gathered an army of demons to bring fear to him. Mara rode at the head of the army on his war elephant, Giri Mekhala. But the goddess of the earth, who we call Nang Thoranee, saw that the Buddha was about to be engulfed by demons. She squeezed all the waters from her hair and sent down a flood to drown the demons.

'So next, Mara sent of plague of rats to devour the holy scriptures. The Buddha created at that moment the first cat in the world. She is called Phaka Waum. She chased away the rats, and preserved the truth of the Buddha's teaching, and to this day we consider it a great wrong to kill a cat.

'Now Mara hurled his most terrible weapon, a great thunderbolt, but the Buddha caught it in his hand, and there and then he turned it into a garland of flowers, like the *puang malai* you see hanging on his neck now.

'Last, Mara sent his three daughters to tempt the Buddha. His three daughters are Aradi, discontent; Tanha, desire; and Raka, love. Well, this was the hardest fight for the Buddha, because now he was fighting the dangers inside himself. But the Buddha resisted their charms, and so today we say: the power of *dharma* – the truth of the Buddha – can save us from the all the dangers inside us and around us.

'So, yes, of course it is difficult to put aside the spirit of Mara. We must learn to turn our desires into beautiful flowers. We must learn to place ourselves above Mara, like the Buddha does. Not only so that we can be above Mara, but so that we can *see* the dangers. They are outside us: desires and discontents. They are no longer part of us.'

'They are part of life.'

'Yes, in one sense. But we Buddhists say, rather, they are part of death. They are part of the world that dies. Mara is a principle of death. That is why he is not the same as *naga*. The *naga* is dangerous, but he is a principle of life. In the Festival of Lights in Thailand, the *Loi Kratong*, it is said that it was a king of the *naga*, Phra Upagota, who finally helped to capture and conquer Mara. This was in the time of King Asoka, who brought the Theravada teachings of Buddhism into Thailand.'

'But aren't desire and discontent a principle of life too?' I persisted.

His lined face looked down at me, a little rabbit-toothed pout. He said cryptically, 'After noon a monk may not eat, but he may take water at any time.'

'I don't understand.'

'Food is what you want, water is what you need.'

He went still for a moment, eyes focussed on something beyond us, mouth still showing two yellow teeth. I started to say something, but Katai laid a hand on my arm, and put a finger to her lips.

I heard the leisuredly rattle of a dried-up teak leaf tumbling from the tall canopy. The temple was called Wat Pa Sak because two hundred teak trees had gone into making its enclosure.

After a bit he looked at me and smiled. 'Your Luther says: *Pecca fortiter, sed fortius fide*. Sin strongly, but believe more strongly. I think that is a good beginning for us all.'

He climbed wearily to his feet, and began to rummage in a wooden chest near by. He brought out a little medallion: a tiny tin Buddha inside a triangular blob of perspex. Katai said, 'It is a *phra kliang* to hang around your neck.'

I made a *wai* and took it from him. Katai too made a *wai*, and I got the feeling she was thanking him for what he done to 'enlighten' me, a poor *farang* who knew nothing. Phra Moonsong received our thanks with a slight bow, but no *wai*.

Katai said quietly, 'He would like you to give money for the temple.' I handed some notes to him. She too gave him money, but she placed the notes on top of the wooden chest. A monk may not take anything directly from a woman's hand.

'Thank you,' Moonsong said, 'for teaching me about Martin Luther, and about Thomas the Becket. I shall tell my pupils.' He thought for a moment. 'So. Is it right: "Who will rid me of this turbulent priest"?'

'Perfect,' I said.

He grinned, impish, pedantic. 'Never perfect,' he said. He ambled off. At the edge of the *sala*, where its shade met the shimmer of the midday light, he met another monk. They conversed for a moment, a faint breeze catching their robes, a few more teak leaves slowly falling, and then they went their separate ways.

Harry was due that night but he didn't show. We sat out on the verandah, burning joss to keep the mosquitoes at bay. I got hungry and suggested we go down to Porn's noodle-shop on Main Street. This had become our regular eating-place. Katai had no desire to 'experiment' in the *farang* way. We had happened into Porn's on the first evening: the atmosphere was friendly, the bean-curd soup delicious, and from then on we took just about every meal there.

Katai said she'd wait, in case Harry came.

'We can leave a note,' I said.

'I'll wait anyway.'

She sat on the floor of the verandah with her chin on her knees. She had put on that same T-shirt again, freshly laundered, the one that read 'Hurts So Good'. Harry had given it to her.

When I got back from Porn's, the light was on in her room. I tiptoed past, but the verandah creaked. Her door opened.

'Oh, hello Charlie.' She tried not to sound disappointed, but I knew she was, and I knew that was why I had tiptoed.

'Harry's not here, then.'

She shook her head.

'He'll be here tomorrow. You'll see.'

She leant in the doorway. The cicadas trilled, the dark smell of the river came up to us: the unseen so close around us all the time. She had a dreamy look. I thought she might cry, and I might have to take her in my arms.

Instead she grinned, put on her cynical Bangkok drawl, 'Yeah. Mad dog come tomorrow. Mad dog say he sorry. I should kick him away, but . . .'

I nearly said, 'Maybe you should,' but I stopped myself. The room behind her, half-seen through the doorway, exuded an indefinable softness, and her voice was soft again as she said, 'Goodnight, Charlie.'

'Goodnight, Katai.'

Her door closed and I went to my room, where old tobacco smoke hung in the air, and my clothes lay where I had left them.

Waking in the little wooden room, chinks of brilliant light in the shutters, strange birdcalls, a rattle of pots and pans in the cooking area, another hot day on the way. A gecko cackled above the door as I walked out onto the verandah.

Katai was down in the yard talking to Suree. She had got the morning organized. We were borrowing a couple of bicycles and going for a picnic.

At the market we bought fruit and beer and Coca-Cola, and a bagful of cooked rice and vegetables, and some quids of *miang* (fermented tea and spices wrapped in a leaf: you hold it inside your cheek, refreshing and faintly stimulant). We set off south, into the sun, past the tobacco factory, across small bridges, the river on our left and the promise of the hills in front of us. Katai wore a wide-brimmed straw hat she had borrowed from Suree. It was a bit too big, and blew off her head as she cycled. She chattered and joked, talking back over her shoulder. I could only hear half of it. She had lost the melancholy of the previous evening. Harry wouldn't come till tonight, she said, so we might as well enjoy the day.

Watching her pedal down the hot dirt-road, hat on her back, baggy black trousers and black singlet, she seemed to me the quintessence of South-east Asia. I thought of a phrase of Harry's: *Indochine, mon amour*.

The heat shimmered in the trees, mostly low and scrubby, occasional giant shade-givers. Passing vehicles set up a cloud of dust which left us choking by the roadside. After a while we stopped to rest and wash the dust out of our throats. Katai grimaced at the taste of the sterilizing tablets I had put in the water. On we went, past Chiang Saen Noi, with its old temple on the hill. The road curved east. We crossed the Kok River, which here joins the Mekong, and at a village called Ban Sae we left the road and followed a bumpy riverside track, skirting an alluvial plain filled with rice stubble.

By early afternoon we were ready for our picnic. We found a track leading down to the river's edge, past scorched plots of tobacco and maize. There was a palm-thatch shed, too small to live in, perhaps a crop-store or a fisherman's shelter. It was shaded by a stand of banana trees, the unripe green fruit clustered, the mauve tendril hanging down like a tassled bell-pull in a Victorian drawing-room. Here we left our bikes. I took a swim. The river was very low: I was still in my depth several metres out. A long pale sandbar basked in the middle of the river. The water was surprisingly cold. Despite the appearance of slowness, the current was powerful as soon as you left the shallows.

We ate and drank. The Singha beer was sweet and warm. I lay back in the grass, drowsy and content, content in a way I hadn't felt for years. Bangkok seemed like another world. Even Harry seemed distant and vague, someone I had known long ago. I wondered if he was really going to turn up at all: part of me wanted him to come, and part of me didn't, and I was too sleepy to work out which part was right.

Then Katai said, 'I want to go across.'

I said sleepily, 'Across where?'

'Across there.' I looked up, squinting in the glare. She was sitting cross-legged beside me, looking across to the hazed, scruffy tree-line of Laos on the far bank.

'You're crazy,' I said. 'No one goes to Laos. They lock you up in a re-education camp if they catch you, and then they throw away the key.' This is the basic lore about communist Laos.

'There's no one there to see us.' She was on her knees now, scanning the horizon. 'Look, there's nothing there.'

'So why – '

'Because I never been to another country before, that's why. Because I got no passport, no money, no way to travel in the world like the *farang*. I want you to take me to Laos, Charlie.'

'And back,' I muttered, still thinking of the warnings I had heard about Laos, but the way she looked at me right then, I would have taken her to the moon.

'Look,' she said, 'We can get to that sandbank there, and then we're almost there.'

'It's deceptive,' I said. 'How well do you swim?'

She didn't answer. Instead she told me to turn my back. When she was ready – a *sarong* knotted above her breasts and tucked between her legs, the traditional bathing-gear for a Thai woman – she put out her hand to me, and we walked together into the Mekong.

We got across to the sandbank without too much difficulty. We could wade until we were about fifty yards from it. Then we had to swim. The current was strong, but the sandbank stretched for a good half mile, and there seemed no danger of getting swept out past it. We let the river take us, swimming diagonally. Katai swam like a child, doggy-paddle.

Our feet touched ground again and we waded ashore. The sand was speckled with fool's gold. It was strangely elastic: our feet sank in, but didn't break the crust. We left no footprints behind us. We walked back along to the upstream apex of the sandbank, and contemplated the second leg of the crossing. It was not much wider than the stretch we had come across, but it looked faster and deeper. This was the business side of the river: the stretch we had crossed was a meander in comparison.

'I don't like the look of it,' I said.

'What does the *farang* fear?'

'Salt, sugar and getting drowned in the Mekong, that's what.'

She looked disappointed. 'Well, I'm sorry, Charlie, but I must go over alone then.'

'You're crazy,' I said again.

She stood irresolutely on the shoreline. I saw birds rising and wheeling above the trees on the far bank. Then I heard a voice behind us, away down the far end of the sandbank. A man had come across on a bamboo raft. He was waving at us.

We walked on down. He was an old man with a wizened monkey face and close-cropped hair the colour of tarnished metal. He was from a village called Ban Suan Dok a few miles further up the riverside track. He had a plot of vegetables here: tomatoes, cucumbers, and a small root-plant that looks like a refined type of potato, and has a sweetish crispy taste. He must have carried earth over to mix with the sand.

Katai asked if he thought we could swim across to the Lao bank. He laughed and wagged his forefinger at her. '*Ra wang*,' he said. 'Take care. The river is very strong.'

'Will you take us across in your *sampan*?' I asked. 'We will pay for the crossing.'

He looked at me suspiciously. He said to Katai. 'Why does the *farang* want to go over?'

'We just want to go to Laos,' she said.

He shook his head, grinning. 'But little girl, you are in Laos now.'

We stared at him. I said, 'You mean this is Laos, right here?' He nodded. He took up his bamboo punt-pole, and ran it along the shoreline of the sandbank.

'*Chai daen*,' he said. The border.

He ambled off to his plot, watered it with scoopfuls of river-water. The opportunism of the peasant farmer: this stretch of land would be covered when the Mekong was in spate, but meanwhile he wasn't going to waste it. After a while he started pulling the raft back down into the water. He asked if we wanted a lift back.

I said, 'It's OK, we'll swim.'

'*Ra wang*,' he said again, and punted off downriver towards the Thai bank.

'So how does it feel to be in another country?' I asked.

She shrugged. 'Same same,' she said.

We should have taken up the old farmer's offer. On the way back to the Thai bank we were careless. We set off from the sandbank further downriver than where we had arrived. We soon found the channel was deeper and the current stronger than before. We tried to push back upstream, but the water was up to our chins, and every step was an effort.

Katai started to get frightened. 'Charlie, I don't like this.' Her voice was shrill.

I said, 'It's OK, if it gets too strong we can go back to the sandbank, try further down.'

'Yes, let's go back, please.'

But somehow we couldn't. The river seemed to have closed in around us. Whichever way we turned the water deepened. Just to stand still was getting an effort: the current wrapping around our legs, the silt squeezing between our toes, pulling us off towards the China Sea.

'We'll have to swim for it,' I said, trying to sound calm. I wasn't at all sure about this – there seemed a real danger of getting swept out past the sandbank, and then we'd really be in trouble – but there didn't seem any choice.

'Charlie, I'm frightened.'

'Swim!' I shouted. We struck off together, towards the Thai bank. The current beat against us, and for a while we were swimming furiously without seeming to move forward at all. I heard her choking, belching. I knew that once someone starts to take in water they get weaker by the second. I trod water, ready to help her, and as I did so my feet touched bottom.

'Look, I can stand!' I shouted. She was looking pretty wild, breathing heavily. I held her in my arms, keeping her chin up, letting us both rest. 'It's OK,' I said. 'We've crossed the deep part. We can walk now.'

Or could we? The topography of the river was strange and treacherous. We were just a hundred yards downstream from where we had set off – I could see our clothes piled on the bank there – but everything was different. As soon as we started towards the bank I felt the river-bed shelve away beneath us. I noticed too that the bank was steep here, red earth and roots showing, a good four or five feet between the water and the level ground.

We were swimming again now, caught in a whipping eddy, Katai spluttering and squawking. I tried to help her, but I'm no life-saver and things only got worse. She flailed, rapped me in the face with her elbow. She was taking in water again.

'Oh no, oh no,' she cried.

Then suddenly the current changed again, and we were bobbing off towards the bank. I saw the farmer's raft in a little inlet. When we were close enough I let go of Katai. The current threw her against the stern of the raft. She grabbed hold of it. I was swept on for a bit, out of sight of her, but soon managed to grab the loop of a root in the bank.

I hung there gasping and grateful. I realized we had nearly drowned. I heard Katai call my name, whether for help or out of concern for me I didn't know. I called back, 'You OK?'

'No.'

She was sitting in the mud, coughing and choking. The old man was kneeling beside her, holding her head down between her knees. She had taken in a lot of water. As she coughed it out, she was crying.

'Oh God, I thought we both gonna die,' she said when she saw me.

'We were OK, Katai, *no pompen*,' I said unconvincingly.

'Oh God,' she said again. She would never have sworn by the Buddha, but she had heard *farang* saying 'Oh God' and 'Oh Jesus' all the time.

The old man was talking to her quietly. I couldn't understand what he was saying to her, and she wasn't about to translate for me. Later she told me: 'The old man say to me I am very lucky girl. He say the river is hungry. That was his word: *hungry*. He say that every year, before the rains come, someone drowns in the Mekong. Last year it was a boy from Chiang Mai: he was a very strong swimmer but the river take him. The people here say that if the river does not take someone, the rains will not come, the crops will die.'

'Like a sacrifice,' I said.

'Yes. It is the *naga* of the Mekong. He must take someone. In return he will bring rain.'

We cycled back down the sandy track to Chiang Saen. The sun was bleached out with a heavy haze. It hung over the river, over our heads. It made it seem like we were pedalling uphill. Katai was quiet and pale. The water had left a greyness on her skin. She cycled very slowly, always keeping behind me.

We stopped to rest. Mosquitoes mustered round my sweating shoulders. Katai stared out at the river and she began to cry again.

She said, 'I wish Harry was here. You take no care of me. You nearly let the river take me. Harry take good care of me.'

Back at the guest house, she ran up the steps and went into her room without a word. The door slammed shut behind her.

Calling the Khwan

'YOU'RE *farang*,' Katai said sulkily. 'You couldn't understand.'

'Try me.'

A couple of hours had passed since our return to Tang Guest House. I had knocked on her door, said I was sorry, refrained from pointing out that it was her crazy idea to cross the river in the first place. She admitted me to her neat little room. She had hung a *puang malai* garland above her bed, and a red *sarong* over the window, which mingled the greenish river-light with a rich pink, gave the room the air of a shady summer bower.

'OK, I tell you. But you won't laugh?'

'Of course.'

'It's what we call *khwan hai*, Charlie. It is the losing of my spirit. It happen today in the river. The spirit inside us we call *khwan*. It is not our life spirit: this we call *winjan*. When the *winjan* goes we die. The *khwan* is something we might lose many times in our life. When you are sick, or when you have the big shock: when this happens we say *khwan khwaen*, which means that your *khwan* is hanging above you.' Her fingers made dangling movements above her head. 'You might lose your *khwan* at some great change in your life, like you get married, or have a baby, or when someone dies who you love very much. The *khwan* is what flies away from us. We call it the butterfly soul, it flies from us so easy.'

'Where does it go when it flies away?'

'That depends. You remember the old man we met?'

'The man we met . . . in Laos?'

She smiled in a way that seemed to say yes, of course it was a crazy idea to cross the river to Laos. 'Well, he tell me the river has taken my *khwan* away. It did not take all of me, I was lucky, but it has taken my *khwan*, and now I am sad and empty.'

It wasn't just the river accident either. Her *khwan* had been in a volatile state for a while – ever since grandfather's death, in fact. 'You remember at Chiang Rai? The fortune stick which told me I had no fortune. And today, when we walk in the sand in Laos, did you see?'

'See what?'

'When we walked we left no footprints.'

'Yes, I did, but – '

'So all these things are telling me I have lost something, that I'm in a bad way, I'm empty. *Jai bau dee*: mind not good, *na*?'

'But you've seemed so happy,' I protested. 'This is your holiday, Katai.'

'Not holiday,' she said firmly. 'It is bigger than holiday. This is the first time I travel out of Bangkok alone. And there's Harry. We got plans, Charlie. This is big change in my life.'

'Plans?'

She didn't answer. She sat down on the bed. 'He won't come tonight,' she said in a matter-of-fact way. 'So we must think about my *khwan*.'

'Right.' I cast around for something to say, some tone to say it in. 'Well. We've got to think of a way – '

She laughed, laid her hand on my shoulder. Her laugh had an edge to it. 'The poor *farang*,' she said, shaking her head in mock sympathy. 'He don't like anything on the inside of people. He always like to stay on the outside, where he can feel big and strong. So. What does the *farang* fear?'

'Salt, sugar and chilli?' (dutifully).

'No. The *farang* fears what is inside him.'

'Oh, for Christ's sake.'

She put her finger to my lips, stopping my anger, cooling my hot heart. 'It's OK, Charlie. I'm sorry. This is not your fault. It is my bad mind talking like this. It is because my *khwan* has gone.' She rubbed her eyes. Her face still had that greyish pallor: the shock of the river still on it. 'Anyway,' she said, 'I know what we must do.'

'What must we do?'

'We must find someone here in Chiang Saen who will perform

the ceremony for us. We call it the *bai see soo khwan*. The ceremony to call back my *khwan*.'

We went down to Porn's noodle-shop. Porn would know what to do. She sat attentively as Katai explained how we had swum across to Laos, how we had nearly drowned, how the old farmer had said that the river was 'hungry' and had tried to 'eat' her, how she felt so strange and thought the *naga* of the river had taken away her spirit.

Porn nodded and murmured sympathy. Yes, of course, the classic symptoms of *khwan hai* were there. Yes, she knew of a *mau khwan*, a specialist in *khwan* ceremonies. Porn's daughter, a pleasant, tubby girl of about fifteen, was despatched in search of this man. She went off into the darkness on her bicycle.

The ceremony would be expensive, Porn warned. The *mau khwan* would have to be paid; the offerings needed would have to be bought and prepared. It seemed that Porn was taking on a managerial role here: she would organize the whole thing. The cost all-in would be seven hundred baht (around thirty dollars).

'That's a lot of money, Katai,' I said. She was careful with money, used to making it stretch.

She said it was worth it. It would be worth it at twice the price. 'It's like paying for an operation when you're sick. Whatever it costs it has to be done.'

'I'd like to watch the ceremony,' I said. 'It would be very interesting to me. Perhaps I could help out with the money. You know: *farang leech* . . .' I mimicked her Bangkok drawl. She always pronounced 'rich' with a sneer, so it came out like 'leech'.

'No, Charlie, thank you. I know you mean it well, but the *soo khwan* ceremony, well, you don't buy the ticket to watch like it was a pussy show in Patpong.'

I started to protest, but she stopped me. 'Of course you can watch. You were in the Mekong with me.' A fleeting warm note in her voice, a sense of something shared, even if it was just a fear – the fear when we felt the primal power of the river, the *naga* force, pulling us away to kill us. She was quickly sardonic again, looking at me through half-closed eyes. 'You think you are the strong *farang* swimmer, but I know you were frightened for a bit there. Perhaps the *mau khwan* will say a few words for your spirit, Charlie. Maybe your spirit is not so good too. But I will pay. This is Katai's ceremony.'

'You're the boss,' I said, and we both laughed.

Porn's daughter came back in, wheeling her bike through the eating area to the kitchen out back. The *mau khwan* was out of town, she said. He had gone to assist at an important ceremony down at Ban Son That: a blessing on a new school house. He wouldn't be back until next week.

Porn wasn't put out. She knew another man, perhaps not quite so expert, but a very competent *prahm*. This word Katai translated as 'spirit-man'. The *prahm* is an all-purpose local ritualist, versed in various ceremonies: the word actually derives from 'brahman'.

The spirit-man lived not far away. Our meal now finished, it was decided that we should visit him without further ado. The four of us walked off down Main Street, leaving the sleepy-eyed servant girl in charge of the noodle-shop. We cut down a couple of shady *soi*, dense foliage overhead, and came round the far side of the town park, to a cluster of wooden houses. In one of these, seated on a verandah, was a small, frail old woman, doing embroidery by the light of an oil lamp. Formalities were exchanged. This was the spirit-man's mother. She sat there serenely as we trooped on up to the *jaan*. I bumped my head on the roof of the verandah. Porn's daughter giggled.

Her son was not here at present. We waited a bit. The old woman sewed: an undulant motif, it might have been a *naga*, aquamarine thread on peach-pink silk. There was talk and there was silence, the Muang women smiling as they spoke, the Bangkok girl sharp and making them laugh, the *farang* on the edge of the circle, nodding like a mascot.

The man didn't come. Was he out doing a ceremony? I asked. No, he was out having *sanuk*, his mother said.

'We all like a good time,' I said. Everyone smiled at my bad Thai, nodded at my profound insight.

Katai said, 'Sure. The good times you have had, it's the one thing they can't take away from you. That's what Harry says.'

A message was left for the spirit-man. The old lady said she was sure he would be able to perform tomorrow morning, unless . . .

'Unless what?' said Katai.

'Unless he's had too much *sanuk* tonight.'

We walked back to the guess how, the streets dark and quiet, the moon over the river crooked with haze. I don't know how she knew, but she was right that Harry wasn't coming tonight. Having got over her disappointment the night before, she seemed to have fallen back on the general Thai view that it's no big deal if someone's a few days late. I saw her eye flicker over the verandah as we climbed the steps, looking for some sign that Harry was here, but everything was dark and still, just a dog barking down the street and our rooms waiting as we had left them, with the untenanted room like a borderline between them.

'It's been quite a day,' I said.

'Oh yes, and tonight we will sleep very well.'

She kissed me on the cheek, so quick it might have been the touch of a moth. She was right too. I lay down on my bed and when I woke up next morning I was still dressed.

It was Katai knocking that woke me. The sound of her knocking joined in with the clucking of the hens in the yard, like the segue into the reprise of 'Sergeant Pepper'. She put her head round the door, face fresh again, saying in sing-song *farang*-speak – as she did countless times up on the fourteenth floor – 'Good morning, sir.'

She had already been down to Porn's. Everything was set up for the *soo khwan* ceremony: it would take place, in the room above the noodle-shop, at ten o'clock. 'I'm going to get my *khwan* back today,' she said, like it was her birthday or something.

She watched me, arms folded, as I sat up. 'Just like Harry,' she said. 'Look *real* bad in the morning.'

I showered with the bucket and scoop. There was coffee and

'scramble-egg' waiting for me. Katai was taking Chinese tea, nothing else. Was she nervous? *'Nid noi.'*

We walked up to Main Street. It was a glorious morning, the sun low and clear, sucking up mist off the river, the sky blue between the old *chedi* and the dark mangoes, blue between the thin grey trunks of the teak grove at Wat Pa Sak.

At the noodle-shop four women were preparing the offerings and decorations for the *soo khwan*. They sat cross-legged on a low wooden dais in the back of the restaurant. Cartons, tools, bicycle-parts, pots and pans had been pushed to the back, and the area where they were working had been swept clean. The scene was fragrant with flowers, bright like the morning. They worked with a quiet cheery expertise: the pleasure of preparing for it seemed a part of the ritual's tonic effect. There was music on the radio, a lilting piece with some string instrument. Katai said it was music from Issan, her father's homeland. She looked as if this was significant.

The women arranged the flowers in bunches, wrapped around with a freshly cut banana leaf. They carefully polished each leaf with a damp cloth, giving it a bright sheen. The mass of flowers – chrysanthemums, frangipani, sugar-cane flowers, a red flower called *sathaan*, and many others – reminded me of the Flower Festival the day I arrived in Chiang Mai, less than two weeks ago, but so far away in the slow elastic time of these Mekong days. There were white lotus blooms too, for the Buddha, though it was explained to me that the *soo khwan* was not a ceremony involving the Buddha. The ceremony was to be addressed to a tutelary spirit, in this case the local *naga*, the river-spirit into whose domain her *khwan* had strayed. We were in the realms of the old village spirit-cults now.

The flowers were to grace the *pha khwan*, a kind of tiered conical structure set on a silver-gilt dish. This is the central item of the ceremony. Its framework was decorated with a serrated ridge of folded leaves. These, Porn said, were called *nom maew*, the teats of the cat. The little coils of leaf around the candles were called *hang nag*, the tail of the *naga*.

The *pha khwan* is a holder for the offerings that are made to entice the errant *khwan* back. As well as flowers, the objects arranged on it were two boiled chicken; a half-bottle of Mekong whisky; sweetmeats of sticky rice, sugar-cane and candied marrow; quids of *miang*; betel leaves and areca nuts; pink birthday-cake candles; and a range of small token gifts, cunningly fashioned out of leaf-cuttings: a bracelet, a wrist-watch, and a cup suitable for an elfin-sized dram of Mekong.

There is something very charming about this characterization of the *khwan* as a flighty, childish creature, won back by these baubles and bonbons laid out for it.

The spirit-man arrived on time. He was a thin, neat man, perhaps about fifty, balding and bespectacled. He was half-Burmese, and had the distinctive Burmese skin, smooth and pale-brown like varnished wood. His short-sleeved white shirt was crisply ironed, frayed at the collar. He carried a couple of exercise books. In his breast pocket was a sheaf of folded papers, a spectacles case, a couple of biros. He might have been a village headmaster, or a moderately prosperous trader, or a minor *fonctionnaire* like Katai's father.

Not – one would have thought, wrong as usual – a caller of spirits, our special envoy to the *naga* of the Mekong.

We went upstairs. There was a thin kind of parlour with cushions on the floor, and a couple of aged armchairs. We were directly above the cook-shop. High on the walls were cobwebbed old monochrome photos in gilt frames. The prints had emulsified, faded to a pale tweedy brown. The King and Queen were there, circa 1960, hung with withered garlands. Down near the street-side window was a big dusty TV set that one knew didn't work. It served as a little family altar: on it were Buddhist statuettes and medallions, jars of spent joss, and also a small collection of dolls: cutesy dolls in synthetic lace, jovial pudgy baby dolls, a Snoopy with a smile badge. Pride of place was given to an ornate pen-holder: two plastic biros shaped like old text-pens, and between them a nickel-plate model of a vintage car which served artfully as a universal calendar. On the base of this object, bearing strange news of another old spirit-cult, was the legend, 'Season's Greetings From Don And Tammy, Tulsa County Autos, Your Caring Car-Mart'.

We settled ourselves, Katai kneeling, the spirit-man sitting cross-legged, me off to one side fiddling with my tape-recorder, the women in the background on cushions, ready to enjoy a morning's entertainment. Porn's husband, who I had not seen before, turned up. He greeted us all courteously, and hovered at the back of the group. He looked like he had recently woken up. I saw the old wedding photo of them on the wall, he with his hair slicked across from a dead-straight parting, Porn with her veily little hat on, the signature of the photographer almost faded out in the bottom corner.

The *pha khwan*, laden with offerings, stood between Katai and the spirit-man. Everything looked neat and succulent and glossy on the silver tray. The bottle of rice whisky had been opened. All was ready for the calling of the *khwan*.

The ceremony began quietly at first. The spirit-man asked Katai to say her name, though he knew it already. He asked her about herself, her place and date of birth. He noted she was born in the *pee katai*, the Year of the Hare. He ran through the circumstances in which her *khwan* was lost. When he spoke it was partly to her, partly to the rest of us. The tone was one of exposition, very matter-of-fact. He might have been opening a meeting of the local PTA.

He touched all the offerings on the *pha khwan*: gentle, fussy movements. A silence fell. Dust moved through the sunlight. He opened one of his exercise books. The pages were filled with neat handwriting, Thai script, on alternate lines. He began to chant. The chant had no tune, just a couple of tones, up and down, a soporific slow-motion sirening. His voice was catarrhal. He stopped to clear his throat. He had the look of someone pausing after effort. When he settled back into the chant there was no sign of that effort, but you felt it was there.

I didn't understand any of it, and a lot of it was unintelligible to Katai when we played the tape back a few hours later. She said that some of it was in Pali, the old ritual language of Buddhism: she recognized a common Pali formula, *Namo tassa sammasam bud-dhassa*, which means, 'I worship the enlightened Buddha.' Some of it was Burmese, and some a language she didn't recognize at all. Some of it was obscured by the noise of trucks and motorcycles on the street below, so much louder on tape than they had seemed at the time.

The preamble went as follows: 'Glory and greatest prosperity. Today is a day of great auspiciousness and purity. On this day the *garuda* will roar. On this day parted families will see one another again. On this day we will recall how King Asoka bestowed the seven blessings upon the people. On this day little children will learn to speak the tongue of their forebears.'

He spoke of the thirty-two *khwan*, which are really thirty-two mini-*khwan*, each a part of the *khwan*, residing in different parts of the body. He spoke of creatures called *ngueak*. These are apparently river-spirits, in serpent-form like the *naga*, but lacking any of the latter's beneficent aspect. They are wicked, predatory creatures, and were doubtless involved in the incident in the river. Any appeal to them would be useless – a different and more difficult rite must be performed to reverse their influence – so the spirit-man was appealing to the higher authority of the *naga* to get the fled spirit back. He spoke of 'Lady Coconut Flower', a kind of wood-nymph, to whom Katai was likened. It was for Lady Coconut Flower that the first *soo khwan* ceremony of all was performed, by Grandfather Tanha and Grandmother Maya, when she was sick and her *khwan* hung outside her.

Then he invoked the *khwan* itself. 'Come, O *khwan*. Let not the *khwan* of the head be discouraged, nor any of the thirty-two *khwan* of the young girl's body. You may return here safely. Be content. Look, we have prepared a feast for you. We have laid out pretty robes for you to wear, a mirror for you to see yourself, though we cannot see you.' (These items were represented in banana leaf: a rich man's *soo khwan* would have real little clothes and mirrors for the *khwan*.) 'We have prepared a splendid feast for you.' He enumerated the tempting goodies on the dish: chicken and whisky, white rice and sugar-cane, betel and frangipani . . .

This went on for about a quarter of an hour. All the while Katai knelt, head bowed, her right hand touching the *pha khwan*. The spirit-man cleared his throat one last time, concluded the chant, and we all sat in silence, a deep silence, for maybe two minutes, like Remembrance Day. I didn't seem to hear the trucks and motor-cycles rolling down the street below. They're on the tape, together with a bird that sounds like it was singing straight into the mike, but I didn't hear them then at all.

The spirit-man sat looking thoughtful. Then he gave a little nod, signifying completion of some sort, and everyone shifted and relaxed, and the normality of the room closed in over the silence, like water over sand. The spirit-man was cheerful, as if the difficult bit was now done with. Katai explained to me later that it was at that point, during that silence, that her *khwan* returned, enticed by the spirit-man's chant and by the knick-knacks of the offering. 'It came into the *pha khwan* then,' she said, 'though not yet into me.' When we played the tape, it was that silence that she wanted to hear again, and the singing of the bird that sounded like it was inside the room.

Next came a very elegant bit of the ceremony. The spirit-man took one of the flowers from the *pha khwan*, dipped it in a bowl of water, and dabbed Katai's hands with it. He repeated the motion several times, sprinkling a bit of water on each of the principal offerings. Then he took a few choice morsels – a bit of chicken-skin, some boiled rice, some sugared marrow, a quid of *miang* – and put them in her hand.

This was food for Katai to give to her *khwan* to encourage it on the last leg of its return. Here the spirit-man recited three brief verses. These are called *kham jam*, 'feeding words'. They are spoken while the *khwan* 'feeds' on the morsels in the supplicant's hand. The word *jam* is used in Thai to refer to the old-fashioned pre-utensil way of eating, by dipping balls of rice into a central bowl of food. Earlier in the ceremony, the spirit-man had invoked Khao Jam, a minor spirit with special responsibility for 'feeding' *khwan*.

One of the *kham jam* went: 'Come, O *khwan*, feed at her hand. Let her be strong and daring, let her be free of illness, let her open her palms and gain what she wishes. Come feed.'

Finally, to seal in the returned *khwan*, the spirit-man tied the 'auspicious thread'. He used a Muang term for this, *faay mongkon*, but the Thai generally call it *sai sin*. The auspicious thread is simply a length of string tied, with appropriate blessing, around the wrist. Its most important use is in rituals like this, but the *sai sin* can be done in a casual way by anyone with the wisdom or status to do it – a parent, an older person, a monk. The tying of the auspicious thread around the wrist is a tying in of luck, health and happiness, and in this case a sealing in of the *khwan*, without which these attainments are impossible anyway.

This wound up the ceremony, but, good to her word, Katai asked the spirit-man to do the *sai sin* for me too, because I had been in the Mekong as well. I knelt before the bespectacled shaman, trying not to dwell on his headmasterly aspect. He spoke a couple of brief formulae, dabbed my hands with petal-water, and tied on the white threads. One of them fell off a couple of weeks later, but the one on my left wrist remained for months, yellowed and tattered, and one night in Bangkok I actually patched it up with sellotape for fear of what might happen to my luck, health and happiness if it broke.

Katai was congratulated, the spirit-man was thanked, Porn was paid, and we went on our way. The day had hazed over. It felt like we had been at Porn's for a long time, though it was little more than an hour. Katai was full of energy, greeting strangers. By chance or design we passed the gates of Wat Pa Sak, and there was Moon-song, sweeping the path to the *sala* with a besom broom, near enough to the road to talk with passers-by.

He greeted me with the words, 'Who will rid me of this turbulent priest?'

We talked about the morning's ceremony. I asked him if, as a monk, he disapproved of the old cults like the *soo khwan*. He said no, on the contrary: at certain times, for instance during ordination, a kind of *soo khwan* was performed by and for monks.

He asked me what the English word for *khwan* was. I said I supposed it was 'spirit'.

'And do you believe in your spirit?'

I burbled a bit about 'life force' and 'psychic energy'. I observed that the state of *khwan hai*, spirit loss, is probably what we in the West would call 'depression'.

He leant on the broom-handle, nodding sagely. 'Hmmm, depression.' He sounded dissatisfied by the word. It seemed like a narrow, stingy sort of word the way he said it. He composed himself, a scholar settling into his subject. 'The word *khwan*, I believe, is from the Chinese word *kwun*, which expresses much the same meaning.' He turned the broom upside-down and traced some lines in the dust with the handle. 'This is the character for *kwun*,' he explained. 'It is composed of two characters: that one means "demon" or "spirit", and this one means something like your breath, or the mist on the river, I do not know the right word. Also when water boils.' His hand trembled in imitation of something light and floating: we settled on the word 'vapour'.

'So, these are the first meanings of *khwan*. It is a spirit, it is a breath or a vapour, it is something inside us that is always ready to fly away. There are also some Thai words that belong with the word *khwan*. One is *ghwan*, which means "smoke". Another is *phan*.'

Here he turned to Katai, as if she could better explain. 'The *phan* is a dream, Charlie.

'Sometimes when you dream,' said Moonsong, 'you go off into the world of the *khwan*.'

Katai said, 'Also *phan* is the word for our sweetheart. When we are in love with someone we say *khwan ta*: you are the *khwan* of my eyes.'

Moonsong stared monkishly into the middle distance, into some space where the meanings and memories of the sensual world lose their awesome power, then he continued, 'When the *khwan* is gone, yes, you feel . . . depression. But look where it goes. It crosses a border, into the spirit-world. And when it comes back, when it is called back in the *soo khwan*, it brings back the air and the touch of the spirit-world. We cannot go across that border yet, but our *khwan* can. To lose your *khwan* is very difficult, very dangerous even, but you *must* lose it. You must let it go, and pray that it will return.'

His hands motioned the freeing of a bird into the air, and his eyes seemed to follow it into the tall canopy of the teak grove.

Mister Harry

THE EVENING of the day of the *soo khwan*, returning to the guest house after supper and a stroll, we came in at the street gate and found Suree, who usually went to bed soon after sunset, sitting out in the doorway.

Katai said, 'He's here?'

Suree nodded. 'Mister Harry is here.'

He was sitting out on the dark verandah, his feet up on the rail. I saw his hat and the glow of the cigarette, heard the clink of a glass and a bottle. He climbed off the chair and stood waiting at the top of the steps as she ran up. I lingered back, gave them some space. There was a moment of almost comic formality as they kissed, a kiss on each cheek but not on the mouth, and stood holding hands at the top of the steps. Katai had – like most Thai girls, contrary to *farang* superstition – quite strict views about public shows of affection: no cuddling and kissing in public, no arm across her shoulders in the back of the *tuk tuk*. Kissing was for when you were alone together.

He said, 'OK, *bway*?'

'OK, *bway*.'

'How you doing?'

'Doing OK.'

They were still holding hands. They seemed incongruous: the jaded dusty traveller and the slim mercurial girl. He said, 'You keep me waiting, Katai. I've been here half an –'

She squawked and beat her fists against his chest. 'You get away. We're waiting for you three days.' He held her wrists and they laughed. They wanted to kiss properly but convention forebade it. She looked back down the steps. 'Hey Charlie!' – a smiling, reproachful hostess to a guest who isn't joining in the fun – 'Come on up.'

Harry disengaged his eyes from her face, shook my hand. 'Really good to see you, man. I see you have taken good care of Katai.'

'I think she's taken care of me, if anything.'

'Teamwork,' said Katai.

'I'm glad,' said Harry. His eyes were back on her now, smiling in a way that was meant be fond but actually looked rather sinister. The scar up his nose showed up, dark and straight, against the pallor of his skin. The pallor, I realized, was dust. I could smell the road on him, and the rice whisky. He hadn't washed or unpacked, just thrown his bags down in the corner of the verandah, and settled down to wait, with a half of Mekong and a pack of Gold City for company.

We took seats. There were two other glasses on the tray, ready for us. He poured a straight soda water for Katai, and a whisky for me. He said, 'I am sorry I am late.'

'What was the problem?' I asked.

He shrugged. 'Waiting. Just waiting. Till I could wait no more. This is the trader's life.' He went over to his bag, pulled out a *pomelo*, a large citrus like a cross between an orange and a grapefruit. He cut it into slices with a big black-handled army knife, and put some slices in her drink.

'Oh, Shangri La Number One cocktail,' said Katai in ridiculous *farang*-speak.

Harry returned to his luggage, took out a bunch of rather dishevelled purple flowers. 'It's for you,' he said. He held them out awkwardly to Katai, as if they were something he wasn't used to handling.

'Oh!' She sounded surprised. 'Oh thank you, Harry.' But she didn't take them. Harry, making a small bow, held them out once more. 'Harry, I must tell you that the flowers are the wrong colour.'

'Hey. I didn't get white because you told me that's for your Buddha, and I didn't get yellow because of some other damn thing. So what's wrong with these?'

'The purple coloured *puang malai* you give to the widow woman, the woman whose man has just died.'

Harry pale, or was it just the dust of the road? He looked at the flowers, then back at her. 'You kidding me, Katai?'

No, she wasn't kidding him.

'Shit!'

He walked over to the rail of the verandah, and flung the flowers out into the riverside scrub. We stood in surprised silence for a moment. He looked from me to her, and then he laughed, 'Hah!', a laugh like a pantomime devil, making a joke of it, but his eyes were still fierce, staring at her.

He plucked up his glass from the floor, raised it. 'We're not dead yet,' he said.

'Yeah, we drink to that,' said Katai, and we clinked our glasses in the moonlight.

Harry was hungry, 'hungry as a bitch'. Katai said we'd eaten but the walk would be nice. Feeling redundant I said, 'I think I'll turn in,' and made to head off for my room. But Katai was having none of it. She insisted I came along too. We must celebrate Harry's return, we must plan our trip into the Golden Triangle.

Harry said, 'But of course,' with a party-spirited gesture. I said they were very kind.

We went to an eating-place Harry knew, a fly-blown little Chinese house in an alley behind the market. A blackened old blanket cordoned off the kitchen. Across the street was a brothel, the courtyard full of teenage boys lounging around a pick-up truck, a low wooden door, a red light, occasional glimpses of girls within.

'Really nice place, Harry,' drawled Katai. 'You know how to pick them.'

'Well, it's not Maxim's, but the *maitre d.* always finds me a good table.' She did not understand the joke. It was for my benefit, the fellow *farang*. Our laugh colluded against her: for some reason he wanted that. He said, 'The food is good and cheap, and everyone minds their own business.'

The *maitre d.* – actually a middle-aged Chinese woman with

blue acrylic slacks and a bad case of psoriasis on her elbows – brought him his meal. Rice, a chicken dish with nuts and vegetables, and the hot chilli salad they call *popaya pok pok*.

Katai said that the phrase *pok pok*, referring to the grinding of the ingredients with pestle and mortar, was also a slang word for sex. In the old days, a wife would send a man's mistress a gift of pestles (*krok*). 'This would tell the mistress to leave off the man, to use the *krok* instead.' She looked up beyond my shoulder. 'The Chinese, you see, have the *ee-kik*.' We turned to look. Up on a shelf sat a squat wooden figure sporting a large and detailed erection. 'It is for good luck and prosperity,' Katai explained. She gazed mischievously at the statue. 'I think it would be very good luck,' she said. Her eyes were laughing at Harry, teasing him, so demure and so loose. He was trying to eat, but he looked uncomfortable. I guessed she was pressing her legs against his, underneath the flimsy little table.

Harry touched the thread around her wrist. 'Where did you get that?'

Her mood changed. She said casually, 'We had the thread tying. They did it for us at the noodle-shop. I thought it would be nice for Charlie to see it.' She turned to me. 'You gonna get the good luck now, isn't that right, Charlie?'

I just nodded, wondering why she didn't want to tell him about the Mekong and the *soo khwan*, wondering why it made me feel so good to share her secret, wondering if there wasn't just a faint metaphorical twitching of the trader's nose, as it sniffed a moment of unease in the air.

Walking back we took a short cut across the dark bus park. In a corner, between a bus and the scrub-hedge, we saw a group of four men, sitting round a small fire of brushwood, passing a bamboo pipe around.

Harry called out a greeting as we passed. One of the men called back, 'Do you want some meat?' That, at any rate, was what I thought I heard him say – *'Aow neua, mai?'*

Harry and Katai looked at one another. *'Neua heng, mai?'* called Harry. The man nodded.

Katai said, 'Harry do you think – ?'

He cut in, 'Sure, just a bit, it's been a long week.' He started walking towards them, saying something I couldn't hear.

I said, 'What's going on, Katai? What's this about meat?'

She explained, '*Neua* does mean meat, Charlie, but also it has the street meanings. *Neua sot*, fresh meat, is a street-girl. *Neua heng*, dried meat, is dope. They are inviting us to take some *neua heng* with them.'

'Oh. What kind of dope?'

'*Ganja*, Charlie.'

We joined the men. There were four of them. The man who'd called us over was a bus driver, and the young skinny one was his 'shotgun'. They had arrived from Muang Nan that evening. The shotgun looked as near to James Dean as a Thai boy could get – not very near, but the intention was obvious: slicked back hair, chewing gum, silver chain on a bare chest. The third man was the shotgun's brother. The fourth man lay with his head on a log, too stoned to talk. A weak smile played about his lips, and from time to time he raised a hand in greeting, as if we were perpetually just arriving.

The pipe consisted of a stout length of bamboo, about three feet long, three inches diameter. Two thirds of the way down it, a smaller, thinner stem was stuck in at an acute angle. Protruding from this, smelling like a bonfire, was a large joint rolled up in newspaper. You smoked by cupping the mouthpiece of the pipe right around your mouth, so that its rough edges bit into your cheeks and chin, and then sucking up the thick smoke through this bamboo chimney.

Harry seemed pretty practised. He got the smoke right in and down, held it there till you thought it was going to come out of his ears, let it out long and slow, went back for another.

'I don't do this stuff as a rule,' he said, passing the pipe to me.

'Me neither,' I said, nuzzling down into the mouthpiece.

Katai didn't smoke. She laughed at us as we huffed and puffed, coughed and grunted. She laughed at our red eyes and our pinched wild faces. She said, '*Farang dag ganja, na?*' The men laughed. *Dag* – meaning to take something greedily – is kind of a rough word. They were surprised to hear her use it.

This was grass from Laos, they told us, Number One *ganja*. The pipe came round again. The world got a little smaller. Everything was shrinking, closing around us until there was nothing but this luminous little bubble of incident. We laughed for no reason, but knew as we laughed that the moment was many-sided. There were hidden permutations in it, things we might not be able to handle. The driver said it was good to smoke with strangers. He said this was the meaning of the word. *Kan* is a word of friendship, as in *duay kan*, which means 'togetherness'. *Cha* is the Thai word for 'tea'. So *kancha* means 'the tea that people take together'.

Harry said, 'It is just the word *ganja*, from the Hindi, but I like his story.'

Harry bought a twist of dope for twenty baht and we went on our way, walking serenely through the lunar streets. Back at the guest house we sat on the verandah, finished off the whisky. The mosquitoes were biting. Katai said, 'I think this is Lan Yung. The Kingdom of a Million Mosquitoes.'

Harry suggested we go and smoke the *ganja*. We went to his room. He had stashed his gear in the corner: the cloth shoulder-bag, the sleeping roll, a plastic bag with fruit in it. His leather satchel he carried with him at all times. He was very self-contained.

Harry made a joint, using a bit of paper from my notebook. Katai lay back on the bed. 'Lao grass,' Harry said. 'You know what they used to call this stuff in Vientiane? The poor man's heaven. Shit, we used it all the time. You could buy a kilo for *nothing*, a few cents. All the money was in opium then.' He lit up the joint, held the smoke down. 'Opium,' he added. 'That's a different story.'

'Do you use opium?'

'In Vientiane, of course, one . . . But not any more, not seriously, for ten years now. Well, we shall see some up in the Triangle, of course. Perhaps we take a taste or two.'

'Where are we going to go in the Triangle?'

'Little place I know. It's about sixty, seventy clicks west from here. We'll find a local guide, *montagnard*. He'll take us over the border.'

Katai looked up when he said that. I thought she was looking at me, thinking of the untowardness of our recent cross-border expedition, but she was looking at Harry, and it would be a while until I understood what her look meant.

We drifted in the poor man's heaven. There were geckoes – the little grey-yellow house-lizard – on the walls and ceiling: watching and darting, patrolling their bland bits of territory. From time to time they called, a clucking two-part trill. The name *gecko* is Malay, imitative of the call. The Thais hear it slightly differently and call the animal *ching chok*.

Katai said it was lucky to have the *ching chok* in your house – or rather, it was unlucky *not* to have them. 'The *ching chok* can tell if something is wrong. So if he is not in the house something is wrong. The *ching chok*, he is very sharp, very clever. He is *pio*, Charlie, like the girls from Nakhon, *na*?' (I noticed it again: when she said something like that, something between her and me, I got the feeling of Harry's nose twitching, his eyes sharpening.)

'Also, if the *ching chok* calls when you are just leaving your house, it is a sign you must not go, a sign there is danger.'

I sat up. Something was troubling me. Of course, the gecko that had clucked at me on the morning of our bicycle ride to the Mekong. They were both looking at me, expecting me to say something, but I couldn't, because for some reason Katai didn't want to mention the Mekong trip, because already we were wrapped in duplicities.

I shook my head as if to clear it. 'Damn strong weed,' I said.

'*Farang* get drunk on the *ganja, na*?' She returned to her theme, told us another bit of gecko lore, how if you had a cut or sore on your body, the gecko would come and lick it while you slept.'

Harry said, 'Shit, come on, Katai.'

He did have a cut on his hand, a couple of inches where a knife he was using had slipped. It had a terracotta stain of iodine all round it. It was giving him trouble. He waved his fist at the ceiling. 'You goddamn little villains, you keep off my hand tonight, you hear?'

Katai laughed. 'Oh yes, Harry, you know, if you have the cut that the *ching chok* licks, it will never get better. In Thailand we say: the crocodile and the *ching chok* are very good friends. You see, they are the same animal really: one very big, one very small, but same-same. So when the crocodile bites you he makes the *big* cut to hurt you. And then his friend the *ching chok* licks the cut when you sleep, to keep it hurting you. It is like our lives, isn't it, when the little bad things come after the big bad thing, so your life don't get better.'

'Teamwork,' said Harry.

'Bad teamwork,' she said.

There was a silence. I sat back against the wall, closed my eyes. It was time to leave, but my limbs weren't getting the message. The ceiling fan droned. Then I became aware of voices down below, at the street entrance to the guess how. Two men, possibly more. A woman's voice answering, Suree's probably.

A sudden noise inside the room made me open my eyes, just in time to see Harry moving like a cat across the room, swiping off the light switch. In the sudden darkness I struggled up, 'What the – ', but Harry hissed me to be quiet. Katai was at the shuttered window, easing it open a crack, listening. Then I heard what they must have already heard: that the voices sounded angry, were demanding something. There was an answering tone of argument from Suree. Harry was moving round the dark room. He had scooped up the remains of the *ganja*, and was getting something out of his bag.

For a moment I was scared. Angry voices in the street, Harry jumping around like a mad dog in a cage, my head swimming with Number One Lao grass: this was enough. But what was really making me nervous was what Harry had got in his hand, catching a glint of moonlight through the open shutter: a knife just like Katai's, the 'wedding knife', with its twelve inches of business-like steel.

'I'm getting out of here,' I said.

'You fucking shut up.'

The voices were getting nearer, preceded by a reluctant Suree. Harry whispered, 'What are they saying?' Katai shook her head, straining to hear. It was only then, in a burst of lucidity, that it occurred to me to reach up behind me, and switch off the ceiling fan. Its noise was so much a part of the room's furniture that we hadn't noticed it. The moment it was off we could hear the voices clearly.

They were *farang*, speaking English badly. They were drunk, and they wanted a room for the night. Suree, protesting saltily, was now in the act of providing them with one, somewhere below us.

We stayed still in the darkness, but the tension had gone. Harry was putting the knife back. We heard one of the men belching below, then a burst of foreign tongue as they conversed together. Katai gave a little giggle. She moved away from the shutter, switched on the light. Harry looked a trifle foolish. It was the first time I'd seen him rattled. In a way I liked him better for it, but I also knew something more about him: the way he'd moved to kill the light, the way he'd gone for the knife. I thought of Guy's warning: 'crazy like a pirate if you cross him'.

Katai slipped out to investigate. Harry said, 'Sorry. It's . . .'

He trailed off. 'It's what, Harry?' I was angry: I saw that my hand was shaking. 'I mean, what's with the knife?'

'It's the *ganja*. You never know out here. It's not like the old days. Now – hell, you know what they do. They give you a bit, set you up. Bad deals like that. It's five years for a thimble-full in Thailand. I thought it was the police.'

I knew he was lying, but he was back in control again now. Katai came back. 'Suree says they are Swedish. They came on the motorbikes.'

She put her hand to Harry's shoulder. 'OK, *bway*?'

'OK, *bway*.'

'I'm going to get some sleep,' I said, climbing to my feet. 'Thanks for a nice evening.'

'We'll have more,' Harry said, reaching out to shake my hand, *toujours le galant*.

Katai smiled, shy and distant now. 'Goodnight, Charlie.'

As I left, Harry was pulling out some cassettes from his bag. 'You don't mind if we play some music?' he said.

They were two doors down but the walls of the guess how were thin. They were playing Dylan circa 1966. Bleak croonings – 'Visions of Johanna', 'Just Like A Woman', 'Stuck Inside of Mobile' – mingled with the slow whispered scuffles of their love-making. The sound of the drunken bikers vomiting came up from the bathroom directly below my room.

My limbs were numb, my head was racing. Why was Harry so jumpy? What was he up to? How far was Katai involved in his business? Why didn't she want to tell him about the Mekong incident? Why was it my destiny to lie alone in a narrow wooden bed thinking about all this?

Groans from the love-nest, groans from the bathroom, then just the clucking of the geckoes, the murmur of the ceiling fan. In my dreams the spirit of Mara danced before me, attired like Honky Tonk Ruthy.

And I said, 'Aw, come on now. You know . . . you know about my débutante.'

And she said, 'Your débutante just knows what you need, but I know what you want.'

The next day Harry announced that he wanted to 'kick back' for a couple of days before we headed on into the Triangle. I had lost any meaningful sense of time, and said that was OK by me. This was, I realized, the perpetual rhythm of his life: heading on and kicking back, on the road and off the road, but never off it anywhere long enough to call any place home. In the *I Ching*, which he consulted often, his hexagram was Lu, the Wanderer. The hexagram signifies movement and stillness, being composed of the trigrams Li (Fire) and Ken (Mountain):

> Fire on the mountain:
> The image of the wanderer.

'I live like a refugee,' he said, the stress on the first syllable, *ref*-ugee, like an American.

His material world he carried in his shoulder-bag and satchel. He had places scattered across south-east Asia where he could call on a bed for a few nights: safe houses, storage spaces, message drops, special currency-changing facilities. He had telex numbers, incoming and outgoing, in seven cities in south-east Asia. But his home he carried on his back, very streamlined. 'Old Chinese proverb: He who travels light sings in the robber's face.'

His clothes were few: mostly cheap cotton stuff bought in the markets. He had one or two pieces of ethnic gear, Hmong ware from his days in Laos: a waistcoat of intricately embroidered hemp-fibre, a leather belt studded with discs of silver. They were worn and dusty. He put them on to show us. 'Strictly for ceremonies only,' he said, whatever that meant. He looked like a small-town bullfighter whose nerve had gone.

The big yellowed tooth that hung round his neck, I learned, was a bear's tooth, from the forests of eastern Burma, given to him by a 'special friend' in Burma.

There was his box of dice: the box silver, the dice ivory. He'd bought it on the Street of Thieves in Hanoi. We played a few games of backgammon out in the yard. He didn't have a board, just scratched out the markings in the dust. We used pebbles for one set of counters, coins for the other. He was good: cunning and strategic. He had the instinct. Whenever he played the back-game he seemed to get it right, swooping like a hawk and racing for home. He would have taken me to the cleaners if I'd agreed to the stake he proposed. As it was, at five baht a point, I was down twenty dollars after one long afternoon session.

There were his cassettes: Holly, Dylan, Brel, Doors. 'Musically I stopped living after 1968.' There was his battered old *I Ching*, his pocket edition of the poems of Rimbaud, a couple of Zane Grey Westerns given him by Khris.

There were his knives: the Karen 'wedding knife' I had seen already, and a big black military knife, with various evil-looking attachments. He called it his Saigon knife. This knife tells a story, he said.

'I won it at a game of stud poker, one night in Saigon, late 1973. This guy was one heavy dude, real fire-and-rain merchant. He'd done the LURP trip: Long Range Reconnaissance Patrol. Those people went into the jungle, behind enemy lines, walked on their nerve-ends for a night and a day. He was the kind of guy we'd say: he's died a hundred times and he's still standing up. Well, that night his luck was out. I took him for all he had: all his dollars and now his knife. He was sore. Out there people got pretty superstitious. I'm sure you appreciate.

'So I told him: Unlucky in cards, lucky in love. You know the saying. He said: Bullshit, motherfucker, that's not the kind of luck you need out in the Nam. But he was wrong, you see. I met him again, maybe six months later. He was on the short stick then: just a few days left before he went back home. He told me something that happened, not long after our game of stud.

'He had this bar-girl in Saigon: I guess you could say he was in love with her, the way soldiers are, you know? Well one day, he was with a bunch of grunts down in Saigon. This was the time of a lot of street action in the city. VC were getting closer every day. They were pulling all kinds of undercover stunts on the streets: bombs, booby traps, all that shit. So he's with these guys, and they're waiting for a bus to take them back to base. There's this shoeshine boy there – shine your boots GI, two dong, very cheap – and some of the grunts are getting their boots shined. Just then, my friend sees his girl across the street. She's waving him to come over and talk to her. He walks over. Just as he's walking over, a boy comes running down the street, pulls off the shoeshine boy's hat. The shoeshine boy runs off after him, the grunts are all laughing, then – shazam! – the shoeshine boy's box explodes. It was a bomb. Ten grunts killed, and my man standing across the street with his mouth open. He knew then: his girl was VC, she'd saved his life. Lucky in love, man, just like I'd told him.'

He paused, looked quizzically at Katai. 'Me, I got the knife. I'm lucky at the cards.'

Harry was unwinding all the time – Katai and Chiang Saen were a tonic combination – but I still felt he was holding me at arm's length, that he was still somehow suspicious of me. He remained tight-lipped about what his current 'beez-ness' was, what had caused the delay, what this 'big one' was that he was after. I didn't know how much he was telling Katai, because I mostly left them to their own devices, but he wasn't telling me anything.

Then one evening he showed me some stones. It seemed a gesture of trust. He had a special compartment inside the leather satchel. Sometimes he carried them inside an elasticated bandage around his calf. He had four sapphires – a couple of 'show pieces', already polished, the others just a bit of raw stock to carry around with him – and a pair of pigeon-blood rubies. The biggest of the sapphires was a thirty-carat stone, a beautiful royal blue. The rough stones were very dark – 'Siamese indigo' – with the light almost black inside them. They were from Chanta Buri. They cost fifteen dollars per carat at source. He could get twice that from the gem-dealers on Majesek Road in Bangkok, and every now and then he found a well-breeched *farang* to sell direct to, for fifty or sixty dollars a carat.

'They call the sapphire the stone of truth,' he said. 'It is blue like the sky of the clearest blue day, and so it is the stone of seeing clearly, of seeing into secrets. They say it is also the stone of maturity, of coming to see things as you get older. Emerald the stone of spring, ruby the stone of summer, sapphire the stone of autumn, diamond the stone of winter.'

I asked about star sapphires.

'It's a phenomenon called asterism. It's a special kind of sparkle that appears in the shape of a six-ray star. The true star sapphire is the perfect work of nature and art. Nature because the stone must have exactly the right crystalline make-up, and art because the cutter must shape the stone exactly right to get the star to shine. The rarest thing is to find a star sapphire with the deep blue colour of the finest blue sapphire. With star sapphires, you get milky blue, grey blue, even grey and white with hardly any blue at all. The star sapphire is called the Stone of Destiny. In Ceylon they call it the Moving Star. It's a lucky stone. It is used to guard against evil spirits, bad kharma. Some people say the star sapphire brings such powerful good luck that once you have possessed one it will go on protecting you even after you have parted with it.'

He was in a mellow mood that night, and over a few glasses of Mekong he told me a bit about his life. He was born in Marseille

around the end of the Second World War: that made him in his
early forties now. His father was half French, half Algerian, his
mother Corsican. He was a mongrel, like Guy said. He grew up in
the tall city of Algiers: grey French tenements built up on the rocks
above the sea, closing round the steep, secretive *kasbah*, the old
Arab heart of the city. His father was a trader. He imported
timber, wine, car parts: anything the *colons* needed. He saw the
way things were going in Algeria, and in the late 1950s the family
decamped back to France, before the war of independence began
in earnest. Harry's mother died shortly after leaving Algiers.
Harry, aged fifteen, his father, and his little sister Jeannot arrived
in Saigon in 1960.

Harry fell in easily with the *louche* world of French Saigon.
'That was in the days when the Rue Catanat was still the Rue
Catanat. Then they changed it to Tou Do Street, which means
Freedom Street: in the war it was the Yanks' cat-house street,
something like Patpong. Then when the North Vietnamese came
in, in '75, they changed it again: Dong Khoi, the Street of the
People's Revolution. My father had a bar off the Rue Catanat, just
around the corner from the Continental. That was where the
sniffers hung out. I knew them all. You remember that song?
Cancel my subscription to the resurrection. That was our song.'

He began 'trading' when he was seventeen. 'You know what
everyone wanted in Saigon in '62? They wanted James Bond
books. I had a friend down in Cholon, book pirate. We were selling
Doctor No at twenty dollars a time.' He drifted round Indo China,
lived in Vientiane for a couple of years, learned the languages,
gathered contacts and expertise. By the time the war came he was
the all-purpose Mr Fixit for anyone who needed anything, legal or
otherwise. He could get dope, girls, documents, guns, transport.
He could get Brut champagne and *paté de foie gras*. Anything that
needed a bit of organization, a bit of Saigon savvy, you got in
touch with Harry Vincent. 'I tell you, man, half the sniffers that
wrote up that war wouldn't have stuck it if it wasn't for me. Hell,
they oughta give me one of those Pulitzers, you know what I
mean?'

It was the sniffers that gave him the nickname 'Mad Dog'. It was a joke on one of the Viet Cong's communist slogans, 'The mad dogs of capitalist imperialism'. They reckoned that if anyone was a capitalist mad dog it was Trader Harry. It was also from this time that he began to be known as Harry Vincent, American-style. He was born Henri Vincent, and that is the name in his French passport, the surname pronounced in the normal French way. His father's bar in Saigon was called Chez Vieux Vincent, which the regulars changed to Vieux Cent Vins – 'Old Hundred Wines', a pun on the family name and on the Chinese phrase, *Lao Bai Xing*, 'Old Hundred Names.'

In Saigon, he said, he was dealing so much with Americans that it seemed best to 'become one'. That way they trusted you more, that way they paid you more. I think also his 'Americanization' was part of a love-hate relationship with France, and with all of Europe. He would never live in Europe, he said. 'I don't want to live in a slum. In Europe you live in the slums of the mind.' In Algiers he had loved the *kasbah*, in Saigon he spent his time down in Cholon, the Chinese quarter. Europe had given him nothing: a certain Frenchified air, a language, a set of codes he knew to be meaningless. 'Colonialism shows you the back-end of civilization. They shit all over a country. It shows you how these codes, this civilized European way, is just a make-believe, a farce, a *rigolade*. The things I saw in Vietnam, the things they did in the name of civilization. Shit!'

As well as his 'trading blood', he got from his father a love of poetry. His hero was Rimbaud, the *poète maudit*, the supreme existential traveller, moving for no reason other than to move. 'You know the last thing Rimbaud wrote? It wasn't a poem. Perhaps you know, he wrote no poems after he was nineteen, after he had been through his "Season in Hell". No, the last thing Rimbaud wrote was a letter to a steamship company. He was lying in Marseille, one leg amputated, the other full of poison. He wrote: "I am almost entirely paralysed, and so I wish to embark early. Please let me know at what time I should be carried on board." Just that, *tout court*. He was going back East. He was still travelling, and he couldn't even move. He died the next day. He was thirty-seven years old, man. Lived two lifetimes already. Shit, I've only just started my first life and I'm the other side of forty. I was born a block away from where he died. I've done that steamship ride many times: to Algiers, to Ajaccio, to Oran. I was born right on the edge of France. Been falling ever since.'

Another hero was Jack Kerouac, the 'dharma bum'. Another was Albert Camus, the 'outsider'. '*Sont tous les marginaux, comme moi,*' he explained: Rimbaud the Belgian, Camus the Algerian, Kerouac the French-Canadian. 'People on the borderline, you know?'

Our last night at Chiang Saen, Harry wearing a *sarong*, sitting on the verandah at dusk, declaiming from his *livre de poche* of Rimbaud, Katai kneeling beside him with her head on his thigh, the words floating off into the shrill of the night:

J'écrivais des silences, des nuits, je notais l'inexprimable. Je fixais des vertiges . . .
Je finis par trouver sacré le désordre de mon esprit . . .
J'avais été damné par l'arc-en-ciel. Le bonheur était ma fatalité, mon remords, mon ver. Ma vie serait toujours trop immense . . .

Pa Kha

THE DIRT road climbed steeply into the foothills of the Shan mountains. With each bend the plain below sank deeper into the afternoon haze, until the paddy fields and tobacco plots and the straggling villages along Route 110 had disappeared entirely, and it might have been the Mekong itself we were looking down at.

We had left Chiang Saen that morning, and hitched a pick-up to the Golden Triangle itself, the tri-border point where Thailand, Burma and Laos meet. A couple of miles before we got to the Triangle, Harry pointed out a few roofs amid the dense greenery over on the Lao bank of the river. It was a small timber station called Ban Khwan. (This means 'Village of the Axe', Katai explained: the word *khwan*, like many Thai words, has different meanings according to the tone used.)

It was here, said Harry, that they fought the famous Opium War of July 1967, a three-cornered battle between the Shans, the KMT and the Laotian military. 'It was Khun Sa's first pitch,' he explained. 'He had bought up all the opium he could lay his hands on, up in the Lahu and Wa States in Upper Burma. I've talked to people who saw the caravan coming down from Kengtung: five hundred mules, man, an opium caravan a mile long. He was bringing it down to Ban Khwan to sell it to General Ouane. Ouane was commander-in-chief of the Royal Lao Army, very big wheel, did a lot of heroin business with Marshal Ky in Vietnam, controlled most of the heroin refineries in Laos at that time. He had a refinery at Ban Khwan, as well as controlling the timber trade here. Now when the KMT heard that this jumped-up Shan bandit was about to do major business with Ouane they decided to put a stop to it. They sent a thousand troops. Everyone met up here at Ban Khwan: big firefight. Ouane won out. He called in a squadron of F-28 bombers, flattened the whole place, collected up all the opium – half a million dollars' worth: a hell of a lot in those days – and sent everyone else packing. One hundred and fifty people killed, village burnt out. It was the law of the jungle in those days.'

The Golden Triangle was beautiful and tranquil. The Opium War has moved elsewhere. The Triangle itself is little more than a long sandbank, reminiscent of the one Katai and I had swum out to the other day. It marks the meeting of the three borders with geometric precision, standing exactly at the confluence of the Ruak river (which forms the easternmost stretch of the border between Burma and Thailand) and the Mekong. The hills of Burma stretch away, green then blue, into the distance. The Mekong makes a broad leisurely curve: looking upriver, northwards, you feel you can practically see China.

The opportunist Thai have cashed in on the notoriety of the Triangle, and its beauty, and made a bit of a tourist attraction out of it. There's a sign which says 'Golden Triangle' in English and Thai, and a straggle of souvenir shops and makeshift restaurants, and some stalls selling Burmese knick-knacks – cheroots, cigarette holders, lacquered betel boxes. There's even a small guest house, the Golden Hut.

A coach-load of Hong Kong Chinese arrived on a day-trip from Chiang Rai, pallid and well pressed, pointing their big cameras at one another.

From the Triangle we took a *song taow* to Mae Sai, a lively little border-town with a bridge across the Ruak to Burma. Thai can cross over here, and buy things in Tachilek, the Burmese town the other side, but not *farang*. Katai went across. Harry and I tried to saunter over with her, but we were stopped and turned back at the checkpoint at the far side of the bridge.

'You go on,' said Harry. 'We'll wait for you.' There was a bar overlooking the river. He said we'd wait there for her. 'Remember what I told you,' he said, and she nodded. As she turned to go, he said, 'You'll come back, won't you.'

'Maybe,' she teased.

We watched her out of sight, then adjourned to the bar. Below the balcony, boys poled bamboo rafts through the littered water.

She came back an hour later, over the bridge, excited from her trip. She brought dolls to take home to her sister, tea wine and green cheroots for me and Harry, blue shoes for herself.

'Everything OK?' asked Harry.

'Everything OK.'

'Now you've really been across the border,' I said, but she didn't hear, because Harry was walking her off, with his hand in the small of her back, so I couldn't hear what he was saying to her.

From Mae Sai we took another *song taow*, south down Route 110. We were the only passengers. Katai seemed listless. She stretched out on the bench of the truck. Harry sat with the traveller's looseness, feet apart, back straight, rolling with the bumps. He was looking hard at Katai, but it was not so much desire in his gaze as curiosity.

I too was curious: what was it between them? Perhaps Katai had the simple answer: 'You can't help who you fall in love with.'

We disembarked at a village called Ban Houai Krai. Here we waited a bit, drank beer in a road-house, sheltered from the afternoon sun. Now at last – our fourth ride of the day – we were climbing up into hill-tribe country, leaving the lowlands to sweat on without us. We could see the higher peaks ahead, dark green in the sun, blue in the shadows. Tonight we would lodge in an Akha village called Ban Pa Kha and tomorrow, all being well, we would find a local guide to take us to see the poppy fields.

The Akha (or Ekaw) are one of the five major hill-tribes that inhabit the uplands of northern Thailand. The others are the Hmong (or Meo), the Mien (or Yao), the Lahu (or Musur), and the Lisu (or Lisaw). All of these tribes have their origin in southern China, and have migrated along various routes into Burma, Laos, Vietnam and Thailand. They are relative new-comers in Thailand, the earliest arriving about a hundred years ago. The Thai call them *khon doi*, 'mountain people'. Each tribe is distinct in language, dress and culture, but they all share certain basic characteristics. They are highland dwellers, preferring to live above 3,000 feet. They subsist on a primitive, shifting, slash-and-burn agriculture. Their religion is animist, with a thin overlay of Buddhism. They sew and weave with genius. And they grow, smoke and sell opium.

A sixth tribe, the Karen (or Yang), probably also originated in China, but they have inhabited Burma and western Thailand for centuries, and have lost all trace of Chinese influence in their culture. They are, in many ways, distinct from the hill-tribes: they tend to live at lower altitudes, they practise a more settled form of agriculture, and they do not cultivate opium.

Also distinct are the tribes of the Mon-Khmer family, who remain from the days prior to the arrival of the Thai. These are the Lawa, the Khamu, the Htin, and the Mrabri. The Mrabri, a tiny and elusive tribe now down to a couple of hundred, are also known as the Phi Tong Luang, the 'spirits of the yellow leaves', because they build their houses out of branches and then abandon them after a few days, when the leaves turn yellow.

The total tribal population in Thailand is now about 500,000: half of these are Karen, and half belong to the various hill-tribes.

The Akha originate in the Yunnan of southern China, where they belong to the tribal group known as the Hani. The first Akha settlement in Thailand was established in about 1903, in the Hin Taek area not far from where we were now. Their population in Thailand is now about 25,000, spread through 150 villages, mostly concentrated in the Thai-Burmese border country north of the Kok river. Much larger populations of Akha are found in China and Burma.

There were two Akha in the *song taow*, shy and saturnine and smelling faintly of old woodsmoke. They sat in silence, close up against one another. The jolting of the truck up the steep rutted track banged me against the tailgate, but produced in them no more than a gentle communal rocking.

Katai spoke with the younger Akha. He had a round nut-brown face, and hair close-cropped like a soldier's. He wore a T-shirt and baggy, blue serge trousers. It is the women who wear the distinctive tribal gear daily: the men only wear it for ceremonial occasions. He was from a village near Fang, he told her. He was travelling up to visit his cousin. We were cordially invited to visit him at his cousin's house in Ban Pa Kha. He and his cousin – like most of the Akha at Pa Kha – were members of the Mawn Po clan, also known in Thailand as the Pha Mi.

It was a good time to travel, he said. The land had been cleared but would not be sown until the coming of the rains in late April or so.

Did he grow opium, I wanted to know. He mumbled a reply. Katai laughed and said, 'He wants to know if we're from the government.'

His caution was justified. The government has been making a concerted effort to eradicate the opium crop this side of the border, and to substitute it with coffee, strawberries, cabbage, potatoes and the like. The Thai opium harvest is now less than fifty tons a year, and officials claim that most of this is consumed by the hill-tribes themselves, rather than fuelling the heroin refineries. Whatever the merits of the eradication programme, the tribes-people inevitably view the arrival of Thai troops in their villages, and the burning of their poppy fields with flame-throwers, as just another chapter in a long history of mistrust.

More recently, another element has entered into the equation. As the hill-tribes' primitive agriculture depletes the soil of the uplands, they have begun to move down to the lower slopes. This brings them into territorial conflict with the rural Thai of the region. It is probably this, rather than opium, that has caused a hardening of Thai attitudes towards the *khon doi*. Since I was there, alarming reports of forced repatriations have been coming out. In September 1987, in a series of dawn raids, some 2,000 tribespeople from thirteen villages were rounded up, trucked up to the border, and handed over to the Burmese army. Given the nomadic nature of the hill-tribes the word 'repatriation' has a hollow ring to it.

After an hour or so, the low, humped roofs of the Akha village came into view. Here for the first time I saw the Akha women in all their finery. The *pièce de résistance* is the head-dress. This is a kind of helmet, festooned with discs of beaten silver, with coins, beads, feathers, monkey fur, discs of mirror, pompoms, and tassles made of the tear-shaped seeds of a savannah grass called Job's Tear. The rest of their clothing – waistcoat, short dress, leggings – is covered with the rich, patterned weaving of the tribe. The Akha style is very sombre, very stately: the colours are dark, reds and blacks, ambers and umbers, smoky colours.

The light was softening. Woodsmoke hung over the village. The sight of the women was thrilling: the thrill of difference in this world grown so similar.

On the far side of the village was the so-called 'guest house', a scattering of bamboo and leaf-thatch huts in a packed earth compound. There were sweeping views east over the hills and down into the plain below. Pockets of thirsty forest could be seen on the steeper slopes, but most of the land below was pale and sparse, the kind of scrubby savannah that is left behind by hill-tribe farming methods.

'Tomorrow we're going on up,' Harry said, gesturing to the darker, greener hills above us. 'Tomorrow we'll see some real forest.'

There was a choice of accommodation: rooms in the main building, or individual huts scattered around the perimeter of the compound. The rooms were no more than wattle cubicles, gloomy and lacking in privacy. We took the huts. They were sparse: a sleeping quarter with a mattress on the floor and a mosquito net; a narrow *jaan*, open on three sides, for sitting out on. There was no electricity. Washing facilities were of the customary bucket and scoop variety.

The place had the air of an extended farmyard. There were chickens and pigs, and piles of old lumber sprouting spiky weeds. There were dogs: the small, sandy-coloured mutts that one sees everywhere in Thailand. It was nearing sunset, and a few guests were mooching around, as if they too were just part of the farmyard.

Currently resident were a pair of pale Frenchmen, here to smoke opium; a silent, sandy-haired Australian backpacker, hiking; a couple of anthropologists – a Dutchman and a Filipina – here to study Akha linguistics; and a few Thai, for reasons unclear.

Three hill-tribe boys ran the place, westernized in dress – T-shirts and jeans – but hill-tribe in features: squat, dark, unexpressive, narrow-eyed, so different from the bland prettiness of the Thais. One of them played guitar. He could sing 'You've Got To Hide Your Love Away' right through, syllable by syllable, without understanding a word of it.

It had been a long day, and I thought the place very beautiful. Harry seemed edgy, though. He fingered the bear's tooth around his neck, he checked the contents of his bag, he peered around as if he expected someone to jump out of the bushes, he snapped at the boy who showed us to our huts (one for Harry and Katai, one for me).

He went up to the washing block to freshen up. I said to Katai, 'What's the matter with Harry? He's jumpy.'

'I know.' She lowered her voice, though he was a long way away. 'It's the opium, Charlie. He says he can smell it in the air. You known he used to *dag fin*.'

'He was an addict?'

'Yes. Long time ago, but . . .'

'Perhaps it wasn't such a good idea to come up here, then.'

'Oh yes, we had to.'

'Had to?'

'Oh, well . . . he promised you, Charlie. He said he'd show you the poppy fields.'

Was it my imagination, or had she meant something else?

Harry came back. He was looking worse. He'd been talking to the Frenchmen – *les deux mecs*, as he called them. They were walking down to the village for a few bowls of opium. They had invited him to join them.

'So of course you say no,' Katai said.

'What the fuck you think I said?' he snapped.

He had a headache. Katai ministered to him with Tiger Balm and cold flannels. I went off to my hut, watched the last of the sunset streaking the hills. A faint tracery of village lights appeared in the dusk below, frail flickering lights, like stars that one guesses are very distant.

Up at the main building there was food of a sort. Twenty-five

baht bought a meal permed out of rice, noodles, eggs and vegetables. There was no beer, no alcohol of any sort. It transpired
that the owner of the place was a Haw Chinese Muslim. The *mecs*
were in one of the rooms, with the door wide open. They sagged
dreamily: they had clearly partaken of their sundowners. One of
them, balding, paper-white face, goatee beard, raised a hand and
gave me a languid peace sign. The other lay chest-down on his bed:
he looked like Pierre Clementi, tall and sultry, with black glossy
love-locks and a red neckerchief. He was staring off the edge of his
pillow, down at the matting on the floor. I thought he was about to
be sick, but he just lay there all the while, occasionally rubbing his
filthy bare feet together.

They had come up on trail bikes: Suzuki 175s. They had been
up here a fortnight, and were so wasted on opium that they were
beginning to wonder if they'd ever get down again.

The anthropologists were writing up their diaries by lamplight.
The Dutchman, blond, thirtyish, with circular rimless spectacles, was a heavy tribal purist. He regretted the advent of the
pick-up truck, the T-shirt, the running shoe, the tin roof. Even
roads and electricity were intrusions. 'Soon they will have the TV
and the video, and then they will be like everyone else.'

Their linguistic study was not going well. They were finding the
Akha uncommunicative. Linguistically the tribe is related to the
Lahu and the Lisu (Tibeto-Burman language-family), rather than
to the Hmong and Mien (Sino-Tibetan language family). They
have no written language, but a strong oral tradition. The tribal
memory of early migration routes is consistent among branches of
the tribe which have had no physical contact for two or three
generations. Like many tribal peoples, their sense of tradition is
expressed as a revering of 'ancestors'. Some Akha are said to be
able to recite a genealogy of fifty or sixty names, beginning with
their own forebears, and going back through clan chiefs real and
legendary, to the 'great father' of the Akha race, Zoeh Tah Pah.

Later that night, sitting on my verandah, coating myself with
Autan, I saw Harry coming out of the next-door hut. He stretched

and rubbed his eyes, went into the bushes to take a pee. Katai had been up earlier and brought back some food. He settled on the steps of the verandah, spooned a few mouthfuls. He was wearing one of her *sarong*.

I saw him turn and stare off into the bushes the far side of his hut. He had that poise I had seen before: he seemed to sniff the air. He got up and walked to the rail of the verandah. He watched and listened, and then he spoke in a low voice. I couldn't hear what he said and I couldn't see who he was talking to. He walked back to where he had been sitting, picked up the plate of food, and laid it on the steps of the *jaan*.

He spoke off into the bushes again, and this time I heard him say, '*Viens diner, donc.*'

Then I saw, emerging from the shrubbery, a low dark figure. It was one of the farmyard pigs. It moved hesitantly towards the plate of food, and began to snuffle up the contents. While it ate, Harry talked to it. He spoke in a low, kindly voice. Every now and then the pig raised its head, quivered its snout in his direction, seeming to keep up a dialogue.

The pig finished its meal and trotted off. Harry called softly, '*Bon nuit, copain.*'

For a while after, he sat on the steps, smoking and staring off into the night. From a hundred feet away I could feel the intensity of his solitude, I could feel that the 'code of the road' is loneliness, as well as freedom.

The next morning Katai went off into Pa Kha and came back with a guide to take us up to the poppy fields. He was a wiry, crop-haired Akha, wearing striped trousers and a loose, round-necked white shirt. He delved into a faded shoulder-bag for regular handfuls of betel. He was in his late thirties, I guessed, but he had the sly, droll look of a street urchin.

His name was Appa. When I told him my name he grinned mysteriously, and spat a blood-red glob of betel into the dust.

Appa spoke no English, and not a lot of Thai, but Katai was a born communicator. All day long she would be at him. Whenever I wanted to know anything she would call out, 'Appa?', in a strident schoolmistressy voice, and he would half-turn back, with a reluctant grunt, to answer another damn-fool *farang* question. One way and another, almost despite himself, he became quite informative.

But for now it was Harry who was doing the questioning. He wanted to know where we were going, whose plantations we were going to see, what the state of the harvest was. He wanted to establish right now that Appa would only get good money from us provided he took us somewhere interesting. Harry was offering a hundred baht for the day, actually a rather stingy sum compared to what one would pay for a guide nearer the tourist centres of Chiang Mai or Chiang Rai.

Appa mumbled answers, eyes downcast, his bare toes fidgeting a pattern in the dust. Sometimes he looked up at us, gave a slow roguish smile. This was usually when he had some information which he thought would disappoint us.

The nearest plantation was about three hours' walk, we learned. We would be crossing into Burma to see it.

'Does this mean we're going into Shan country?' I asked.

Katai conferred. 'Yes. We see Shan poppy fields.'

'Is that safe?'

'He says the Shan are his friends '

'I hope he's right.'

Harry laughed. 'Relax,' he said. 'This guy knows what he's doing.'

The biggest disappointment, the broadest smile, was that we had missed the opium harvest. It had been early this year, at least in this part of the Triangle. It had finished a week ago.

'Sorry about that,' Harry said.

'Well, it's a pity we had to hang around in Chiang Saen so long,' I grumbled.

He spread his hands, plausible Gallic Harry. 'But the poppy harvest is not consistent. I'm sure you appreciate. There are many micro-climates here, variations even from one valley to the next. Further west, they probably haven't harvested yet. There are Lisu villages, up past Pai, I know the people there. I'll tell you all about it. Let's enjoy ourselves now, shall we?'

We stood outside the gate of the guess how. After a while a pick-up truck came labouring up the hill. Appa sat up front with the driver. We joined a couple of tribesmen on the benches in the back. They were going up to a village near the mountain temple of Doi Lang. We watched the scenery out the back of the truck. Harry said, 'I saw a movie one time. There's this guy and a girl riding in a car. The girl says, What are you running away from? And the guy just says, Look behind you, and there's this shot of the road moving away behind them.'

After a few miles we stopped. Appa motioned us out of the truck. There was a village below us, a precipitous track leading down to it. We paid a few baht to the driver, and the truck went off with its dust-cloud, the two Akha in the back staring out at us.

We set off east, Appa leading the way, barefooted and agile, Katai following tall in black, Harry in his waistcoat, bag slung cross-wise. In his bag he carried a water-bottle, a knife, a compass, a length of rope, a *sarong*, cigarettes and matches, oranges, Tiger Balm. He looked ready to walk for a week.

We skirted the ridge above the village and quickly entered woodland. The trail was clear and well-trodden. It rose and fell steeply, down across shady creeks, up into hot open stretches that laid the hills out before us. The upper peaks were dark green, shading off into blue: we were looking out across Burma, out into the Shan hills, the heart of the Triangle. The lower slopes bore the scars of clearance: blackened tree stumps, dull yellow savannah, plumes of smoke rising from a further valley.

At one of the creeks I stopped to splash water on my face. Appa turned and said something. Katai said, 'Appa says there is good water further on. We will stop there.'

'This water looks pretty clean to me.' I said.

'He says the spirits are good at the place further on. We know these water spirits, *na*, Charlie?' She winked, maddeningly con-spiratorial. She skipped across the stepping stones and slid her arm into Harry's. He was fiddling with the bevel of his compass. He growled at her to get off. She laughed and began to move up the steep slope the other side.

Harry looked up from the compass. 'We're moving north-west,' he said thoughtfully.

The trail wound up steeply, densely hedged with bamboo and teak saplings. Appa was far above us, perched on a boulder. He watched us with mild curiosity as we panted up the slope after him. The path was slippery here: the stream ran down across it and turned the leaf-mould to mud. Ten minutes later, we came down into a luxuriant little hollow. Here we found the approved water-source. There was an ingenious conduit, made of halved sections of bamboo, channelling off clear brook-water. Two cups, also made of bamboo, hung from a convenient branch. We slaked our thirst and rested. The trees seemed to stretch up for a mile above us, smooth pale trunks with an azure mottling of lichen, telescoping up to the canopy.

On we went, Appa forcing the pace. He was silent and grudging, but sometimes, as we walked ahead, he would give a quick, furtive glance down off the trail, and when we got up to that spot, there would be something of note – a design carved on the rock, a cache of old poppy pods, the corpse of a buffalo with a horde of black insects swarming around the gaping red crater of its belly.

A village came into view in a saddle of the hills below us. The round thatched roofs radiated out over the cleared ground like the leaves of some spreading plant. I hoped we were going to stop and visit the village, but Appa kept on walking, and we soon passed the fork in the trail which led down to it.

'He says we can visit there on the way back,' Katai called back, anticipating my whine of complaint.

Poppy Fields

NOTHING MARKED the border except a line of trees running down the hillside, across the trail, and down into the river valley far below. Each tree was scorched, or truncated, or marked in some way, but they were too widely and irregularly spaced to be noticed as a line unless you were shown it.

'Pah Ma,' said Appa modestly. We were in Burma.

What exactly this meant seemed as nebulous as the demarcation itself. Not much to Appa, whose clan – the Mawn Po – was spread indiscriminately across Burma and northern Thailand. Not much in terms of modern nationhood, either, since the Burmese government's writ ran out a good hundred miles from here. Almost all of northern and eastern Burma is rebel country, though in this case 'bandit country' would be more accurate. A few Shan armies are genuinely involved in the secessionist war, but for the most part they are involved only in as far as it enables them to get on with their drug business unhindered.

However, it certainly meant something in terms of opium. The poppy fields began just a few hundred yards across the border, and after twenty minutes' walk they stretched up and down the slopes as far as we could see. The trail wound off into the distance like a farmer's track through a field of green corn.

The poppies were all without petals. As Appa had forewarned, the harvest had finished a week ago. The bare pods bore the score marks of recent tapping. Traces of dark sticky gum adhered to some of the cuts: raw opium. When first tapped, the sap of *Papaver somniferum* is grey and glutinous, like fresh rubber, but it swiftly oxidizes to a deep marmite-brown. A special knife is used for cutting the poppy-heads, with a curved blade like a miniature bill-hook. The incisions are made vertically: some tribes slit the pod with a downward motion and some with an upward motion, each adhering to its preferred method as doggedly as the big-enders and little-enders of Lilliput. Harvesting is usually done by the women of the tribe. Great care must be taken in the cutting of the pods. If the cut is too deep, the sap will spill out onto the earth. If the cut is too shallow, the sap will not ooze, and will harden inside the pod.

We left the trail and walked up the side of the field until we came to a patch of boulder and scrub. Here we could look over the whole landscape, but could not be easily seen ourselves. Appa claimed the Shan were his friends, but it was best not to advertise our presence in their opium fields. Here we would rest up for a while.

Appa scraped some opium off with his fingernail, and nibbled at it thoughtfully. He gestured for us to follow suit. Harry smiled and took out his Saigon knife.

'Maybe you shouldn't do this, Harry,' said Katai.

'Maybe I shouldn't,' he said, working gently on a poppy-head. He sniffed at the dark gum on the blade. He nodded expertly. 'What you've got here,' he said, handing it to me, 'is the raw material for some of the best heroin in the world.'

It had a strange woody taste: sickly but agreeable. I felt my stomach loosening, my heart slowing, an ease spread through my limbs. Harry gathered a nugget for Katai and finally one for himself. One by one we sat down, and then lay down, in the tall yellow grass at the edge of the field.

Appa took Harry's knife and examined each appliance with great care. He smiled as he handed it back. The knife was a language he understood: he had little use for words, but this strong and useful thing spoke clearly to him.

We sat in the sun, gazing over the stalky landscape. No one came, nothing happened. Katai murmured, 'Mai mee arai nai gaw pai': there's nothing in the bamboo. This means: no problem, nothing to worry about. It seemed strange that it should be so. Millions of words have been written about the global evils of heroin, and yet here at the heart of the empire all was serene, the green poppy-heads swaying in the breeze, the Shan hills laid out before us, the silence over everything.

For maybe an hour we lay there, talking desultorily. Then I saw Harry roll over onto his front and scan the hills below. 'We've got company.'

Two figures were moving slowly up the trail, coming from the Thai side. We watched in silence. 'Just two,' said Harry softly. He looked over at Appa, who was crouched at the edge of field, poppy-head in hand, also watching the moving figures. He smiled and nodded back. There seemed no cause for alarm, though it was now clear that each of the figures was carrying some kind of rifle over his shoulder.

Harry was looking at me, that note of challenge in his eye. 'Shall we go and talk to them?' he said. 'See what the man has to tell us?' He drawled out 'the man' like he was talking about some ounce-dealer on the Upper East Side, right down the other end of the global trail. I suddenly had a strange flash of paranoia: that Harry had wanted to come up here all along, that we were all of us part of some devious mad-dog drug scam, that he had actually intended all along to meet these guys, third field down after the border.

He said, 'OK, listen. I'll go down with Appa first. You two stay up here. If there's any kind of monkey business when they see us, if they start moving their guns around, you get your butts down behind the rocks here and keep low. OK, *bway*?'

'OK, *bway*,' said Katai.

'After we've spoken with them, if it's cool, I'll wave up to you. Don't show yourselves till then. We don't want to make them jumpy.'

The two men were about a hundred yards from where they would pass on the trail below us. I said, 'You'd better move then, otherwise you'll be coming at them from behind.'

Harry said, 'Right. Come on, Appa.' Appa looked sheepish, pretended he didn't understand Harry's bootleg Thai. 'Katai, tell him we want to talk with these men.'

Katai spoke slowly and reasonably. Appa climbed to his feet, spat on the floor, smiled none too warmly. 'It's another fifty baht, Harry,' said Katai.

'No fucking *pompen*.'

They moved off down the hillside, Harry in his hat just a shade taller than Appa. They walked easily, arms and hands loose, demonstrably free of weapons. Harry had his Saigon knife in his shoulder-bag, Appa the small machete in his, but these were nothing against a pair of rifles – 'M-2s: old but pretty damn serviceable', as Harry punctiliously put it later.

The men saw them as soon as they started walking down. They stopped and stared. The taller shielded his eyes against the glare. I found myself crouching guiltily behind the long grass, hoping they couldn't see us.

Harry gave the men a short greeting wave. Katai said, '*Farang* so sweet when he's a bit scared.'

The men were waiting at the crossroads, where the edge of the field – a rocky defile, a water-course in the rainy season, dried up right now – met the trail. The two pairs joined up. I strained to pick up body-talk. The still air carried their voices, but they were talking tribal language. I saw Harry proffer his water-bottle: the language of things, as spoken on the border. The shorter man drank first. He was older than the tall one, I thought.

After a bit Harry waved and we walked down to join them. I tried to saunter. Harry was all smiles, keeping everything light. The taller one was scarcely more than a boy: fourteen perhaps. The other was about the same age as Appa. They had a Chinese look to them, the older man broad, with black spiky hair falling at an angle across his forehead. The teenager was more slender, and his hair was thicker and wavier, but he had the same high cheekbones and slit-eyes. They wore dull, coarse clothes – dun-brown, overall-blue – and plastic thong-sandals.

We all nodded at one another. Katai said, '*Sawadee, chow*.' They bowed their heads brusquely and mumbled, '*Sawadee, kap*.' The boy was looking a bit nervous. Perhaps he thought we were from the Narcotics Assistance Bureau. I saw a buttery kind of grease about the firing pin of his rifle: this was a well-maintained fire-arm. I didn't want him to get the wrong impression. Better take it easy with the questions.

'So what do you want to know?' she asked.

I was about to start in with some gentle openers. Who were they, where did they come from: the rote-questions of my trade.

But it was Harry who moved in, Harry she was talking to. 'OK,' he said, talking to her behind his smile. 'I've established that they're Shan, that they don't understand anything I say, that I can't get through to them at all so far. So . . . ' He turned to me. 'Offer them a cigarette, Charlie.' The offer was accepted, the meeting shaped round the given length of a smoke.

Harry said, 'Ask them where they come from, Katai.'

Like Lao, the Shan language has close family-links to Thai, and much of the basic vocabulary is the same. The boy answered her question with a mumbled name.

'Again?' said Harry.

Katai asked again. The boy said, 'Wan Sen Pawmong.'

'Is it the nearest village Burmese-side?'

It was.

'How far?'

'Two hours' walk, Harry.'

'Are there any roads out?'

There was some difficulty here. The linguistic cross-currents were strong. Harry persisted, the soul of courtesy. Katai persisted, the born communicator. The men knitted their brows and leant towards her as she spoke. Appa stood to one side, a little embarrassed by this outburst of *farang* inquisitiveness.

What Harry was after, it seemed, and what he eventually got, was an idea of how this village of theirs communicated with elsewhere in Burma. Tortuously it emerged. There was no vehicle access to Wan Sen Pawmong, or to any of the villages round about, but there were mule-trails all through the mountains, and reliably guided you could reach, in two or three day's good walking, the small trading town of Mong Hpayak. There you could pick up the road north to Kengtung, one of the major towns of the Shan States and a border trading-post with China.

Harry mused, 'So from here to Kengtung . . . five days?'

The Shan assented. Harry was looking at Katai. She returned his gaze. 'And back makes ten,' she said.

'Ask them if there are army blocks before Kengtung.'

They didn't think so. It depended. The old man added that he hadn't been to Kengtung for years.

I was completely nonplussed. 'Why do you want to know all this?'

Harry ground his cigarette out in the dust, gave a tight smile. 'Never know when it might be useful.'

'Useful for what?'

'Do you want to ask these guys some questions?'

I did, of course. The Shan had finished their cigarettes, too. They were beginning to think about moving on.

I asked, through Katai, whose poppy fields these were.

The old man said, evasively, 'Village fields.'

'His village?'

'No another village.'

'Was the harvest – ?'

Harry cut in, 'Hey, don't push it on the opium. They won't like it and they won't tell you.'

I took his point, and changed tack. 'Ask them where they are travelling from today? Have they been in Thailand?'

They had. They were in fact coming from the Akha village we had passed on the way. They traded with a *jeen haw* – a Haw Chinese trader – who lived in the village.

'What do you trade?' I asked.

Harry again: 'Shit, man. What do you think they're trading just after the harvest?' He was getting restless. 'We've asked them enough. Don't want to make fools of ourselves.' With diplomatic charm, protestations of *shoke dee*, he eased us out of the meeting. We all shook hands, very merry. The Shan shouldered their M-2s and went on their way. We went on ours, and twenty minutes later we crossed back over the invisible border, back into Thailand.

On the way back we called in at the Akha village. The path led down to the traditional Akha gateway: a wooden arch about ten foot tall, two stout trunks and a squared cross-bar. The wood was decorated with carved shapes, triangles and diamonds. The patterns were the same as they use in their weavings and appliqués. Each shape has a meaning: river, mountain, rice, poppy, and so on.

Strung to the uprights of the arch were several small articles of bamboo, fishbone-shaped, a series of thin stems woven into a vertical spine. Appa called these *da leh*. They are charms, he explained. They are to prevent bad spirits coming into the village. If a person carries bad spirits they will get tangled up on the little branches of the *da leh* as he passes.

'What kind of spirits?' I asked.

Appa grunted a few items. Katai translated: 'Many spirits, Charlie. The hawk spirit and the tiger spirit, the spirits of sickness and madness, the spirits of drought and flood. And, oh yes, the spirit of the *kio*, the vampire. You remember I tell you: the *farang* is a vampire.'

Passing through the archway, Appa's grim eye upon us, I half expected some signal to break the silence, some arcane kind of bleep, as my cache of bad spirits was detected.

We walked down into the village. The reddish earth of the paths was smooth and powdery. It was mid afternoon, a quiet time. Few people were out and about. Faces watched from smoke-blackened interiors, from supine positions in the shade. At the centre of the village was a wide empty space of bare earth: it is convenient to call it the village square, though nothing about the village was remotely rectilinear. The houses were round tumps of bamboo and thatch. They seemed a product of accumulation rather than construction. The walls sagged, the paths curled, the forest looped down into clearings, smoke seeped out of the shaggy roofs like morning-steam on a flock of mountain sheep.

There was a single larger house with some pretensions to lines and corners. To this Appa led us. An old man walked onto the verandah. He greeted us courteously but without obvious pleasure. He was clearly not Akha. He was slender in build, quite tall, with a small cadaverous face. He had an immensely long white hair dangling from a mole on his chin. He wore a blue cotton shirt, and trousers cut off below the knees.

He waved us to come up the steps onto the verandah. Katai made her Chinese *wai* – knuckles upmost, rather than fingertips – and said, '*Kam sha*.'

We sat on the verandah. The old man went inside, gave orders which were answered with a woman's tired-sounding voice. Inside his house, through a bead curtain, could be seen jumbled goods: gunny-sacks of grain, a spigotted tank of paraffin, coils of rope, iron rods, hoes and axes, handles and hafts, candles and soap and a carton bearing the name 'Buspro', which turned out to contain sachets of Burmese Aspirin.

Harry stretched and leaned back on his hands. 'This is the Haw trader the Shan men told us about. It's the rule in South-east Asia. Wherever there's people selling and people buying, there's a Chinese trader in between. He'll cover all the area within a day's walk. Right now he'll be buying up a lot of the opium round about. That's what our Shan friends were doing here.'

'So they brought their opium here?'

He nodded. 'They get about 200 dollars a kilo from a guy like this. But your Chinaman probably won't have paid out in dollars. All through the year he sells to the tribesmen on credit, and now he'll be calling in the debts in the form of opium. Black gold, man. Hell, there have been Chinese I really loved. Back in Cholon: some very good people. But in business . . .' He winced and shook his fingers in a cautionary, once-bitten way. 'Don't matter where you look. Drug trade, gem trade, skin trade, name it, the Chinese are there. They're the spider right in the middle of the web. You take care with Chinese. Because you're caught in that web even though you don't know it.'

He sat up and added, 'But right now I love them, because this tea is going to taste like the goddamn elixir.'

An elderly lady, hair knotted behind her head, was carrying out a tray with four small cups on it. He was right: the tea was bitter, hot and totally tonic.

As we sat on the verandah, the village women came quietly across the square, a few carrying stuff to sell – clothes, bags, jewellery, weavings – others just to take a look at the *farang* passing through. They wore the strange helmets and rich weavings of the tribe.

They were proud of their head-dresses, and bent their heads for us to inspect them. The different clans of Akha wear different

shaped head-dresses, I later learned from the Dutch anthropol-
ogist. The rounded, helmet-shaped style worn by these ladies
showed that they were Mawn Po, like Appa. The Loi Mi clan
favour a smaller, flatter head-dress, while the A Jaw clan (called
the U Lo in Thailand) wear a taller, more pointy number.

Amid the festooning of silver coins on one old lady's helmet
Harry recognized, with an exclamation of delight, some old
piastres from the days of French Indo-China. Others were Burmese
kyat, Indian rupees, Chinese dollars, Laotian kip: all the coinage
of this mongrel realm.

Something else on her head-dress caught his eye. 'Will you look
at this?' he said, speaking to himself. There were two beads: one
blue, one green.

'Precious stones?' I asked.

'Not exactly,' he said, peering at the head-dress as closely as
politeness would allow, given the old lady beneath it. 'They're
glass beads, no doubt about that. But I'll lay money that they're
worth a bit. They're European: could even be Venetian. They
were brought over by traders into China, centuries ago. I've seen
them around before, but these are beauties.'

The women laid out a few wares. We bargained at a leisurely
rate: bags and necklaces and waistcoats. None of the helmets was
for sale. All the gear they were selling was old-looking. Whatever
they had they would offer, including clothes they were wearing.
The woven patterns are appliqué on a background cloth of home-
spun cotton. The cloth is dyed in indigo from plants grown in the
village. A woman said the cloth must be dyed every day for a
month to get this deep beautiful blue. That is why she must ask a
hundred baht (though the waistcoat in question would have cost
five hundred in the night bazaar in Chiang Mai).

They are individually shy, but in a group the Akha women were
more communicative and alert than the men we'd met. I found this
the general rule in hill-tribe country. The men are gruffer, slower,
deeply reserved: they can be kind and hospitable in their actions,
but in their manner there is this sullen-seeming tribal machismo.
This goes hand in hand with the debilitations of a heavy opium
habit. Very few hill-tribe women smoke.

Inside the Haw's gloomy store-room Appa was purchasing opium. I watched through the bead curtain. The trader had a fat black wedge of the stuff, two or three kilos, wrapped in banana-leaves and polythene. I guessed it was produce the Shan men had sold him. He tore off a small piece, showed it to Appa, said something which sounded like a price. Appa nodded.

Harry was at my shoulder. 'Let's go in. He won't mind. This is just a casual deal.'

They looked up when we walked in, but they didn't say anything. Harry asked to look at the opium Appa was still holding. He said to the Haw, '*Chandu, mai?*' The Haw nodded. He asked how much for this piece. The Haw said, 'One hundred baht.' Harry said he would buy some too.

'Is that a good idea, Harry?'

'You wouldn't want to leave without tasting some of the local produce would you?' He said it lightly, but I saw the skulking look in his eye. There are some battles you never win.

Chandu, Harry explained, is proper smoking opium. The raw opium, the stuff we saw on the poppy pods, is dissolved in hot water, strained through a cotton cloth, then the water is boiled off. It is one stage purer than raw opium. From *chandu* they then make morphine base, and from that heroin, but neither the hill-tribe grower nor the Haw trader would have anything to do with those later stages.

The trader took down a wooden case, teak, shaped like a small violin case. Inside was a set of iron balances, and, each nestling in a separate compartment, half a dozen weights sculpted in the plump shape of the Chinese Buddha. He chose the second smallest. It squatted in the shallow iron bowl of the weights. I remembered the shrine at the Gipsee Rose strip-club: you meet the Buddha in the strangest company, and I suppose that is one of the beauties of Buddhism.

Actually – as Katai soon pointed out – Buddhism is not at all in favour of intoxicants. Monks, of course, may take no drugs or alcohol, though they can and frequently do smoke tobacco. She told of the legend that the Buddha, when he was struggling towards the light of *dharma*, cut off his eyelids to stop himself from falling asleep. Where his eyelids fell there grew the first opium poppy, a symbol of the falsehoods – false rest, false visions – that the *bodhisattva* must cast aside on his quest for the true light.

We walked to another village, an hour's walk, then a steep climb. This was a Lahu village: less colourful than the Akha – in none of the Lahu villages I visited did I see people wearing traditional costume – but very friendly. Here we were invited to drink and eat. A huge *burri* of local tobacco was tamped into a bamboo pipe and passed around.

One of the Lahu boys got out a musical instrument. It was a kind of banjo, wood and hide, with three wire strings fastened to pegs at the neck. He played a mournful, striding sort of tune, three chords, hill-tribe blues.

Inside, the women were preparing us a meal. Strips of pork fat were torn from a row of meat hanging from the rafters. These were fried in a wok on the fire. In another rice-cakes sizzled. I passed round the tea wine that Katai had given us – 'a present for my two *farang*' – when she came back all breathless across the bridge at Mae Sai.

The hut was filled with lumber and rags, broken farm-tools, cobwebs and shed-dust. Appa was quiet, aloof. Perhaps he was just relaxing. Perhaps, though I couldn't really believe this, he was tired. We ate our meal. The Lahu squatted on the balcony opposite, watching each mouthful with pleasure.

One of them told a mischievous story about the Akha, how in the 'early time', the Great Creator's sons and daughters all paired up, and out of their unions came the various hill-tribes: the Lahu and the Lisu, the Meo and Yao, and so on. But the Akha boy had no partner, so he was forced to marry a monkey in the jungle in order to found his dynasty.

Appa laughed, showing betel-blackened teeth. In his village, he said, they told the same story about the Lahu.

Harry and I sat side by side on a low bed in Appa's house at Pa Kha. He had invited us back to smoke the opium we had acquired from the Haw. Katai had declined and returned to the guess how.

Appa's wife brewed Chinese tea in a kettle. She squatted by the smouldering fire, muttering at it as she fanned up the embers. She was a small, quiet, amiable woman. She wore no head-dress, just a scarf of cloth on her head, but she wore the embroidered leggings, and the short indigo skirt with the long sash hanging down, for modesty's sake when she sits or squats.

Their son was there too, a stocky boy in his teens. He wore a T-shirt that said, for no apparent reason, 'Block Bust'. He was shy at first, though later he talked with us.

The house was dark and low and redolent of woodsmoke. Chinks of light glowed through the bamboo walls. Apart from the low doorway, curtained off with blankets, these were the only source of light in the hut. It was a 'ground house', built on a floor of packed earth, rather than up on piles with air underneath. We were up at about 5,000 feet here, the higher altitude range for hill-tribes. The mornings can be misty and chill, and these low-built houses retain the warmth better. In terms of tribal status, elevated houses are more up-market, because they're harder to build. There were some of these at Pa Kha, but not Appa's.

There was a raised area to the right of the doorway as you came in. There were two mattresses here, covered with blankets, and between them lay the blackened clutter of Appa's opium kit: bamboo-stem pipes with small metal bowls, a wick-lamp, dibbers and needles and a small rusty knife.

Also among the impedimenta were several sachets, one or two revealing white powder inside. For a moment I thought it was heroin, but I knew this was unlikely. The hill-tribes have nothing to do with heroin as such. I saw more of the white powder scattered around, mixed with the black ashy detritus of previous sessions.

I asked Harry what the powder was. He looked down at the sachets. Something seemed to surprise him. He reached out to pick one of them up. 'I don't believe it,' he murmured.

'What is it?'

'It's Old Longhead!'

'What do you mean, Old Longhead?'

He laughed. 'It's just aspirin. Chinese headache powder. They mix it with the opium.' I asked him what for. 'It's mostly to bind the opium. When its fresh, it's a bit too wet, unstable. They put the aspirin in, like straw into the mud to make a brick. Some people say the aspirin also stops you getting a bad head after you've smoked.'

He handed me the sachet: it had smudgy Chinese characters on it, black on green, and a line-drawing – done in the timeless, tacky, joke-shop style – of a man with a hugely elongated forehead.

'The strange thing is,' Harry said, 'I haven't seen Old Longhead for maybe twenty years. When I was a smoker, in Vientiane, the rickshaw boys used to mix it in. It was always this brand: the guy with the great long headache. So after a while we – not the Lao boys: I mean the French – we used to make it our word for opium. Monsieur Tête Longue. *Allons visiter Monsieur Tête Longue . . .*'

He tossed the sachet back onto the tray, laughed drily. 'Well, here I am back again, *mon vieux.*'

Appa lay on one bed, propped up on his elbow. We sat on the other, drank the tea his wife gave us – muddy and luke-warm, nothing of the pungency of the Haw lady's brew – and watched him preparing the first bowl of opium.

First he scraped out the bowl of the pipe, made a small pile of the black residue: ash and oxidized opium from the previous session, the 'tailings' as Harry called it. He explained that they often mix this with the opium, to make an inferior but cheaper smoke. Tonight we would be smoking pure *chandu*.

Appa gently tore a small piece off the wedge of opium. In the lamplight I saw the rich colour of the opium, where it was stretched and pulled. It was a deep reddish-brown, the colour of a young conker, the colour of plum jam. He kneaded the piece between his fingers, mixed in some of the powdered aspirin. He now had a rounded pellet the size of a large pea. He impaled it on the end of a dibber, a thin metal spike about six inches long, and heated it over the meagre flame of the wick-lamp. He held it so that the ball was just at the fringes of the flame, never quite touching. He kneaded it some more, his fingers grimed with opium and carbon. It was now ready for smoking. He pushed it into the shallow bowl of the pipe, held the bowl at an angle over the flame, and wrapped his lips around the bamboo mouthpiece. Still the opium must not touch the flame. It sizzles and sweats but never quite burns. He used the dibber to prod and tease the melting pellet, to keep the airway open, to keep the smoke coming. He took the smoke in, slow and level, in one long grateful draught. The mellow, sickly smell spread through the dark hut.

The light faded unnoticed. After a few bowls everything takes on a loose, underwater feel. If you close your eyes you can easily imagine that you're floating, that these ripples of sensation are carrying you off through the darkness, and when you open your eyes again you'll be somewhere else: but where?

Harry quotes Rimbaud, of course: '*Comme je descendais les fleuves impassibles* . . .'

Everything is now done in the horizontal position that opium exacts. Appa is propped on one elbow, smoking, preparing, face close over the lamp, restful and intent. When your turn comes round, you crawl into the smoking position, lying on your side, head resting on a pillow of old clothes . You are like a child in your posture. Someone could come and cover you with a blanket, and you'd smile and say 'Thank you' without looking up. Your eyes are on the pipemaker, his grimed hands nudging the gear into the bowl, his face up-lit from the wick-lamp, his Chinese eyes with the pin-prick pupils. He swings the long stem towards you, the opium sputters, you suck the woody smoke down as slow as you can (though taking three or four draughts where Appa only took one). You can taste the smoke but hardly feel it, it's so mild. The taste is sweet. The taste is bitter. Your eyes are still on the pipemaker. You fear that if you look too long into his eyes you will disappear into them, tumble slowly down long black tunnels, like Alice down the rabbit hole. But nothing matters, least of all your fears.

Harry said this was high quality opium, this was stuff the tourist trekkers would never get. I said benevolently, 'You get it right, don't you, Harry? You get the best out of things.'

He said, 'Code of the road,' and we laughed.

Harry told me I would probably be sick some time. This was natural, because I didn't 'have the habitude' for opium. I had already felt twinges of nausea, but found that as long as I didn't move too much, as long as I lay still, with my eyes shut, the sickness remained somehow apart from me. It was happening in some distant region: my body. Most of all you don't want to stand up. Your two-legged self, upright and uptight, has gone off somewhere, and left this smiling cadaver with enough motor energy to talk, to light cigarettes, and to crawl into place for the next bowl.

We lay side by side on the bed. We talked up to the ceiling. Harry drifted into reminiscence: his 'smoking days' in Vientiane, back in the sixties.

The Laotian capital in those days probably had a heavier concentration of opium dens than any other city in the world, he said. 'The spooks at the US embassy had done a survey. Kind of a market survey, you could say, considering the stakes the Yanks had in the opium business in those days. They found there were a thousand *fumeries* in Vientiane, give or take. That's about one for every fifty men, women and children in the city.

'There were *fumeries* in the centre of town, and all around The Strip, but the best opium I ever smoked was out on the edge of town. You'd get a rickshaw boy to take you there, to the places where they smoked themselves. These were rough places. I mean, these were the shanties, nothing fancy. But the opium was so sweet, man, so strong. You could spend a night and a day in there, never realize the time.

'In the next shack there's the rickshaw boy's coffee-shop. Here they sell you *café électrique*. That's strong black coffee with amphetamine laced in. Speed coffee. So the boys would come in, have a few bowls, then a shot of *café électrique*, and then they go out to work again. The rickshaw boys, they never slept.

'The *fumeries* in the residential quarter were something else. They were high-class dens. Like Madam Chang's. That's where you went if you wanted to discuss a little something, some *beez-ness clandestin*, perhaps. It was a very cosmopolitan clientèle. You'd meet the *colons* there, the good old trading boys. I remember one old man, his name was Mazarin, so of course we called him the Cardinal. He was a teak merchant, had a Lao wife or two, knew the country better than his own village back home. He was what we call *un vrai Indochinois*. He'd be there every night at Madam Chang's, had his own pipe, his special pipe-maker: she was a lot prettier than this guy here, I can promise you!

'I remember he said to me once: the first time you smoke the opium, he said, it is like the first time you look into the eyes of a beautiful woman, and you *know* you're going to regret you ever met her.

'Sometimes I'd smoke it up in the hills, with the *montagnards*. The Hmong tribe: they call them Meo in Thailand. They had a kind of legend about the opium poppy. There was once a Hmong who fell in love with a fair-skinned *farang* girl. The girl died and out of her corpse there bloomed an opium poppy. The *montagnard* says: The sap of the poppy is sweet, as she was; the sap of the poppy relieves my sorrow, as she did.

'There is another opium legend too, but perhaps you do not know. It is the story of Narcissus. The flower *Narcissus* is not the daffodil, as we have it. It is the opium poppy. It is from the Greek word *narke*, numbness. My friend the Cardinal told me about this: he was a scholar of such things. Narcissus is the opium smoker. He stares into the black pool of the opium reverie. He sees there his own face, his own self. He finds it beautiful. When you smoke the opium you look inside you. Some people, they don't ever want to look outside any more. They fall in love with the dream. They die beside the pool, like Narcissus.'

After eight or ten pipes we were no more disposed to talk. We lay sprawled on the bed, like Narcissus beside the pool. When I shut my eyes I started to get the visions.

I see faces, but not my own. I see the faces of Appa, and of Harry and Katai, and of the Shan men who grew the poppies and the Haw trader who sold the opium. Then the portrait gallery takes on a random life of its own. I see my mother and father as I knew them when I was small. They are sitting in the Old Hillman brake that got stuck on the one-in-three at Lydford Gorge. Faces come up of people I haven't seen for twenty years, the mathematicians and carpenter's wives of my life, and now here is L'Italienne, the beautiful woman you regret you ever met, seen exactly, in a certain garden, wearing my check shirt, laughing as I tell her in my teenage poetic frenzy that she's like the Hyacinth Girl in *The Waste Land*. But now the faces are beginning to speed up. They are taking on elasticity and movement. Some of these people I definitely don't know. They are twisting and deforming. They are growing pustules and carbuncles. They are doing Les Dawson faces. They are entering cycles of decay and putrefaction before my eyes.

Then I start to think I might be dying. This is the movie, the roll-call, passing before the drowning man. It strikes me that, of course, it *has* to speed up like this, to get it all in before you go. Drowning is what this death would be like, drowning in the black pool. This is for a moment a real fear, but so distant, like a voice calling far enough away to be ignored. The fear passes, as everything passes, serenely across and out of mind. Perhaps when you die you are silently inwardly laughing at these visions, as I am now: laughing at this Keystone Cops caper, laughing scared through these crummy ghost-train tunnels, laughing so hard your lips don't even move.

I know I can snap out of it if I want to. All I need to do is flick open my eyes. I look up into the rafters, try to make out the shapes up there, things stored, rags and bones and corn-cobs. I close my eyes again, and now there's nothing there, just these ripples spreading through my body when my hand moves to scratch an insect-bite, or when Harry shifts beside me, or even when there is a murmur from Appa or his wife: the tiniest disturbance registering on the quiet black waters.

We slept where we lay, like drunken peasants in a Breughel painting. Once in the night, as Harry had warned, I had to get up and be sick. There was a convenient spot not far from the hut. It was hardly like being sick at all: it came easily, copiously, painlessly. Out there in the moonlight I knelt and covered my vomit with dust and leaves, and in the morning there was no trace of it at all.

The Kingfisher

WE WOKE early. I felt as fresh and clear as if I'd had nine hours' sleep, though it was probably half that. Appa and his family seemed to move straight out of sleep and into the day. Appa was rooting for something in a pile of old ironware in the corner. He found it: a couple of rusty spikes. He carried them outside. The rough woollen curtain parted to reveal a stab of rose-pink morning sunlight. The blanket fell back into place, and the hut resumed its sombre, smoky half-light. Appa's wife was fanning up the fire beneath the kettle.

I have watched the hill-tribes in their homes, and I am always struck, as I was then, by a sense of the continuousness of their lives. The women particularly seem to live out one long, un-differentiated chore: cooking and washing, sewing and weaving, milling and winnowing, suckling and mothering, and so on. I'm not saying this is good – I'm not like the Dutchman, who wanted his tribespeople picturesque and underdeveloped – but it seems to be a part of the tribal psychology. The *farang* life is measured into compartments: work, leisure; day, evening; what I am now, what I will be later. The tribespeople just keep on keeping on, slow and practised and implacable, expecting nothing more than the turn-ing of the day, and of the seasons, and of their lives, after which brief turnabout they join the wider omnipresent wheeling of the 'ancestors', whom time no longer needs.

We got up. I felt like apologizing that we'd just crashed out there on one of their beds, but Harry told me not to bother. It was expected, he said. The invitation to take opium at Appa's house was an invitation to sleep at Appa's house.

Back at the guest house we found Katai sitting on a bench outside the eating-place listening to the musical youth singing

'You've Got To Hide Your Love Away'. The anthropologists were writing their diaries. It was all they ever seemed to do. The Frenchmen were slouched in the shade, staring at their motor-bikes, putting off leaving for another day.

Katai looked up, bland face, not smiling. 'Hello boys,' she said. 'You have a good time last night?'

'It was first-class *chandu*,' said Harry stiffly, trying to sound in the right.

The hill-tribe guitarist moved into a rendition of 'Follow the Sun'. Katai watched his fingers, watched his face. Harry said, 'Order some breakfast for me, I'm going to clean up.'

She didn't look up. 'Order it yourself, Harry. I'm listening to the song.' As Harry strode off she muttered, '*Farang* need a maid, *na*?'

For a couple of days I didn't see much of Harry and Katai. I had a touch of fever, a liquid stomach, a heavy dose of lassitude. I slumped in the shade, making desultory efforts to write. My pen was too heavy, the lines trailing downwards. I didn't know what I was supposed to be writing about. It was unseasonably hot. At night the air was sweetened by breezes, but by day it was leaden. The plain below was swathed in haze. The hot season was coming in early, Harry said. That's why we had missed the poppy harvest.

I was beginning to think about leaving, resuming my heavily broken journey to the forest temple. I didn't want to go back down into the heat, but I was getting restless. My sickness seemed like a preparation for a new journey. I was grateful to Harry and Katai: they had shown me things, in their separate ways. But I needed something more.

Farang always need something more.

Harry and Katai seemed busy. They were out for long periods of the day, they could be seen conversing earnestly on their verandah. Katai kept an eye on my welfare, brought me water, bathed my brow. Harry more or less ignored me.

Then one evening – I suppose it was forty-eight hours after our opium session – she came down and sat on the steps beside me. She seemed moody, listless. I asked how things were going, what they had been up to. She said, 'Oh, you know: walking around, talking with people. The hill-tribe people, so interesting.' She spoke in a tired, unconvincing sort of way. I wondered if she'd gone and lost her *khwan* again.

'Where's Harry?' I asked.

'He's not here.'

'Where's he gone?'

'Back down the hill, Charlie. He's gone to meet someone.'

'Who?'

'A friend of his. A Shan.'

'Look, Katai. What the hell's going on?'

She stared sulkily out into the evening air. There was no sunset, just a vague pink wash over the scrubby hills. I could see figures moving down on the slopes below, a couple of pack-horses walking up a trail, laden with what looked like maize. Again I asked her: what was Harry up to?

'It's his plan,' she said softly. 'You know, the big one. I shouldn't talk about it. You know what he's like.'

'Tight as a rat's arse.'

'I'm sorry Charlie. It is Harry's way. You'll have to ask him. I think now he trusts you.'

'Big of him,' I said, and turned over to sleep again.

The next day, nearing dusk, Harry returned in a *song taow*. With him was his friend, the Shan. His name was Gochok. He was a slow, tubby, scruffy man of middle age. His hair flopped down over his forehead. He pushed it back with a movement that became a stretch and a yawn. His handshake none the less was firm. He said, 'Any friend of Harry's is a friend of mine.'

Gochok went off to eat. Harry stayed behind. He had been smoking opium every night at Appa's place – so Katai had told me, crossly – and he wasn't eating much. He had brought some rice whisky up from the store at Ban Houai Krai. I declined his offer of a drink: I was still feeling a bit ragged from the fever.

'Instead of giving me a drink, Harry, why don't you give me a break?' He hoisted an eyebrow, playing it cool, but he knew what I meant. 'Come on,' I said. 'Can't you trust me?' He smiled but made no answer. I said, 'OK. I'll tell you what I think. I think you're setting up some kind of drug deal.'

In the sour ruminations of my fever I had concluded that this was what he was up to. At times I wondered who else was involved: the two Frenchmen, for instance, who lounged the day away in the shade and walked into Pa Kha three times for their fix of opium. The men we had met at the border, the Haw trader, Appa. And, the worst of it, Katai. If Harry was doing a drug run she was a part of it.

But Harry snapped back, 'I told you, that night in Chiang Mai. I don't mess with drugs. OK, I like to visit Old Longhead from time to time, but the scag-trade, that's not my style.'

'So what then?'

He looked at me for a while. 'Well, I suppose it can't hurt to tell you. I have my rules about sniffers, as you know, but, well . . . you're OK.'

'Thanks,' I said, sarcastic. I wasn't feeling too good: stomach empty, metallic taste of fever in mouth, tired of this man holding me at arm's length.

He lit a cigarette, let the smoke come out his nostrils. 'Let's just say for now that I'm in the position of *entrepreneur*. What the Yanks call the honest broker. I have my clients. One client here, one client here' – poking the bamboo floor with a stick – 'and me doing the running, the leg-work I think you say, between. But of course it is not just running. There are difficulties. The borders . . . certain sensitivities . . . problems of communication. You know.'

He stopped there, as if he would like to leave it at that. I said nothing, waited for the silence to edge him on.

'In particular, my man in Burma,' he said cautiously. 'He is the problem right now. I have to make contact with him: certain arrangements. For this it is necessary to contact him in Kengtung.'

I struggled into sitting position. 'So *that's* what you were on about when we met those Shan.'

He nodded. 'If I can't get through to him in Kengtung this whole deal is going to fall apart.'

'So if it isn't drugs what is it?'

He looked at Katai, smiled. 'I'm trying to catch a kingfisher,' he said. 'The feathers are so beautiful, man.'

'Catch a – What are you on about?'

Katai said softly, '*Fe t'sui*. The feathers of the kingfisher. It is Chinese, Charlie. It is how the Chinese call jade.'

Harry leaned forward, face glistening in the twilight. 'This is the big one, man. We're talking about Burmese jade. We're talking about some of the finest in the world. It's from the Kachin State, way up in the north of Burma, from the hills around the Chindwin River. They've been mining it there for six, seven hundred years. There's plenty of the stuff, but it's hard to get hold of. You get your hands on a few good pieces of Burmese jade and you're a rich man.'

'And your . . . client has got some to sell?'

He nodded. 'He's got plenty.'

'Who is he?'

'Well, listen. Some of the jade mountains are mined by the Burmese government. State Mining Corporation Number Two, to be precise. Head office in Yankin. Director General, Mister U Myo Nyunt.'

'You've done your homework.'

'Yeah, didn't do me much good, though. I tried to buy some jade, all tidy and legal, a few years back. But no one wants to play dice with an independent like myself. Government-owned jade is a very closed book. There's a special dealer's session in Rangoon, once a year, but you need to go with a fancy business card and a lot of currency in your wallet. Besides, I had a bit of trouble in Rangoon a few years ago. Tried to take out some Buddhas. They're a bit tight about that, as you may know. I spent a week in the slammer before the French consul got me out.

'What I'm talking about here is strictly unofficial. That's why you have to be careful. Eyes open, mouth shut: you know what I mean?'

I nodded.

'The government doesn't own all the jade, you see. It probably doesn't even own half of it. A lot of the jade mountains are in the parts of Kachin State controlled by the tribal rebels. The KIO:

Kachin Independence Organization. The rebels are anxious to sell this commodity, of course. All they need is someone to help them do it.'

'And that's you.'

'Bravo.'

'And you get to keep a bit of the jade.'

He smiled, but didn't answer. 'They've got plenty of deals set up already, of course. They sell a lot across to China, along the old trading routes. But I've got a very special contact.'

About six months ago, he explained, he met a man called Ne Lin in Bangkok. 'Met him through a sniffer, in fact.' Ne Lin was a Kachin, and he was a representative of the National Democratic Front, the rebel alliance. He in turn had a cousin, another Kachin, name of Captain Tuja, also a big wheel in the NDF. Ne Lin told Harry that Tuja had access to large quantities of jade, mined in rebel-held parts of Kachin State. Harry made an offer of some sort – he wasn't too specific about what – and Ne Lin said he would communicate with Tuja. Nothing much happened for a while: Harry was busy down in Chanta Buri, and when he got back to Bangkok, Ne Lin had gone. Then, about a month ago, Harry received word from him. They had a meeting, up near the border at Three Pagodas Pass. He went up there with Khris, partly to check out the rumours about the sapphire fields at Bo Ploi, and partly to meet with Ne Lin. They were coming back from there when I saw them on the platform at Lop Buri station.

The gist of Ne Lin's message was that Tuja was interested in doing a deal. He was up in Kengtung. He would wait for word from Harry. Kengtung is the easternmost town of any size in the Shan States. It is a trading post with China, and an important point on the illicit jade route. Tuja had a base of some sort there, though his actual headquarters were up near Myitkyina in Kachin State itself.

That's why we were up here now. Harry had intended to come here all along, as I had begun to suspect. He wanted to find a good spot for his 'little bit of border business'.

He reckoned it was just about right here. 'It's a kind of indefinite area here,' he said. 'Further west and you run up into Khun Sa's country, around Mong Tung. Anything happening there is going to run into trouble. Further east and you're up against the border with Laos: more trouble. This is a good corridor here. You see, I thought it was a good sign that the Shan men came to sell some opium to the Haw. It means that this area is not controlled by Khun Sa, or not totally controlled anyway. So yesterday, Katai and me, we went back over, to where we went with Appa. We walked on for a couple of hours till we got to the Shan village they told us about: Wan Sen Pawmong. It was fine. We met a few Shan, but nothing heavy. We walked right into the village. They were mighty surprised, I can tell you, but they were cool. So you see, we have a . . . forward base, as the grunts used to say in Nam. We have somewhere to do business with Captain Tuja. We have a cage for the kingfisher, right?

'So now we are entering on the last stage. This is very delicate. We have to get the message up to Kengtung. This is where our friend Gochok comes in.'

Gochok was himself from Kengtung, but he lived in Tachilek, the border town just across from Mae Sai. Katai had left a message for him, when she went across on her little shopping trip to Burma. Gochok's speciality was black market transport: consumer goods coming up from Thailand, Chinese goods coming across from Jinghong. His work brought him in contact with the NDF offices in Kengtung. He was the ideal person to run Harry's message. He would travel up to Kengtung, make contact with Captain Tuja, and, if all went well, bring him down to Wan Sen Pawmong.

'So now you know all about my beez-ness. Now you know why I got the border fever. You feel better now?'

Harry had known Gochok the Shan from way back. He was an 'old campaigner', a veteran of the Burmese civil wars. He had fought with the Shan National Army, the first of many rebel armies from the region.

The Union of Burma, it is well known, is anything but a union, and ever since the British handed Burma back to the Burmese in 1948, there has been discontent among its many ethnic minorities.

Ethnically, the government represents only about two-thirds of the population: Burmese lowlanders living in the rice-rich flatlands of the Irawaddy delta. All around that central swathe, and particularly in the highlands of northern and eastern Burma, are the various tribal groups – Karen, Kachin, Shan, Kayah, Mon, Wa, Arakanese, Lahu, and others. They are fighting for independence, or at least for federal self-determination.

The Burmese government – a one-party socialist state, ruled since 1962 by military strongman General Ne Win – has consistently refused to deal with their demands. Divided, the tribal groups posed no real threat, but since the NDF alliance was formed, about ten years ago, the threat has grown. Eleven tribal groups are affiliated to the NDF: a total fighting force of about 20,000 men. While this is only a tenth of the size of the Burmese army, the guerrillas have certain inbuilt advantages. Their strongholds are in rugged terrain, they command strong support in the tribal villages, they control areas rich in mineral resources, and – since the tribal lands run almost the entire length the Thai-Burmese border – the flow of contraband goods that fuels Burma's black-market economy must first pass through rebel 'tax points'.

Of all the tribes the Shan are the most fiercely independent. A combination of geographical remoteness and political toughness has resisted all attempts to colonize their mountain domain. Despite the inroads of Burmese socialism, Shan society remains reactionary and feudal. Its traditional base – fiefdoms governed by an overlord, the *sawbwa*, and his private army – looks back to the mediaeval pattern that once prevailed in northern Thailand, with its factious *muang*. Some of the fiefdoms are tiny, but the biggest, Kengtung, covers 12,000 square miles. When the British annexed northern Burma in the 1880s, they wisely chose not to tangle with the *sawbwa*, and throughout their rule in Burma, the Shan States remained largely autonomous.

'The Shan people,' said Gochok, 'are the friends of many, but the servants of none. We have dealt with the Chinese, the *Thai noi*, the British, and, yes, even the Burmese. But none of them has ever controlled us. Even in Taunggyi' – the capital of the Shan States, and nominally under government control – 'we are free in our hearts.'

Gochok told us about the early days of 'The Struggle'. He had joined the Shan National Army 'soon after the Inglorious Fourth of January'. He was referring to 4 January 1958, the date that had been fixed for the Shans' secession from the Union of Burma. 'This was the promise the Burmese made when the British handed over the country to them in 1948. They said that in ten years the Shan people will be free, independent of Burma. But then they try to take away the powers of the *sawbwa*. They trick the *sawbwa* to coming to Rangoon and then they lock them up. The Fourth of January passes. Nothing happens. They have forgotten their promise. What can we do? They will not give us our freedom, so we must take it.'

By 1960 the Shan rebellion was in full swing. The Shan National Army had seven battalions: a fighting force of 5,000 soldiers, controlling most of Kengtung State. The first commander of the SNA was Sa Gnar Kham, a former Buddhist monk. His deputy-commander was U Ba Thein. Both were Kengtung men.

'We lived on the run,' said Gochok. 'We ate the fruits of the jungle: leaves, ferns, wild honey. We cooked the *chakachan*, the jungle cricket, in honey. That was our meat. The opium kept us from hunger, kept us brave.'

Was the SNA, I asked, an opium army, like Khun Sa's bandit army today?

Well, yes and no, said Gochok. Opium was its wealth but not its reason for fighting. For centuries the power of the *sawbwa* has rested on opium. The Shan always preferred to live in the highland valleys, which are best for cultivating rice. They left the hilltops to other tribes: Palaung, Pa-O, Wa, etc. The *sawbwa* took tribute from the hill-tribes, the main one being opium. So naturally the SNA looked to opium as its major source of funds.

Gochok quoted the words of the old KMT leader, General Tuan. 'Necessity knows no law. An army must have guns. To buy guns you must have money. In these mountains the only money is opium.'

The SNA set up a series of arms-for-opium deals with the Lao general and heroin magnate Ouane Rattakone, whose exploits at Ban Khwan Harry had recounted. Ouane was, of course, bolstered by the Americans in Laos, and indeed U Ba Thein, the SNA's arms-procurer in Laos, worked closely with the infamous Harold Young, the American missionary who organized anti-communist agents for the CIA in these sensitive border areas close to China. So, ironically, it was with American backing that the Shan insurgents went into the opium business – just as it was with American backing that the Kuomintang had set themselves up as anti-communist watchdogs in the 1950s, and thus established their slice of the opium and heroin market.

The other main contender in this nexus of insurgency and drug-trafficking also had a government to thank: not in this case the Americans, but the Burmese government. In the early 1960s, following the disbandment of the *sawbwa*, the Burmese began to authorize the formation of local militia to combat the Shan rebels, and to suppress the activities of the KMT inside Burma. In order to arm and equip these militia, the government authorized them to traffic in opium. These militia were called Ka Kwe Yae, or KKY, and two of the first commanders of the KKY were destined to become opium millionaires. One was Lo Hsin Han, who controlled the Shan opium trade for about five years up to his arrest in 1973. The other was Khun Sa. By 1964, he had a well-armed militia of 800 men. He severed his ties with the Burmese army, shifted his base from Lashio to Tang Yang, built a crude refinery, and set up as a freelance opium warlord.

The success of the Shan National Army was shortlived. In 1964 their charismatic commander, Sa Gnar Kham, was shot and killed at the SNA's forward caravan post in Thailand – Ban Houai Krai, the village just a few miles down the hill, where we had changed trucks on our way up here to Pa Kha – and by 1966, the SNA was virtually washed up. Its seven regional commanders were either dead or had split off to form independent opium armies.

There are now two main militias active in the Shan States, the SUA (Shan United Army) and the SSA (Shan State Army), but they are very different. The SUA is Khun Sa's fighting force, now based along the Thai-Burmese border between Mong Tun and

Doi Lan. It is exclusively concerned with opium trafficking, even though it claims to be a freedom-fighting organization. In 1985, Khun Sa teamed up with General Moh Heng, the commander of yet another private army, the Shan United Revolutionary Army. Together they have formed the Tai Revolutionary Council, with an office in Chiang Mai, and a flag featuring a white tiger on a map of the Shan States. This has all the appurtenances of a 'legitimate' nationalist army, but everyone knows that Khun Sa is the real power, and heroin the real war-cry, behind the organization.

By contrast, the SSA shuns any connection with the opium and heroin trade. It is a member of the NDF coalition, and the NDF, struggling for recognition in the outside world, is very strong on its non-involvement with opium. Two of the major tribal groups within the NDF – the Kachin and the Karen – claim to exert the death penalty on anyone caught dealing in opium.

Twenty years later, said Gochok, the natural successor to the Shan National Army he fought in is not Khun Sa's SUA, but the smaller, more idealistic SSA. The difference between them, he said simply, is that the SUA fight for money, the SSA for freedom.

There is deep enmity between the two armies. This is partly territorial rivalry: Khun Sa has winkled the SSA out of the key strategic points along the rivers and caravan-trails that bring the opium down from the Shan and Wa poppy fields. It is also partly a result of a cynical collusion between Khun Sa and the Burmese military. At a meeting at Mong Tun on 7 March 1984, General Aye San, regional commander of the Burmese Army, offered Khun Sa a deal. Government troops would leave Khun Sa's drug business alone, if he would undertake to control the Shan rebels. In effect they were asking the heroin bandits to act once more as their hinterland militia. With that typically Burmese sense of political stagnation, the deal seems to mirror the events of twenty years earlier which first set Khun Sa up.

At this time, Gochok said, the Shan State Army was in disarray. Territorially, it was caught in a crossfire between the armies of Khun Sa in the south, and those of the Burmese Communist Party in the north. Its soldiers were defecting in roughly equal numbers to both sides. He did not know what would happen next, and that was one of the reasons he was now more closely involved with the more dynamic armies within the NDF: the Kachin and the Karen.

The following day, Harry, Gochok and Appa journeyed back up to the border, and across to Wan Sen Pawmong. I wanted to go too, but Harry said we would be too many. He didn't want to attract attention. It was just a reconnaissance trip, so Gochok would know the lay of the land. Gochok would be able to go up to Kengtung by road – he had a trader's pass that enabled him to cross over the border bridge between Mae Sai and Tachilek – but when he travelled back down with Tuja they would have to go cross-country, probably by foot, along the trails that the rebels and smugglers used, to avoid the army checkpoints along the highway.

Katai and I walked out in the afternoon haze. There was a spot of high ground about half a mile east of the village, with a stunning view over blue hills and vaporous valleys. We lay down in the tall scrub-grass, watched a pair of buzzards wheeling over the rugged limestone scarps.

She said, 'You know, if it hadn't worked out with Gochok, I would go across myself. I would go to Kengtung.'

'That would have been very dangerous,' I said, sounding like a boring elder brother.

'I would do it, Charlie. I would do it for Harry. I told him so. It make me frightened to think of it, heart go boom boom boom. But it make me feel so good too. I would love to go across the border, to feel free of everything and everyone, to travel in the night like a thief, to run like the *katai*. I am good at that, Charlie. I could do it. But Harry . . . he don't listen to me.'

There was a silence. When I looked at her I saw there were tears in her eyes. I put my arm round her, her head on my shoulder. 'You shouldn't be sad,' I said.

'Harry making me very sad right now,' she said. 'He don't care nothing about me. He just think about the big one, nothing else. He worry all the time. He tell me to shut up. I come all this way to be with him, but he don't want me. He don't want to listen to me, he don't want to make love with me. Right now all he wanna do is smoke the opium and dream about the jade.'

'It's important to him, Katai. He's . . . well, he's not too young anymore, right? I think he's staking a lot on this jade deal.'

Smiling through the tears, putting on her tough voice. 'Yeah, he's an old man. What's the young girl like me falling in love with him for?'

'Don't ask me.'

'I *am* asking you, Charlie. He's just a mad dog. Why don't I kick him away?'

I said, 'If things had been different . . .' But she put her finger to my lips. She was right: it was not a sentence that ought to be finished.

That night I decided I would leave. I was running short of time, and maybe short of purpose too. I would have liked to stick around to meet Tuja the jade-man, but Harry reckoned it would be at least a week or ten days before he showed up (to which I mentally added: if he showed up at all). If I was going to get to the forest temple, and stay long enough for it to mean anything, it was time to leave right now.

Early the next morning they waited with me till a *song taow* arrived, rattling down the dusty hill, empty in the back. Harry shook my hand. 'Good luck, my friend. I hope you find what you're looking for.'

'You too, Harry. I hope you catch your kingfisher.'

'One day, when this is all over, when I am rich, perhaps you'll see me taking tea in the Ritz.'

'I'll look forward to it.'

Katai didn't want to say goodbye. She toughed it out instead. 'Hey, Charlie, don't look so worried,' she said. She made a curious scratching movement at the back of her neck. 'You know what that means, Charlie?'

'No, I don't.'

'It is the Thai joke. It means: the *farang* carries his worries with him like a dog carries fleas.'

'Thanks, Katai.'

'When you get to the temple you will forget your worries.' And as she kissed me on the cheek she added softly, 'And you will forget Katai, *na*?'

I shook my head in answer and climbed aboard the truck.

I watched them out the back, Katai waving, Harry standing still beside her, the powder of dust around them. A sense of ending: the strangeness of the last few weeks came upon me, now it was over. The first bend came. Harry had already turned away, but Katai was still waving.

Down in the valley, Ban Houai Krai, I drank Coca-Cola and waited for a truck to take me down Route 110 to Chiang Rai.

Tupu's Cave

WAT THAM TUPU, the Temple of Tupu's Cave, is a patch of rugged tropical forest, four square kilometres in area, in the southern foothills of Thailand's highest mountain, Doi Inthanon. It is not a temple in the architectural sense. There are no stone buildings of any sort, no *prang*, no *chedi*, no images of the Buddha, no spirit houses. This is the first precept of the forest temple tradition: the forest itself *is* the temple.

It is about four miles from the nearest village, Ban Wang Nam Yat, an hour's walk going uphill. In the dry season the track is passable to four-wheel-drives and motorcycles, but it is unlikely any will be going. If you have been travelling on trucks and buses for the best part of two days, and the daylight is fading, and you're feeling exhausted but also slightly smug about getting this far, then this last little stretch of foot travel will seem a longish one.

After a while you pass a sign announcing the temple – you are now on holy ground, though there is no visible fence or boundary to confirm this – and about ten minutes later you arrive at a scattering of wooden buildings. Two are the size of small houses: one is a meeting house, with kitchen and washing area, another is the *sala* or meditation hall. The rest are small, bare, grass-thatched cabins, called *kuti*, which are the temporary homes of monks on forest retreat. All the buildings here, you are firmly told, were built from the wood of fallen trees. Not a single healthy tree has been sacrificed in the interests of human comfort. The *kuti* belonging to the abbot of the temple, Ajahn Pongsak Tejadhammo, is the smallest and scruffiest of all. I thought of the story in Basho's *Narrow Road to the Deep North*, about the Zen priest who scratched a poem in charcoal on the walls of his hermitage:

> This grassy hermitage
> Hardly any more
> Than five feet square,
> I would gladly quit
> But for the rain.

It was dark when I arrived, and at last met up with Geoff, a twelve-stone Englishman with a ruddy face and a stumpy black beard, who was indirectly the reason I had first heard of this temple. At certain times of the year the temple is quite full. Monks come on their *tudong* – part pilgrimage, part retreat – as well as novices, students, laymen, *farang*: anyone eager to lose the material world for a while, and to listen to the gentle teachings of Ajahn Pongsak. But now it was a quiet time, in the depths of the hot season, with the rains imminent, and the place was almost deserted. Apart from Geoff, the only other residents were a nun from Hong Kong, and a pale American called Neil, a novice monk from the forest temple of Wat Ban Anachat. The nun was called Mae Chee Sudhamma. (Mae Chee, 'white mother', is the appellation for nuns, who wear a white robe; Sudhamma is her Pali name, meaning 'good teaching'.) She was in her early thirties: spectacles, bright eyes, shaven head.

I was welcomed without fuss, given a bowl of noodles, and shown to a hut. It had a roof and a floor, and that was about that. Later we sat on the verandah, watching the fireflies flicker on and off like tiny warning lights. The night air was cool: we were at about 4,500 feet here. One felt straightaway the simplicity and silence of the place. I mentioned my desire to learn about Buddhism. Geoff growled, 'Don't look at me to teach you anything, chum. I'm just learning like the rest of us.' He added, 'But the Ajahn will be here tomorrow, and if you don't learn something from him, you might as well give up right now!'

I met Ajahn Pongsak the following morning. He was a shortish, stocky man in his mid fifties. His face and shoulders and shaven head were smooth and evenly brown. He looked strong and fit, walking up a forest trail with a rolling gait, or sitting bolt upright in a lotus position on the floor of the verandah. A man of deep understanding, a scholar of Pali, a true *ajahn* (teacher), he had nevertheless a peasant's toughness. He was a poor farmer's son, born in the small town of Tham Nop, in Nakhon Sawan Province, in the central plains. In school he studied only up to Pathom Four, the equivalent of primary Grade Four. Throughout his teens he worked in the rice paddies on his father's farm.

Over the days I plied him with all sorts of questions. He never once made me feel I was a nuisance, though I think it is true that he gently steered the discussion onto matters he wanted to tell me about, which weren't always the ones I wanted to ask about. The patient Geoff or the Mae Chee translated my questions. He would listen carefully, murmuring his understanding, and then it would seem that he 'recognized' the question, saw into it, and he would give a big smile and make his answer. He spoke in a light, even, flowing voice. The answers seemed easily given but they were subtle and precise, sometimes difficult to translate, difficult to understand. He would watch me, smiling still, as the answer was translated to me, and he saw my reaction to it. He seemed always to go to the heart of the matter.

He smiled a lot. At first I thought there was something cryptic about his smile, something significant, but actually it was just that he had recently had three false front teeth fitted. He was embarrassed about them, Geoff said, and no longer smiled for photographs. This seemed a touching chink of vanity in a man so free of all that sort of lumber.

Sometimes we went for walks up into the forest behind the temple. He walked easily and lightly, carrying a walking staff. He seemed intimate with the forest, at home with the touch of earth, the smell of the leaves, the murmur of the rivers. The sun filtered down onto his bald head, his dull orange robe. The trail led out past the *sala*, which they called the Meeting Place of Compassion and Silence. There was a huge wild mango tree near the *sala*, with little stone seats in a litter of leaves and windfall mangoes. Here, of an afternoon, the Ajahn sat and gave his talks.

The tradition of the *wat pa*, or forest temple, looks back to the
wanderings of the Buddha himself, and to his retirement into the
forest of Uruvilva to seek enlightenment. 'There have always been
two types of Buddhist monastic tradition,' explained the Ajahn.
'The tradition of the village or town, and the tradition of the
forest.' In Thailand the forest tradition goes back at least to
Sukhothai times, five or six centuries ago. It was at this time that
the semi-legendary monk and wiseman Tupu came here, and
lived in the cave. The cave is a few miles from the temple, but
visible from it, in the limestone hills rising up to the north. The
stains of bat guanp below the cave have formed a shape which the
villagers say is the silhouette of Tupu himself.

In those times, the Ajahn said, no one except the monks wanted
to live in the forest. Everyone else was unable, or too frightened, to
live in the wilderness. It was only a couple of decades ago that a law
was passed forbidding people to settle in the forest without
permission. Before that it was unnecessary: no one wanted to,
except a few hill-tribes coming in from China and Burma. The
word *pa*, 'forest', carries pejorative overtones for the Thai. It is
used to describe the 'wildness' of undisciplined or immoral people.
Things that are contraband, or bootleg, or legally dubious in some
way are called *khaung pa*, 'things of the forest'. Used figuratively,
pai pa, 'going into the forest', means to defecate. It is also used,
curiously, to mean entering a cemetery. The actual dangers of the
forest are translated into an idea of what lies outside social bound-
aries: criminality, bodily functions, death. Those who live in
isolated country areas are called *khon nauk wiang*, 'people outside
the walls'.

An idea of nature's beauty seems foreign to the Thai, and if they
do want to express admiration of some natural scenery they use a
recently borrowed word. It sounds like *wioo*, but is actually a
version of the word 'view'.

The forest temple is a monastic retreat. It is a place for study, for
training in the techniques of meditation, for achieving inner peace
and 'mindfulness'. In the forest 'you learn to draw up the *tri pitaki*,
the three baskets of Buddhist knowledge: *vinaya*, the basket of
discipline; *sutra*, the basket of the Buddha's sermons; *dharma*,

the basket of truth.' But though it is a retreat it is also – and especially for Ajahn Pongsak – an involvement. He sees it as the practical, physical side of the Buddhist tradition. It is linked closely with the whole idea of the *tudong*, the monk's wandering pilgrimage. Both the *tudong* and the forest temple are, he said, 'for monks who like to see for themselves'. The *tudong* is physically arduous. When a monk goes on *tudong*, he should take only a parasol and a mosquito net. In the evening he sets up the parasol, hangs the mosquito net down from it, and sleeps the night on the forest floor.

'In the forest,' said the Ajahn, 'you do not learn from books and scriptures. You learn from nature and from the necessities of life. The forest is not only the temple, it is also the teacher.'

Pongsak's actual teacher was a famous monk called Ajahn Buddha-dassa, the abbot of the forest temple of Wat Suan Moke, and one afternoon, sitting beneath the mango tree near the *sala*, Pongsak recounted how he had come to Wat Suan Moke and found his 'spiritual home' in the forest.

He was twenty-three years old when he went on his first *tudong*. He had entered the monkhood three years before, studied at Nakhon Sawan, and at Wat Mahatat in Bangkok, a famous centre for the teaching of Buddhist meditation practice. Restless with 'theoretical studies', he went on *tudong*, first to a cave near Fang, and then to the forests around Doi Wang Na, one of the old sites of Lan Na.

'In the forest I practised meditation, with constant perseverance, following the precepts I had been taught at Wat Mahatat. And so I reached the moment when the *chitra* (consciousness) was released. It was no longer aware of the body, and stayed suspended by itself.

'But when I came out from the forest, I found that the mindfulness and concentration I had achieved there began to slip away again. I was restless. My *chitra* was sliding backwards. The mind was still shifting. It had advanced no further. I felt that perhaps I had not practised enough, that I did not know the path thoroughly, so I returned once more to Wat Mahatat in Bangkok.

'It was now the year 2500 BE.' (The Buddhist Era is reckoned from 543 BC, the presumed date of the Buddha's death: 2500 BE is 1957 AD.) 'This was a very auspicious year for Buddhists, marking the halfway mark in the present cycle of five thousand years. My teachers were caught up in the great celebrations, and were busy blessing images and amulets and lustral water, fortune-telling, and all the rest.

'I began to study Pali. I could see no further way forward in my practice of meditation. The teachings at Mahatat seemed to offer me nothing new. I was beginning to have great doubts about my belief. I had got used to living in the peace of the forest, where even if there was no great growth in my understanding, there were at least no problems to trouble me. But now, returning to the city, observing the ways of the city monks, I began to be uncertain. Some of the monks seemed concerned only with their advancement: they studied in order to pass exams, they were ambitious for promotion and preferment within the Sangha. In December, when preferments are made, the successful monks threw a great celebration. There was feasting and jollity lasting all day, four or five hundred monks together, huge amounts of food brought in from the Chinese eating-houses near Wat Mahatat. To me this extravagance did not seem right.

'For perhaps two years I grew deeper in doubt about the way forward. I was easily angry. I could not sleep. In order to sleep I tried to practise concentration, to calm myself, but I was distracted by the sound of the radios in the other monks' rooms. I began to have trouble with constipation, and had to take laxatives. On some days I could not eat at all. If anyone said something which I disagreed with, I flew into a rage.

'During this time my mind was being tugged this way and that, never still. I had been a monk for seven years now. I began to think it would be better to disrobe rather than go on like this. But then I thought of the peace I had known in the forest, the peace of living surrounded by such purity, and I felt it would be a pity to turn my back on that.

'It was at just this time, this time of great wavering, that another monk, a classmate in my Pali studies, first told me about Ajahn Buddhadassa and his forest temple, Wat Suan Moke. He told me of the wisdom of the Ajahn, and of the beauty of Suan Moke. It stood beside a river, deep in a cool forest full of wild animals. Just hearing about it I instantly felt soothed.

'The monk fetched me a book he had, written by Ajahn Buddhadassa. It was a transcript of the first talk he gave to monks who had asked for his teaching. The title was *The Principles of Buddhism*. On the fourth or fifth page the question was asked: "What is Buddhism?"

'The Ajahn answered, "Buddhism is the principle of knowledge and the practice of knowledge in order to understand truly the way things are."

'Reading these simple words was a revelation to me. "Ah, so that's it!" I said to myself. Up until this moment, you see, I had thought that the purpose of practice was to get something, or to arrive somewhere. But it is only this: to understand truly the way things are.

'From that point on I knew what I must do. In a single month I read three or four more of the Ajahn's books. Then I travelled to his temple, Suan Moke. I arrived there at the end of March 2502 BE, and was warmly welcomed by Ajahn Buddhadassa.

'I had only been there seven days, however, when Ajahn Buddhadassa left to give a series of talks in Bangkok and Chiang Mai. I thought I too would visit Chiang Mai, to see some friends up there. I intended to see Ajahn Buddhadassa there, and to ask his permission to return with him to Suan Moke. But our journeys crossed, and when I got to Chiang Mai he had already returned south.

'Once again my state of mind began to become agitated, and a few months later I decided to go once more to Wat Suan Moke. But this time Ajahn Buddhadassa did not give me a warm welcome.

'He was upstairs in his old *kuti*, taking his meal. He sent a novice down to me. The message he sent down was, "Tell that monk there's nowhere for him to stay." When the novice came to me, he recognized me from my previous stay. He said, "Oh dear, *tahn*, the Ajahn says there's no room for you." I was immediately very downcast. The novice suggested I should go to the *sala* and rest after my journey. In those days it was two days to Suan Moke from Bangkok: a long train journey to Chumporn, and then the local train the next morning, to Chaiya, and then a walk to the temple.

'The *sala* was a long low building in the forest. It was used by the monks for meditating, for chanting and for *tham boon* (merit-making) at the time of the full moon. I stayed there all day. In the evening the novice brought another message from the Ajahn: "Tell that monk I am not ready to see him yet."

'Again I felt downcast. I could not understand the Ajahn's attitude. But then I realized that the Ajahn was wise, and was seeing how firm my intentions were. If I persevered, surely he would not turn me away.

'For two days I waited, my fears and worries that I would be sent away constantly surfacing in my mind. Then, on the third morning, the novice came again to me. This time he brought the message that the Ajahn was now ready to receive me.

'I went to pay my respects, but Ajahn Buddhadassa looked away as I made my prostrations. "There's nowhere to stay," he said.

'"Tahn Ajahn," I replied. "I can stay anywhere, even in the space underneath the *sala*."

'He looked at me quickly. He was still in thought for a moment, and then he said, "There is a small hut, round the back of the hill, where Tahn Sawai used to stay. There's no one there now. You can stay there."

'And so I settled in at Wat Suan Moke. I learned much from Ajahn Buddhadassa, whose teachings, as I have told you, are based on the *tri pitaka*, the three baskets of wisdom. My peace of mind was quickly restored to me. From that time I lived in the forest for five years, until 2507 BE.'

Often, if one asked Ajahn Pongsak something about the philosophy of the forest temple, he would answer by recalling the teachings of Ajahn Buddhadassa.

'What I learned from the Ajahn was what we call in Thai *tham matak*. This means to live according to nature, to act truly, without pretence in any form. He lived in a truly natural way. If it was time to speak, he spoke. If something funny happened, he laughed. If a monk did something wrong, against the teachings, he was strict. A reprimand from him was not just a passing thing. It went deep into the heart.'

It was from Ajahn Buddhadassa that Pongsak gained his deep respect for the forest, a respect expressed in both spiritual and practical ways. Buddhadassa would always lecture the monks severely if any of them committed some small violation of the forest. One, for instance, had chopped down an old and beautiful tree to use its trunk for the main pillar of a *kuti* he was building. Another had stripped a number of trees, to boil up the bark to make dye for the monk's robes.

'Ajahn Buddhadassa was very strict about this. He gathered us together, after our daily meal, and lectured us on the right attitude to the forest we were living in. He told us: "Nature is beautiful. Nature is pure. How is it that we, as monks, fail to see this beauty and purity? If a man cannot see this, why is he practising meditation? Trees are beneficial to mankind. They have a value in our lives, a value for the earth. Why is that we, as monks, have no understanding of the value of trees? We lack true gratitude to trees. We do not understand what the forest gives to us. All monks should recognize the gratitude they owe to all trees and all plants."

'That was the precept that Ajahn Buddhadassa taught us. It is not one of the normal precepts. It is not something everyone knows.'

It was the translation of these precepts into practical action that created Wat Tham Tupu. Pongsak is a pre-eminently practical man. In some senses he's the serene forest hermit I had hoped and expected to find. But also he is very political, very *engagé*. The Temple of Tupu's Cave, though consecrated as a temple and serving as a retreat for monks, is also – sometimes it seemed primarily – a focal point for a radical and remarkable experiment in conservation.

He first came to the site of Tupu's cave about fifteen years ago. 'The whole area below the cliff was thick wild forest, with tall trees, many of them a metre or more wide. There was a hut below the cave where people used to stay. In the mornings the hills all around were hidden with mists and clouds. The air was cool and sweet. There was so much dew it looked like it had been raining. Just walking around you would be soaked. That's how wet it was, especially up on the ridges. That's why the weather was so cool in those days. It was so very beautiful, it is hard to put it into words.'

Seven years later he returned to the area and found the forest beneath the cliff had been clear-felled. He was heartbroken. When he returned again, in 1983, he found further devastation. Not only was the forest itself being ruined, but the whole area was beginning to suffer as a result. Two of the rivers that water the valley – the Mae Tim and the Mae Pok – were drying up through loss of tree cover at the watersheds. A third, the Mae Soi, was still flowing, but only at about a quarter of its natural rate.

The enemies of the forest are many. There are the big teak-logging interests which can decimate an area in one year. Officially the Royal Forest Department sets quotas for each area of forest, a 'maximum allowable cut', but inevitably there is a huge amount of clandestine logging, particularly of teak (mai sak) and of the huge, resinous dipterocarps called in Thailand *mai yang*. Just before I was there, in the nearby forest round Ban Hot, a police officer had discovered 300 illegally felled teak trees. The economics are powerful: those 300 logs would be worth about 5m baht ($200,000). It is said that the FIO (the Forest Industry Organ-ization, Thailand's state company for forest products) is soft on illegal logging because it gains by it. The wood-poachers go into a patch of virgin forest, and deplete it to such an extent that it is past recovery. Then the FIO goes in and clear-fells the entire area, profiting both from the timber and from selling the cleared land for agriculture. Many local FIO officials have been implicated in bribery scandals, as have administrators of Thai National Parks.

Another major problem is the hill-tribes, whose primitive slash-and-burn agriculture is ecologically ruinous. Behind them lurk the opium wholesalers, mainly Chinese, who encourage tree-felling to ensure sizeable poppy plantations. We took a pick-up truck up into the hills above the temple to see for ourselves. The greatest damage is being done by a group of Hmong villagers of the Kae clan. They settled in the high ground around the Mae Tim watershed some fifteen years ago. To begin with there were about fifty families, but now there are three hundred. They cleared a lot of the forest to plant opium. Since the military crack-down in the late seventies, much of the opium crop has been substituted. The Hmong here now mainly grow cabbages, which they sell for one baht a kilo. It was for this that the forest was destroyed.

The Hmong are also decimating the pine forests on the ridges above the valley. Some of these are huge, two-hundred-year-old trees: native pines, *merkusii* and *khasya*. The tribesmen gouge the lower trunk with axes, then burn the wound to kill the tree. It is then felled and split up, and the resulting wood is sold for kindling at five baht a bundle.

Down below, the Thai villagers add to the onslaught, nibbling away at the skirts of the forest, turning it into agricultural land for crops like dry-rice, peanuts, lentils, onion and chilli, or for fruit orchards of mango and longan. They also fell trees for timber, and for charcoal, and because the ashy soil after the forest has been burned off produces in abundance the edible plant called *paak waan*.

Confronted with this devastation, said the Ajahn, 'the first task was educational: to convince the villagers that they needed the forests, to show how the health of the forest affected the health of the village, particularly in the provision of water for the paddy fields.' This idea of 'health' came up often when he spoke about conservation. It seemed to be the bridge between his monkhood and his new eco-political role. Spiritual health and bodily health – trees, water, rice – he sees it as a single whole. 'The monk's duty is *sila tham*, practising the rules of Buddhist morality. Conservation is *sila tham* in action.'

His aim is to establish here a 'Buddhist conservation park', a protected forest reserve covering seventy square kilometres around the temple area. He has had to battle hard with certain regional authorities, most notably the *nai amphoe* (sheriff) of Chom Thong. The project is still in its infancy, but has so far succeeded against many odds. The villagers have pledged their wholehearted support. They will enclose the reserve and protect it with voluntary twenty-four-hour patrols. It has already been fenced at its critical northern upper boundary, to prevent the Hmong tribesmen on the ridge from entering. Firebreaks have been cut throughout the area. Nearly four miles of three-inch metal water-pipes have been laid, running down the ridges on either side of the Mae Soi watercourse. These provide water to irrigate the forest, to protect it against fires, and to feed the paddy fields of the valley. Where the forest has been worst damaged, there has been reafforestation: five thousand seedlings, eucalyptus on the high ground, mango and longan trees lower down.

All this the Ajahn described with his mixture of gusto and modesty. And perhaps more important than its immediate local influence, Wat Tham Tupu is providing a role-model for this powerful fusion of Buddhist morality and practical conservation. Thailand's forests, like all of South-east Asia's, are deeply threatened. Primary forest is disappearing at a rate of a thousand square kilometres a year. It may well be that the influence of Buddhism is the only force powerful enough to halt this destruction.

One night I had a dream. Katai was in it, of course. She was doing that scratching joke, as she had when we said goodbye at Pa Kha. 'Farang carries his worries with him like a dog carries fleas.' And then she took a bottle of Mekong whisky and poured it into the glass I held, but when the glass was full she kept on pouring. I watched the golden liquid splashing into the dirt. When I woke up I was pleased to realize that it was a sort of Buddhist dream. It came from a story I had heard about a Buddhist master called Nan In. Nan In received a visitor who was very eager to learn the secrets of Buddhism. He served tea, and – like Katai in my dream – kept pouring after the cup was full. He said to the visitor, 'You are full like this cup. How can I show you the truth unless you first empty your cup?'

I tried to empty my cup, so the Ajahn could fill it, but I wasn't sure how. He didn't seem at all keen to teach me anyway, or not in my *farang* sense of 'teaching' anyway. Sometimes he would phil-osophize and sometimes, when earnestly asked, he would give advice, but much of his advice boiled down to something direct and simple, something that bounced the question straight back, because the only one who could solve your problems was you. A favourite phrase was *sabai jai*: have an easy heart, do what you feel is right, or – as Geoff translated it – 'Hit 'em from where you are'.

In the end, one realized, it was what the Ajahn *did*, and what he had done, that told the truth. That was his philosophy: '*sila tham* in action'. One time he quoted a saying of the Buddha's: 'A man in his own refuge'. By this I think he meant that attending to what you are and how you behave, even on a mundane level, will always help you. This is related to the Buddhist idea of *loka sacca*, the 'worldly truth', which governs our conduct towards others. It is distinct from the *sacca dharma*, the 'absolute truth' as taught by the Buddha and aspired to by monks.

At whatever level you come in at, Buddhism makes its wise, nonchalant offer. As little or as much as you want, it will help you, in the simple words of Ajahn Buddadhassa, 'to understand truly the way things are'.

On the morning I was to leave Tupu's Cave, looking for the Ajahn to say goodbye, I found only his staff leaning up on the verandah of the meeting house, and a book lying open there, weighted down by a stone. It was a breezy morning. The thin pages rattled like an insect's wings. The book was well-thumbed, smudgily printed in grey ink. It was a collection of *sutra*, the Buddha's sermons, in Thai script. On the open page a single sentence was heavily underlined. I asked the Mae Chee what it meant. She translated it as follows: 'In order to travel the Path, you must become the Path'.

I didn't quite know what these words meant. The truth hides beneath them, sneaks up round the back of your mind like an ambush. They seemed to key in with a mood of recrimination that was on me that morning. When I first arrived at Wat Tham Tupu I flattered myself that I'd been on a long and circuitous journey – a crazy kind of *tudong* even – to get here. But over the days, listening to the Ajahn tell of his wanderings, of the steadfastness that brought him to where he now was, I came to see what a long way there was to go. His quiet strength seemed a reproach to my shallowness. How foolish I had been, thinking I could just arrive, and be blessed with the peace of the forest, as if on some spiritual package-tour. I had travelled the path, I suppose, but not become the path. There was another kind of journey entirely, one I hadn't even begun.

Then the Ajahn turned up, quietly out of nowhere, his orange robe damp at the hem from forest dew. He wished me luck and *sabai jai*. The sun was climbing over the top of the mango trees. He asked if I had water for the walk. As I set off he said, smiling broadly, 'The journey of a thousand miles begins with the first step.' He said it lightly, really just a joke about the hour's walk down to Wang Nam Yat, but I felt he was looking right inside my mind.

Kayah

MEETING UP with Harry again was either pure chance or heavy kharma, I don't know which. Harry would no doubt incline to the kharmic view, that it was all somehow on the cards, part of some hidden pattern, the 'code of the road'.

It was early April in the small border town of Mae Hong Son. I had no particular reason for being there. It was a time of no expectation, deep in the dry season: the land hot and withered, the air thick with the smoke of forest fires, another long afternoon settling over the rooftops. I tried not to sleep in the afternoon. It brought no refreshment, only sweats and fever dreams, and waking at dusk with the taste of quinine in your mouth.

Ever since leaving Tupu's Cave I had been drifting, floating down the days as if they were some kind of river, travelling by bus or truck or foot, moving because moving was better than stopping, because if I stopped I might never start again. I walked from village to village, through high teak groves and down along broad shallow rivers. I saw the cave-swifts emerging from the mouth of Tham Lod at sunset, blotting out the light like a biblical plague of locusts. I saw a pool full of *bra moung*, huge blue carp a full metre long. An old Shan man said the fish were magic. In what way? 'Because no one can eat them.' In a Hmong village hut I saw little geometric patterns, animist charms, nailed to the wall, and a heap of blackened bones in a pot near the fire. A couple of times on the trail, I thought I heard gunfire, but the people said no, that's just the bamboo cracking in a brush-fire. Then once, not far from Khun Sa's stronghold at Doi Lan, it really *was* gunfire. It sounds so thin, so insignificant, so different from a movie soundtrack. It floats off into the air, hangs there for a moment, ricochets off the far side of the valley. But the sound I remember best is the soft dulled resonance of the wooden bells round the water buffaloes' necks.

Sometimes I slept on the floors of hill-tribe huts: a supper of rice and pork fat, a few bowls of opium, a night of blissful ease, the howling of dogs at dawn. Sometimes I slept in cheap roadside guest houses, places that offer little and ask little in return. Waking in the night, staring into the darkness, you feel not loneliness – you could handle that – but rather the opposite, a sinister sense of populousness in the room: all those people who have passed through here, their grease around the light-switch, their smell on the pillow, the close air smudged with their presence.

There was no particular reason for being in Mae Hong Son. It was nine-tenths gravity that pulled me there, and the rest was just the rattling of a dry-season brain.

There's not a lot to the place. It is the *chang wat* – provincial capital – of Thailand's most north-westerly province. It has a high school, several beautiful temples in the Burmese style, an airstrip, and about 10,000 people. Mae Hong Son Province is one of the most sparsely populated in Thailand, and over half its population is non-Thai – hill-tribes, Shan, Burmese and Chinese. The town is a crossways. The one and only highway through this part of Thailand – known at different points as Route 1095 or Route 108 – runs through north to south. The Pai River, flowing west, intersects with the highway just south of the town, before running across into Burma. Since Khun Sa set up his western headquarters at Doi Lan, a mountain stronghold just across the border about fifteen miles due north of Mae Hong Son, the town has grown in importance as a heroin clearing-house, but to the outsider it remains just a small, pleasant crossroads town: a few dusty streets, some concrete buildings on the two main drags, the rest the usual rusty-coloured wood and tin roofs. The market is filled with consumer gear bound for the Burmese black economy: jeans, T-shirts, kitchenware, mosquito netting, sunglasses, bedding, and the churn-sized 36-hour drinking-water thermoses which are something of a status symbol out here. Out from Burma come cattle and rubies and, of course, opium and heroin. Like all smuggling towns, Mae Hong Son has a high vehicle population: Japanese jeeps, trucks and limos, and thousands of motorcycles.

My hotel, the Mae Tee, looks out onto Main Street. There's a noodle-shop on the corner, and next to it a repair shop with Texaco and Firestone stickers, and behind the roofs the tall conical hill with the white Burmese-style *chedi* of Wat Doi Kong Mon. I'm leaning on the windowsill, watching a skinny boy in a T-shirt wiping his hands on an oil-rag. He turns back to say something to someone in the dark workshop. In that shadowy interior, I now see two men walking outwards, towards the street, talking as they go. The sun falls on their faces. One of them is Chinese. The other, in the rattan hat, is Harry Vincent.

I resist the desire to call out. Harry's doing beez-ness, that is clear. There must be something special afoot: I remember him saying, 'I never mess with Chinese, it's a rule I have from way back.' I can hear their voices, but I can't make out what they're saying. Everything Harry does, everything he is, seems just out of earshot. They shake hands, confirm some arrangement. Harry makes a joke, some wrinkle-eyed *drôlerie*, and the Chinese man laughs. The mechanic smiles, continues to wipe his hands on the oil-cloth.

Now Harry's coming across the street, hand resting loosely against the cross-slung leather bag. He pauses for a pick-up to pass. A snatch of rock music from the cab, teak planking roped to the flatbed. He's walking straight towards me. I call his name. He looks up, squints into the brightness. He lifts his hat to shade off the sun, looks for all the world like an old *boulevardier* about to compliment a pretty lady on the balcony. He sees it's me.

The eyes narrow. A thin smile slips onto his face. 'Well, if it isn't the French lieutenant!'

There's a natural superiority when you spot someone first, when you're prepared and they're surprised, but Harry's greeting was so cryptic it threw me into confusion. I blurted out, 'What brings you to Mae Hong Son?'

His eyebrows flickered in that pained way he had when you had offended some protocol or other. He looked around him, at the people going to and fro. Whatever had brought him to Mae Hong Son, he wasn't about to discuss it out in the midday sun on Main Street. He said, with a slight air of resignation, 'Why don't you get dressed, and we'll take a beer? I'll be round the corner, at Panit's. You know it?'

'I'll be there in five minutes.'

He turned to go. I called after him, 'Where's Katai?' He must have heard me, but he didn't look up. He just kept on walking.

A few minutes later I found him, sitting with his back to the wall, in the small noodle-shop called Panit's. On the jukebox Carabou was singing the song of *Phu Ying Yai*, one of Katai's favourites, 'about the people with the open heart'. As I came in he called out, *'Noo, noo!'* – just like that time at the Noi in Chiang Mai – and ordered a large cold Singha for me.

He asked, 'When did you get into town?'

'Last night. Came in from Pai.'

'Did you get to your temple?'

'Yes.'

'Find what you're looking for?'

I shrugged. He nodded, drank some beer. He wasn't looking too good: strained around the eyes, yellowish. We were all getting a bit yellow, smeared with that greasy sheen that is as near as you get to a tan in the baleful sun of the dry season.

I said, 'Where's Katai, Harry?'

His face was bland, but his eye met mine, cold and hard. 'So the French lieutenant's a bit worried?'

'What's all this French lieutenant stuff?'

'You seen that movie? *The French Lieutenant's Woman*. I saw it in Panang once. He goes away and there she is on the sea's edge, *toute en reverie*, looking where he's gone. Just like Katai . . .'

'What are you getting at?'

'Don't fuck with me, man.'

I was angry, got up to leave, sat straight down again, and said, 'Don't *you* fuck with *me*, Harry. I never laid a finger on the girl. And even if I had it would have been all your fault. You shoved us together so you could go off on your bloody beez-ness. You left us alone together for three nights in Chiang Saen. Did you think I was a fucking monk, or is it just that you didn't give a shit?'

People were staring at us, most with amusement, but a couple of men, silently sharing a half of Mekong, watched humorlessly from behind shades. They looked like people who considered this to be their patch, and didn't appreciate any trouble in it, even it was just a couple of *farang* arguing about a girl.

More quietly I said, 'Look, she's a beautiful girl. But I swear nothing happened. She was in love with *you*, Harry.'

He looked old now. You could see the white of his scalp through the thinning black hair. He was fingering his ear-lobe in that abstracted way. 'So,' he said flatly, neither agreeing nor disagreeing, 'nothing happened.'

I shook my head. 'Nothing of the kind you're . . . Look, what's all this about, anyway. What made you think –? Where the hell is Katai?'

'She's . . . She's nowhere. I don't know where the hell she is, man. She went. That's it.' He flicked his fingers. 'The lady vanishes. *Comme ton Eetchcock . . .*'

'Where? When?'

'Up at Pa Kha a couple of days after you left. I walked up to the Shan village – you remember? – to see what was going down, to see if there was word from Captain Tuja. When I got back the girl is gone. No letter, no word, nothing. The Akha boys say they don't know nothing about it, don't even know which direction she went. They were lying, of course.' He frowned, added meaningfully, 'The girl had everyone on her side.'

He lit a cigarette, left it in his mouth, watched me through the smoke. World-weary Harry, the butt-end of the affair. He was always playing a part, half in and half out of some movie in his mind, somewhere between *Johnny le Flambeur* and *Pierrot le Fou*. Perhaps he was in a song now: Jacques Brel, the cynical romantic of *Les Chiens et les Femmes*, Harry's favourite.

'So you know what I figured?' he said. 'I figured she had gone after you.'

'But why did you think – ?'

'She was sad when you were gone.' His hands moved in a Gallic

way, cuffing out the words he didn't like to say. I let it melt me for a
moment: the sweet retrospective thought of Katai pining for me.
But I knew the real explanation.

'You're a damn fool, Harry,' I said. 'She was sad because of you.
I talked to her about it, the day before I left. She said you didn't
care about her, you'd never stay, you were only interested in your
jade deal, you were getting back into opium, the whole shebang.'

He stared at me for a moment, then he smiled. 'Well, my friend,
we are none of us perfect. Only the stones are perfect, and they've
been working on it for a million years.' I thought: I've heard all this
before. He stubbed out his cigarette, bear's tooth dangling down.
'Maybe you're telling the truth,' he said. 'Maybe not.'

'Oh for Christ's sake. Look, the important thing is: what's
happened to Katai?'

'Yeah. Important.'

'She might have done something crazy. She wanted to go across
the border, you know. She talked about it. She had this thing
about being free.'

'So why worry about her? She is free now.'

I had no answer. There was silence between us. Then he said,
'So what was all this about the Mekong? About her butterfly soul?
About' – he imitated Katai's pidgin English – 'me and Charlie and
the *soo khwan*?'

'That? That was nothing.'

I explained about the incident in the river, the loss of the *khwan*,
the ceremony. I wondered as I was explaining why Katai had made
such a thing of it, made it something between us, something that
Harry had picked up on and worked into another shape and
meaning entirely: a Desdemona's handkerchief. 'That's all it was,
Harry,' I concluded. 'It was an important thing for her, I suppose.
I just happened to be there.'

'*Merde.*'

Another silence. I wondered what had happened to Katai. I was
worried for her, but the worry was somehow distant. I had lost my
capacity for worrying. Wasn't that what I had wanted?

Harry said, 'It's always going to go like this. How do you keep it
from going? That one little time, when you're dancing with a

stranger, and you know you're really touching someone, and they're touching you, and you say to yourself: I'm alive after all, my heart's beating so fast I *gotta* be alive. Worth all the gold on earth, that moment. The rest is just . . . You're not dancing any more. You're just two people. I guess we live for the little moments.'

He shook his head, shook the whole thing off his shoulders. 'I'll catch up with her. You'll see. Let's have another beer.'

Sitting in the shade halfway up the hill of Doi Kom Tong, the tin roofs below us, the lakeside temple, the airstrip nosing right up to the edge of town, Harry told me the answer to the question I had injudiciously asked when I first saw him: what he was doing in Mae Hong Son.

He had waited ten days at Pa Kha, taking solace from opium in Appa's dark den, walking up to the Shan village every other day in the hopes that Gochok had got back with Captain Tuja the jade man. When finally Gochok did come, it was with bad news. Captain Tuja was no longer in Kengtung at all. He had moved south to Kayah State.

Well, Harry was very down when he heard this: his girl gone and the 'big one' on the rocks. But back in Chiang Mai, checking out a couple of friends who knew about the rebel armies, he found that the news was not so bad. If Captain Tuja was down in Kaya State, he was almost certainly at the Kachin 'bureau' there. Since the formation of the National Democratic Front, the Burmese rebel armies have been collaborating as much as possible, and most of them have some kind of representation in the other tribal states. In the case of the Kachin, their bureau in Kayah State is specifically designed to give them access to Thailand (with which Kachin State has no border). Their bureau stands, in fact, on the Pai River, less than ten miles the other side of the border. This afternoon, Harry said, he was going to meet up with a Shan lady called Rin. For reasons not clearly specified, she knew her way around the border. She could provide a boat and a pilot, and the necessary logistics to get across the border and down the Pai River to the KIO bureau.

Later we met Rin, just a couple of doors down from the motorbike garage where I had seen Harry. The man he was talking to there was her husband. She was a good-looking woman, broad-faced in the Shan way. She was thirty-seven, the mother of a teenage boy, but looked younger. Her right forefinger was done up in plaster and lint. 'A monkey bit it,' she said, laughing, and I didn't know whether to believe her or not.

We went over the plans. Early the next morning we would take a *song taow* a few miles south, to Ban Houai Dai, on the Pai River. There we would pick up our boat, and head downriver to the border post at Nam Phiang Din. There were two obstacles to getting across the border: the first was the Thai border post, the second was the Karenni guerrilla army that controls the area. Both of these could be ironed out by the provision of cash. Harry was as short of readies as usual, and I had no illusions about why he was, as he put it, 'including me in'. Rin figured the cost of the ride at three thousand baht: half of this for her and the boatman, half for border backhanders.

Under an early morning mackerel sky, we met up at the town market. Rin bought pineapple and yellow watermelon, hard-boiled eggs and *satay* sticks, some of this for gifts along the way, some to sustain us. We rode out of town in the back of a pick-up, but soon stopped at a small shrine. There was a cave, half-obscured by leaning bamboo, and in it a statue of Leou See. From a distance he looked like a Buddha but close up you see he's burly and bearded, and his eyes are shut. Rin offered him a *puang malai* made up of little white flowers like stitchworts. He is a major spirit, she said. A magic man. A 'friend' of Buddha.

'If you are lost in the jungle, if you run into trouble, if you have an accident, you make a prayer to Leou See. He closes his eyes and thinks of you. He protects and cures you. You see: his eyes are shut.'

The boatman was waiting down at Ban Houai Dai, a tall, handsome young Shan. He wore baggy black trousers rolled up to his thighs, a white singlet and a grey cricketer's sunhat. He carried a shoulder-bag, thin red stripes on oat-coloured wool. The boat was there – a twenty foot *hang yao*, a 'long-tail' boat – but there were mechanical problems. We sat on the bank while the boatman tinkered. The sun rose behind us, hitting the tangle of greyish forest on the far bank.

Rin told us something about the country we were heading for, Kayah State. Its inhabitants are the Karenni, also known as the Bwe. They are a small sub-group of the Karen. They are somewhat distinct from other Karen groups – the Sgaw, the upland Pa-O, and so on – but the creation of two distinct states, Karen and Kayah, was doubtless a calculated move by the Burmese government to fragment the tribal opposition. About a quarter of a million Karenni live in Kayah State. It is a small state, less than a tenth of the size of the Shan States.

Like the other Karen groups, the Karenni have taken strongly to Christianity, partly from British missionary influence during the days of the Raj, and partly because a certain religious eclecticism seems a hall-mark of the Karen. They happily mingle their old animistic cults of *awkse* – 'feeding the ancestors' – with various strains of Thai Buddhism, evangelical Christianity, and millennial sects prophesying the coming of a great Karen king. Many Thai-dwelling Karen belong to a sect called Telekhon, and around here, in Mae Hong Son and Chiang Mai provinces, there is the cult of the White Monk. This sprang up in the 1970s, around a charismatic Muang monk, who left the Buddhist priesthood, took the sobriquet of Kruba Khao, the White Monk, and proclaimed himself the high-priest of the Karen in exile. He was an active social reformer, founded schools and development projects, and was followed by many Muang Thai as well. He promised the refugee Karen in Thailand that he would lead them back to their homeland in Burma, that he would find them rich farming land, and ensure their prosperity by his control of spirit forces.

The problem with the boat was fixed. We set off down the wide, green river. The water was very low. The long angled prop-shaft of the *hang yao* allows the shallowest of draughts, but once or twice the propellor hit bottom, crunched on the gravelled bed. The pilot veered from bank to bank. The vegetation beside the water was lush, but the hills rising up beyond were dry and pale. You could see the tawny ground in among the thin trunks, like an animal's hide beneath bristles. The line of the hills was undulant: like a *naga*, I thought, and wondered again about Katai.

After half an hour we reached the border post at Nam Phiang Din. It was just a few open-sided wooden houses and one brick-built office. About twenty people live here: policemen, wives and cooks, under the supervision of a moustachioed captain. His moustache was unusually successful for a smooth-skinned Thai. He was very mellow, and grew more so upon receipt of a couple of hundred baht in payment for turning a blind eye to our crossing. He must be doing pretty well, I reckoned. The crossing is used by Karenni rebels getting supplies from Thailand, by border traders of all sorts, and by the occasional boatload of anthropological adventurers coming to see the Karenni sub-tribe called the Pa Dong, the 'long neck women' whose necks and wrists and legs are hooped about with iron rings.

The young policemen lounge in the shade. A woman is spinning. The enterprising captain has a small silk farm going. The little cocoons of silk are white and yellow, thimble-sized, like the furry buds of pussy willow. They are light to pick up. The dead worm rattles inside when you shake it. Trader Harry tells the captain he may be able to do business, wholesale the raw silk, he has the contacts in Chiang Mai. The captain is interested. They shake hands. 'We'll talk,' says Harry, and we clamber back down to the boat.

A few more minutes downstream, we spied a floating wooden building, connected to the right bank of the river by a duck-walk. This is the Karenni border post. Rin had already taken down our details: name, nationality and profession. She had told me not to say I was a writer. My old stand-by, 'researcher', as in my passport, was OK. Harry gave his nationality as French, his profession as 'trader'.

Rin climbed up onto the jetty. Inside the dark little shed was a man in green fatigues, with the letters NDF sewn on his shoulder. A girl was leant against the wall of the hut talking to him. She had the *tannaka* spirals on her cheeks – a sandalwood paste the

Burmese wear to protect their skin from the sun. She had an army cap on, peak facing backwards, guerrilla chic.

The soldier checked our papers, scanned us briefly. Just a couple of *farang* with a touch of border fever. Rin climbed back down into the boat. She said we must now go to the Karenni Ministry of Foreign Affairs. 'Well, that's what they call it. Really its just the place where you pay them some money for coming into their territory. Just like all the other countries.'

The ministry, it turned out, was a couple of bamboo huts in a clearing on a bend of the river. Inside, the walls were papered with old pages from the *Bangkok Post*. There was a Thai Airways calendar, a cheap woman's umbrella in pink and black. A portrait of a soldier in smart military cap turned out to be the Karenni leader, Saw Maw Reh, in his younger days. He is now a venerable figure: bespectacled, white haired, portly, schoolmasterly. They proudly told us that at the Second NDF Congress, held at the Karen headquarters at Manerplaw, Saw Maw Reh was elected president of the NDF for this year.

The Minister of Foreign Affairs was in Mae Hong Son, we were told. His assistant – described as the 'half minister' – was a taciturn, middle-aged tribesman. I paid him 1500 baht, about sixty dollars: 'entry tax' for the three of us. The boatman didn't count, apparently. We were now free to travel into the rebel country of Kayah State.

Half an hour further downriver, on the left bank, we came to the rebel army's training camp. There was a landing-stage stacked with sacks. They looked like defensive sandbags, but they all contained chips of some grey stone. Harry bent down to examine them. There was a shiny grey flecking on the rock, which came off on his fingers. He said, 'Raw tin, unless I'm mistaken.' It turned out that he was right. The area of Kayah State controlled by the rebels includes the tin and wolfram mines around Mawchi. The tin was bound up river to Thailand, a source of income for the hard-pressed guerrillas.

A soldier met us. He wore a white vest and camouflage trousers, and a chunky wristwatch with a silver bracelet. He seemed to know Rin. He led us up the sandy track to the camp. There was a parade-ground, hacked out of the forest, with a score of huts around the perimeter. Most of the huts were rough, hasty structures of bamboo and grass-thatch, but one or two were smarter, with close-woven walls and leaf-thatch roofs. We saw them roofing one of the huts, weaving the big brown leaves onto a thin wooden frame, each row a separate frame. Leaf-thatch is used a lot in north-west Thailand. The leaves used are teak, cabbage palm, and a forest hardwood called *mai tung*.

Soldiers sat and lounged in the shade. Some of them were very young. Some smiled, some were sullen. They smoked cigarettes, wore wristwatches, looked old before their time. A soldier posed for me to take a photo, cross-legged on a verandah, holding his semi-automatic rifle. Children played listlessly in the doorway, dressed in cheap Western clothes, no doubt from the market in Mae Hong Son.

In the middle of the parched square a flag hung limply on a bamboo pole, showing the Karenni emblem, a big drum. There was no breeze, no sense of movement of any sort. It was midday and all was silent. The war, such as it was, seemed far away.

We were led to the mess-hut, and here we met a Karenni captain, the highest rank in the camp at the moment. He explained that many of the Karenni soldiers were on detachment further south. They were fighting alongside their Karen cousins, facing the Burmese Army's 102nd Regiment down near a town called Mesana. The Karenni Army is small, he says. It has three main objectives: to support the Karen, who are receiving the brunt of government attacks; to maintain control of the tin-rich mountains around Mawchi; and to harass the government troops protecting the big hydro-electric plant south-east of Loikaw, the capital of Kayah State.

Most important, he said, Kayah State is a liaison point, a conduit between the Karen and the tribal groups of the north. Among the soldiers we met there were a group of handsome Indian-looking men from the ALO, the Arakan Liberation Organization. Arakan State is way over on the western border, up against Bangladesh. It takes six weeks to get here, moving along secret trails, across the government-occupied lowlands. They train here for a few months, and then they return.

The Karenni captain had a little folder of photos showing the successes of the army: prisoners of war, enemy wounded, and so on. In joint Karen and Karenni actions the previous year, he claimed, 1,100 enemy soldiers were killed, including 23 officers, and 2,300 wounded. Rebel losses were 155 killed, 217 wounded, 15 surrendered and 16 captured. The figures were probably untrue, but they give an idea of the relentlessness of the war. Since the formation of the NDF, the government has vowed to crush the Karen, seen as the mainstay of the rebel alliance. They call this operation the Four Cuts, its aim being to cut off Karen supply lines, to cut off civilian support in the villages, to cut off border trade with Thailand, and to cut off the heads of all rebels.

Harry asked about the rebels' weaponry. The captain said that in the old days they got American weapons out of Vietnam, but nowadays they have to make do with what they capture – or in some cases buy – off enemy troops. Again he had the figures: a net gain over the year of 13 heavy weapons, 50 small arms, 95 handgrenades, 2,300 shells, 316 mortar bombs, and 110,000 rounds of small arms ammunition. There was a room full of old guns in the mess-hut, stacked higgledy piggledy. Most were aged single-shot rifles, plus a few semi-automatics, G-2s and G-4s. Strangely, the room had a dusty, woody smell that made me think of an old cricket pavilion.

We took lunch here, sharing what we had with the captain and a couple of the Arakanese. As well as what we had purchased in the market, Rin had brought Shan food with her: jungle venison in thin strips, pork in peanut sauce, jackfruit and chilli salad. The soldiers ate ravenously. Harry picked. He was beginning to get restless. It was time to move on, downriver to the Kachin bureau, to meet, at last, Captain Tuja the jade man. We headed back to the boat.

In one of the huts a boy was playing on a wooden flute. The tune sounded like *Auld Lang Syne*. He spoke a bit of English, and I asked him what he had done that day.

'Three-inch mortar training,' he said, but it transpired that they were using wooden models. All the real hardware was in demand down at the front.

He was seventeen. He had joined the guerrillas six months ago. I asked if he had seen any action. He shook his head. I asked if the government troops ever come up here. He said they didn't. They had never been closer than Ywathit, at the confluence of the Pai and Salween rivers. We were safe here, he said.

Since then, things have proved otherwise. In April 1987, the Burmese Army launched a major offensive into Kayah State. During a two-week operation, they torched ten villages deemed to be sympathetic to the rebels, press-ganged two hundred locals to act as porters, came up the river in motor-launches, and burnt to the ground the rebel camp we were now standing in.

No doubt it has been built again. The war, like much in Burma, has a slow, stagnant, perennial feel to it. Little is gained, little is lost. There are long build-ups, brief firefights, and without a doubt, there are atrocities. The Karen have the reputation for not taking prisoners, but the evidence shows that it's the government troops who commit the war's nastier deeds, and the innocent villagers of the region who bear the brunt of them.

I asked the boy why he was fighting for the Karenni Army. He answered, 'Because I hate the Burmese. Because there is nothing else.'

The Kachin bureau was a pair of smart, newly-built huts on the right bank of the river. It had an air of neatness and purpose entirely absent from the Karenni camp. A tall boy greeted us. He wore a *longyi* – the Burmese *sarong*, worn knotted at the front, rather than tucked in. In another hut, set back from the river, I saw a group of soldiers. One of them came to the entrance. He wore dusty green fatigues. He had a semi-automatic rifle, held loose in the crook of his arm. Another joined him, picking his teeth. They looked down at us, keeping an eye on things. They were thirty yards away, but I felt their presence. I had the feeling we were in a more serious neck of the woods here.

The boy spoke no English but he had a bit of Thai. Harry asked for Captain Tuja. The boy shook his head. Captain Tuja was not here, he said. Harry stayed calm, but I saw the muscles tighten at his eyes. Another missed connection seemed on the cards.

'Where is he?' he asked.

The boy looked down at the ground. He was young, but he looked tough. 'Why do you want to see him?'

'I have business with him. He is expecting me.'

The boy nodded slowly. 'I can take a message,' he said. 'Who are you please?'

Harry said quietly, 'You tell him Harry Vincent has come to see him. You tell him Harry Vincent has come a long way to see him.'

'OK. You wait.'

We settled down in the shade of a tree by the river bank. The boatman tamped some black tobacco into his pipe. Harry tipped his hat down over his eyes, nestled against the trunk of a tree, and was silent. I asked Rin how she knew the people at the rebel army camp. She said her husband supplied them with certain things. 'What sort of things?' I asked. She smiled and said, 'What they need.'

The boy came back after an hour. 'Captain Tuja will see you,' he said. Harry smiled.

It was now four o'clock. Rin said she was going to have to get back across the border tonight. Harry said, 'That's OK, Rin. You go now. I'll find my own way out.' He turned to me. 'You want to go back with her?'

I looked from one to the other. This time I knew that Harry wanted me to be with him. 'After all this,' I said, 'I'd hate to miss the show.'

The three of us set out, moving away from the river, the tall boy leading, his machete held loosely by his side. We heard the engine kick into life, and the boat heading off back upriver. We were quickly into the forest. It narrowed around us, closed like a door behind us.

Captain Tuja was not what I had expected. He was about thirty, tall and urbane. He stood at the door of a small wood-built house, one of three in a clearing surrounded by immensely tall trees. He had a Chinese-looking face: high cheekbones, glossy black hair. He wore a white sweatshirt and fawn lightweight trousers. He did not look like a soldier at all. As he later put it, he was 'on the logistical side'. He spoke excellent English: he had been educated by Baptist missionaries. His Christian name was Robert.

Harry walked towards him, hand outstretched, saying 'Captain Tuja, I presume,' which made me laugh.

'Mr Vincent.'

'Please, call me Harry.'

They shook hands. Harry introduced me, his 'associate'. We took off our sandals and climbed up the steps onto the *jaan*. Unseen birds whooped in the forest canopy.

Harry said, 'I am very glad to meet you, Captain. I have been trying to get in touch with you for a long time.'

Tuja smiled. 'I am always on the move. It is our new policy. We move, we co-ordinate, we communicate. We do not have the numbers. The government has ten soldiers to every one of the NDF. So, we have tactics instead.' He had his base at the KIO headquarters, he explained – the political HQ at Na Hpaw, the military HQ at Pa Jau – but his 'liaison work' took him down as far south as Three Pagodas Pass, a distance of some seven hundred miles as the crow flies, and considerably more over the clandestine routes the rebels have to use.

The boy brought us little tin cups of Chinese tea. We settled ourselves on the floor of the verandah. Harry offered Tuja a cigarette, but he declined. He let us relax, acclimatize. The sun was getting low. The trees glittered. Then he made a gesture to Harry which meant, 'Shall we get down to business?'

Harry put his fingertips together. 'As you know, Captain, I met your cousin Ne Lin in Bangkok. He tells me you are the man to deal with in the matter of jade. He tells me that you are interested in finding new markets.'

Tuja nodded. 'Of course.' He turned to me, as if to explain. 'We have our traditional market. For many centuries we have traded with China. In China they call my country *Yu Thian*, the Land of Jade.' He returned to Harry. 'Yes, we are interested. We are aware that there are many markets for jade: in Hong Kong, in Singapore, in Bangkok. If someone could help us to penetrate these markets we would be glad to do business.'

I thought it strange that we were sitting here in the middle of the Burmese jungle, and they were talking to each other like a pair of corporate whizz-kids.

Tuja poured more tea. 'My cousin tells me you have many contacts in the gem business in Bangkok.'

Harry smiled. 'I have been in this business twenty years, Captain. In Bangkok, the name of Harry Vincent . . .'

He trailed off modestly. Privately I wondered just how much enthusiasm the name of Harry Vincent would generate in the gem circles of Bangkok, but Bangkok was a long way away and there was no voice of dissent.

'Well, Mr Vincent, you have come at a good time. Perhaps you understand, our mines are still rather . . . primitive in their workings. We have our mining season. It is not a long season. Before March we cannot work because the mines are flooded from the rains. After May the heat is too great: much fever. We do not work much after May. But right now, the mines are open. They are on-stream, I think you say.'

Harry said, 'Do you have some samples?'

'Of course.'

Tuja called out to the boy, spoke to him in the Chinese-sounding tones of the Kachin language. The boy gave a broad grin, hurried off into the hut behind us. He came out carrying something heavy wrapped in a sack, and laid it in front of Tuja. Tuja unwrapped it. There was another sack inside, and out of this came three large pieces of rock.

This also was not what I had expected. I had only seen the finished product before: this was jade in the rough, 'raw jade'. It was not green at all, but a dull reddish-brown, with clumps of mud and small pebbles adhering to the surface. This is called the 'skin' of the jade. The biggest piece was about ten inches long, and was coloured a kind of tomato-red. There were black scorchmarks on the surface, and gouges which looked like they'd been made by a chisel.

In the middle of this piece was a small rectangle where the skin had been polished away. This showed a rich, deep emerald green. This was the 'jade window'. Harry had told me about this. When you buy jade in the rough you have to make your decision on the evidence of this 'window' alone. It gives you a glimpse – but only a glimpse, maybe a misleading one – into the 'heart of the stone'.

Harry was still and silent. The three pieces of rock sat on the bamboo mat, sat between the soldier and the trader. Harry didn't even seem to be looking at them. He was, as he put it later, 'letting the stones speak to me'.

Tuja seemed to understand this, because he made no comment, no effort to push Harry in any way.

Harry asked where they were from. Tuja said they were from the mines near Mawkalon, in the valley of the Uru River. Harry nodded. Only now did he reach out and touch the biggest of the stones. He laid his hand gently over it, iike it was a small animal he was soothing before picking it up. Then he pressed his finger against the little green 'window'. He nodded as if the touch of it pleased him.

He picked it up, held it out to me. 'Feel it.' I did as he had done. The bit of polished jade had a chilly, marble-like smoothness.

'True jade,' Harry said. 'Always cold to the touch.' Tuja nodded at this piece of lore.

Harry looked the piece over. He pointed out the black marks on the weathered skin. 'See the miners' marks? They use the old methods up there. They build a fire on the rockface, and then they split out the vein with a hammer and a wedge. What you see inside the window there has taken a million years. What you see on the surface is the mark of a moment. Every stone tells a story.'

He bent his eye to examine the jade window. 'The colour is very beautiful,' he said.

'This is the finest green,' said Tuja. 'The glass-green, trans-lucent: we call it *mja yay*.' He turned to me. For both of them I seemed a way of widening the arc of the meeting, diffusing its intensity. 'You have seen the Emerald Buddha in Bangkok? That is

Burmese jade, *mja yay*.' He picked up one of the smaller pieces.
'Here we have also the clouded green, which we call *lat yay*. Not so
fine but somehow very attractive. It is used for making buttons and
pins, that sort of thing.'

There are two chemically distinct types of jade, Harry explained: nephrite and jadeite. All Burmese jade is jadeite. The
green of jadeite arises from the presence of chromium – as does the
green of the emerald – whereas the darker 'spinach green' of
nephrite is due to iron in its composition.

Harry took out his Saigon knife. He gestured to Tuja as if to say
'Do you mind?', and Tuja gestured back to say, 'Go ahead.' He
turned the rock over. 'Look,' he said, pointing with the blade of the
knife. In three places on the underside the skin had been scraped
off, though these were small, irregular scratchings, not like the
window. 'Three people have checked this piece before me.' He
scraped off a small bit of the skin, till the jade shone dully through.
Then he made a few swift nicking motions with the blade against
the green surface. He proffered it to me. There was no mark on the
green. A simple test, he explained. On the Mohs scale – used by
gemmologists as an index of hardness – jadeite measures 6.5 to 7.
Common steel, like the blade of a pocket knife, measures around 6.
So the blade makes no scratch. This is useful to know when buying a finished article. Potential fakes – glass, green soapstone, most
kinds of sandstone – will scratch, but so too will true jade that has
been buried for a long time, or burned heavily.

He replaced the piece on the mat. We sat in silence for a while.
Dusk was falling, and this stage of the proceedings seemed to be
over.

The talk turned in a more general way to jade. The Kachin have
been mining jade for centuries in the hills around the Uru and
Chindwin rivers. 'It is in my blood,' Captain Tuja said. 'It is the
same with all the Kachin of that region. We say we have green
blood.' His father had been a minor local chief in a village near
Hweka, one of the chief mining centres. The Chinese had their
buyers at the mines. In those days the chiefs levied a ten per cent

tax on all jade mined. The jade was then either taken down to the trading town of Mogaung, where a tax of as much as a third of its value was levied by the government, or – to avoid that imposition – it was smuggled across the border into China.

Tuja remembered the jade auctions. It was sold in the rough, with the little jade window offering up its tantalizing secrets. The actual bidding was conducted in silence. The auctioneer received bids from the merchants not by word of mouth, but by having his hand or wrist grasped in a certain way.

He saw the jade carvers at work, practising the ancient and secretive art of *cho mo*. It is not so much carving as a slow patient grinding process. The carver had a polishing-wheel, powered by a foot-treadle, and he applied water and various different 'sands' to work the jade to the desired shape. There was *huang sha* ('yellow sand'), *hung sha* ('red sand'), *hei sha* ('black sand') and *kuang sha* ('Canton sand'). These were abrasives based, respectively, on quartz, crushed garnet, emery and carborundum. For polishing they used a grey powder called simply *pao yao*, the 'precious powder'. All sorts of legends circulated about the constituents of this – it was supposed to contain crushed rubies, tiger's bone, and so on – but in fact it was simply a mixture of corundum with a fine grey earth. Traditionally the earth for the *pao yao* was sieved silt from the alluvial plains of the Yellow River.

The main Chinese jade-carving centres now are Canton, Peking, Soochow and Shanghai. The latter two cities specialize in the whiter jades, known in Burmese as *kyauk atha* and *pantha*. Harry said he had recently seen a Soochow incense burner in white jade, very beautiful.

The Chinese have worshipped jade from time immemorial, though all the oldest pieces are nephrite rather than jadeite. This was mined in the Kun Lun mountains between Tibet and Turkestan, in what is now Sinkiang Province. Burmese jade deposits were discovered about seven hundred years ago, but because the countries were at war, it didn't reach China in any significant quantity until the eighteenth century. It was brought out of Burma through the Yunnan. So the Chinese call it *yunnan yu*, to distinguish it from nephrite, which they call *chen yu*.

Tuja quoted the words of an ancient Chinese book called the *Shou Wen*, describing the 'five virtues' of jade:

Its lustre and brilliance is warm. This is the way of kindness.

Its true nature may be seen from the outside. This is the way of rectitude.

Its note is tranquil and strong. This is the way of wisdom.

Its form may be broken but cannot be twisted. This is the way of bravery.

Its sharp edges are not intended for violence. This is the way of purity.

The tea cups were filled, the birds called, the sun set. Everything felt right, strangely harmonious. After all the expectations I had loaded onto the forest temple, it was here on the edge of a war that I felt most at peace. The two men sitting cross-legged on the bamboo mat: the chunks of precious matter between them: the *farang* trader and the rebel tribesman. And me off to the side. The sniffer? The travel writer? A more pleasing, more ancient word occurred to me: the witness. Every scene must have its witness, and that's why I was there. There was much I didn't see, even more I didn't understand. But just being there was like a little jade window, a glimpse into the heart of things.

When darkness fell, the tall boy – his name was Saw Ni – brought us a dish of rice and vegetables. We ate by the light of a paraffin lamp. Harry and I were shown to a hut: a mat and a blanket each. We lay in the darkness, occasional chuckles in the forest behind the hut.

I said, 'Will you buy some of his jade, Harry?'

'That depends on the price. We haven't talked money yet.'

There was a silence.

'Harry?'

'Yeah.'

'How are you going to pay for it?'

He sighed, turned over, face away from me. 'When the time comes I'll pay. There are many currencies up here on the border.'

'What do you mean?'

'Go to sleep.'

The following morning I woke to find Harry and Tuja already taking breakfast tea on the verandah. Harry said, 'It seems there's a boat calling at the KIO bureau, on its way upriver. Maybe you should take it, get back across the border. There might not be another one for a few days.'

'And you?'

'I'm going to stick around for a while here. Sort a few points out with the Captain.'

An hour later I was ready to go. Saw Ni would guide me back down through the forest. I shook hands with Tuja, thanked him for his hospitality. For the second time I said my goodbyes to Harry.

He said, 'Thanks for keeping me company up here. You're a useful guy to have around.'

'Well, thank *you*.'

'You English! What you got thank me for?'

'All of this,' I said, gesturing round. 'You've taken me somewhere I would never have been.'

'Mind how you go, my friend. Remember the code of the road.'

'Tell me, Harry. What *is* the code of the road?'

He grinned. 'Damned if I know,' he said.

Experience Flows Away

A COUPLE of days later, hot, dirty and exhausted, I arrived in the outskirts of Chiang Mai in the back of a *song taow*. The truck stopped at a traffic light. There was a band of small boys by the side of the road, holding a bucket of water. I saw them running towards the truck, but it was still something of a surprise when they emptied the entire contents of the bucket over me.

'It's the beginning of *songkran*,' the driver called back. 'You'd better get used to it.'

Songkran is the traditional Thai New Year, celebrated on and around 13 April. With their natural disposition to *sanuk*, the Thais have readily taken to the *farang* New Year on January 1st, and the Chinese New Year in the beginning of February, but *songkran* is the special one, and nowhere more so than up here in Lan Na.

Songkran is a water festival. It comes at the height of the dry season. It is a propitiation of the rain gods, a carnival squandering of precious water, a cleansing at the start of a new seasonal cycle. The word *songkran* in Thai means literally a 'move', a 'change'. Historically, the festival seems to have come east from India. Its prototype is probably the Hindu *holi*, celebrated around the same time. In Burma, the same festival is called *thingyan*: like *songkran* the word signifies a change. One of the games associated with *thingyan* is the tug-of-war. The Burmese rain gods, called *thain*, are quarrelsome deities, whose battles produce thunder and rain. The tug-of-war is to encourage them to resume their celestial skirmishes. The importance of *songkran* in northern Thailand may be an inheritance from the Mon, the indigenous pre-Thai inhabitants of the region. In Bangkok, where the tradition is much less strong, it is a small Mon community in the outlying district of Phra Pradaeng which mounts the most splendid celebrations.

A refined aspect of *songkran* is the ceremonial bathing of Buddha images with scented water. This is called *song nam Phra Putha rup*. It is also traditional to pay respects to elders of the family, or venerable monks, by sprinkling scented water on their heads. After this the elder receives a gift – typically a *pha khao ma* (the everyday *sarong* worn by a man), or a bottle of *paeng sot*, 'fresh powder', a preparation of talc and scented water which is smeared on the skin to keep off the harmful rays of the sun, like the *tannaka* used by women and children in Burma.

The more general aspect of *songkran* is the throwing about of huge volumes of water in a communal street mayhem called simply *len nam*, 'water play'. For three days Chiang Mai is awash. No one can venture onto the streets without immediately getting drenched. The soakings vary. Sometimes it's a bucketful thrown from one of the pick-up trucks that roam the streets, ghetto-blaster roped to the back of the cab, celebrants crammed in the back with a few plastic bins full of filthy *klong* water. Sometimes it's a more gentle, more courteous sprinkling. People carry little plastic scoops which you can buy at the roadside. As you promenade – and all the world promenades through the shining streets of *songkran* – you encounter many people, and every so often one of them stops you, lifts his or her little scoop full of water, and politely and slowly pours the contents over your head or down your neck. They murmur the New Year greeting, '*Sawadee pee mai*'. You are careful to thank them. Theoretically it is possible to ask someone not to soak you, but then you will have to pay a forfeit. This would get expensive, and anyway it's hot enough for the water to be pleasant (though by the third day you might just be getting sick of it.)

At the heart of it is the old sympathetic magic. There is provision for further water-throwing ceremonies two or three weeks after *songkran*, if the rains have not come by then. In southern Thailand the New Year festival, the *wan wang*, involves no water-pouring, probably because in the plentiful wooded and watered south, there is less need to propitiate the rain gods. The abandon and abundance of *songkran* stands, as carnivals so often do, in apposition to hardship and dearth.

The sight I remember best was on the first day of *songkran*. In a temple courtyard somewhere in the old town I came upon what looked like everybody building sandcastles. This is another *songkran* tradition. They were not sandcastles, but *phra chedi sai*, 'sand pagodas'. The builders were mostly women and children, all spruced up in their best clothes. They brought the sand into the temple in small silver bowls. (At other times of the year I have seen people carrying in a bowlful of sand or earth to a *wat*, but that is a different custom. It is done because when you walk out of the temple, you will have some particles of sand or earth stuck to your feet. That earth is consecrated, and should not be taken out. It is bad form to take anything *away* from a temple: it is a place to bring things to, not to take things from. So the devout person brings in some earth to replace, in advance, what he will take out.)

Two offerings are traditionally buried in the sand pagoda: a coin and a fig leaf. So the *phra chedi sai* imitates the real *chedi* in microcosm. The coin imitates the precious ornaments placed in the *chedi* before it is bricked up. The fig leaf is the relic, the memento of the Buddha. It symbolizes the legendary 'bo-tree' under which he sat. This tree was actually a pipal, or giant Indian fig: *bo* is a Singhalese corruption of Sanskrit *bodh*, 'enlightenment'.

When a team finished building a pagoda, they sprinkled it with the scented water they call *nam ob*, decorated it with flags and pennants, stuck in candles and joss, and placed balls of boiled rice before it as an offering. Around the base they tied a cloth, red or yellow. Some of the more meticulous edifices were enclosed in a little lattice fence, made of balsa wood. This is in imitation of the *racha wat*, the traditional wood-built enclosure of the temple grounds.

Once built, it seemed accepted that the sand pagodas were fair game for attack. Marauding bands of small boys went around, trying to break them down and get the coins out. The builders defended stoutly. The whole thing was done with that wonderful Thai blend of solemnity and festivity, a lightness of touch that comes from strength not shallowness.

In the north you can see them build similar structures on the sandbanks at the edge of the river, or on little bamboo rafts that they let float off. These are called *phra chedi nam lai*, pagodas of the running water.

The essence of both the sand pagodas and the water pagodas is their fragility. They are built in order to disappear. They belong to this first day of *songkran*, a day of purification. They are one of the rituals that come under the heading of *song khau*: expelling adversity. These fragile pagodas carry away what is dead and gone: the hopes and fears and experiences of the past year. All this is expressed in the traditional name for the first day of *songkran*, which is *wan sangkhan laung*. This can be translated as 'The Day that Experience Flows Away'.

And so – at the turning of the year, at the end of the journey, somewhat refreshed by the green thoughts of the Ajahn, somewhat revived by the splash of water in the streets – my thoughts began to turn to Bangkok, and home, and also to the question that had nagged and puzzled me since I had met up with Harry at Mae Hong Son: what exactly had happened to Katai? There were times when I'd thought of looking for her up along the border, but I was too tired to try, and knew it was pointless. I kept my eyes open for her in Chiang Mai, but nothing. Perhaps she had gone home to Bangkok, or at least there might be news of her.

Back in the City of Angels, money running low, I took a room down on Khao San Road. This is the backpacker's ghetto. Rambling wooden town-houses lurk behind the grille-fronted shops and restaurants. The budget travellers are packed in like rats here: two dollars a night for a cubicle with beaverboard walls, two dollars for fried rice and a beer in the restaurant out front.

I called up the Shangri La, and asked to speak to Katai. They put me through to Housekeeping, who put me through to the Supervisor on the fourteenth floor, who told me, 'Katai doesn't work here no more.'

'How long?'

'Since she went on her holidays.'

It looked like there was no choice: I was going to have to go and meet the family. It wasn't that I didn't want to meet them. I just didn't know how I was going to explain – as the possibility seemed strong I might have to – how one night, somewhere on the border, their beloved daughter and sister had disappeared without trace.

The address she had given me was just off the New Road, a stone's throw from the Taksin Bridge where she had waited for Harry on the night of their first date. I took a river ferry down as far as Chinatown, then walked along the wharfs near Yaowarat, long-nosed trucks parked bumper to bumper, dark little warehouses each giving out their particular smell to the street: sacks of flour and grain, gunny-bags of garlic and chilli, crates of fruit for the canneries. In an upstairs room I hear voices, and a rustling sound, like sea over shingle. They are playing *mah jong*, 'washing the tiles' before starting a new game. A pair of geese waddles up a rutted alley, watched over by a small boy. The waterfront is visible at the end of the alley: an old jetty, sludgy banks of river mud, a bar of grey brightness like in a painting by de Stael. Water is Bangkok's saving grace: the great Chao Phrya and the quiet backwater *klong*.

New Road was clogged with monoxide, but behind the packed sidewalks, behind the fruit stalls and tailors' shops, is a network of little *soi* or alleyways. The openings are so narrow you would hardly notice them, like the covert beginning of a trail in the forest. Inside it is another country, that hidden world behind the thoroughfares. It is immediately quieter, shadier. There is earth underfoot, and the swampy smell of *klong* water, and secretive little shrines at the cross-ways. A dog with a question-mark tail trots ahead, seeming to lead me in. Three old women are sitting out in a doorway, shelling peanuts. They break off their conversation to watch me as I pass.

'Sawadee, kap.'

'Sabai dee lah, ka.'

Somewhere in this maze, after many courteous but erratic directings, I found the house of Katai's family, surrounded by a makeshift wooden palisade. I knocked on the door. I felt eyes on my back from across the way, but turning found it was only a bird – a big brown Indian mynah, as common as crows in some parts of the city – sitting on a branch of a jackfruit tree.

A young man opened the door: I wondered which of her brothers this might be, the lazy one who changed TV channels with his toe, or the industrious student. I guessed it was the former, whose name was Phom.

I said, in my best schoolboy Thai, 'Good morning. I am looking for Katai.'

Phom shook his head. 'I am sorry. She is not here.'

'Is she still . . . on her travels?' He didn't seem to understand quite what I meant, so I said, 'She hasn't come back yet.'

'No, she hasn't come back yet.'

'Oh dear.'

He looked me up and down, faintly suspicious. I could see the facial resemblance – wavy hair, lion nose – but none of her spark. 'Are you a friend of hers?' he asked.

'Yes, I met up with her in Chiang Mai.'

'Ah, so you are a friend of Harry?'

'Yes.'

'Katai has told us about him.'

He smiled the bland, all-purpose Thai smile, the kind that leaves you feeling down on points before the game's even started. There was a woman's voice behind him. He turned. I saw an elderly lady in a yellow and black *sarong* standing on the stairs at the back of the yard. They spoke a few words – I heard the word *farang* – and then Phom stood back from the door and gestured for me to enter. The ground floor was a shady, cluttered kind of patio, stone-floored, with a table and chairs, and then the cooking area, and then the stairs leading up to the *jaan* above.

Courtesies were exchanged, and I was given a seat at the table. The woman, Katai's mother, opened up the fridge, mostly empty, and brought me a can of Coke. She spoke to me in single words and sign language. When I said things to her in Thai she didn't seem to recognize the words. After a bit she shuffled off, upstairs, leaving me alone with Phom.

He asked me about myself. He told me of all the English pop stars he liked: George Michael, Sting, Paul Young. But not Boy George: no, not Boy George.

I wondered just how I was going to tackle this. I was going to have to tell them what I knew. There were going to be bad repercussions: the police, perhaps; long stories to tell; Harry's dodgy beez-ness to be explained.

I said, 'Have you heard from Katai at all?'

'Heard from her?'

'Yes. Since she went to Chiang Mai.'

'But Katai is not in Chiang Mai.'

Taking a deep breath, sounding strangely like the obtuse policeman in a whodunnit, I said, 'I have reason to believe she has gone into Burma.'

'Burma?' His face split into a wide grin. 'She is not in Burma. She is here in Bangkok.'

I stared at him. 'Oh, I see . . . Oh well, that's alright then.' He laughed at my strange relief, shook his head at the congenital loopiness of the *farang*.

'She is at work right now. She will come back at about seven.'

'She's got a new job, then?'

'Yes, she is working at the sauna. Do you want to go and see her? It is not far.'

He gave me an address off the Phetcha Buri Road. I thanked him and left. I took a bus up to Siam Square, the smart new precinct where the *dek bou* promenade. From here I walked the few blocks to the Phetcha Buri Road. As I walked I thought: she's given in, she's selling her body, a diamond for the monkeys. Sauna, Turkish bath, massage parlour: they all mean the same thing in Bangkok. Even in the barber's shops you're liable to get offered more than a shave and a trim. And now I'm going to visit her, just another *farang* with dollars to spend and itches to scratch, just another Heinz looking for his 'little place' on the Phetcha Buri Road.

The directions took me into the residential quarter behind the main drag, down narrow duckwalk streets, and eventually to a wooden building that looked much like her family's house. There was a handpainted notice in Thai and English: 'NUMBER ONE SAUNA'. I hesitated before going in. I didn't know if I wanted to go through with this. The air was close. My shirt was wet with sweat. I couldn't get it out of my mind: what it would be like to make love to her, and what it would be like to hand over the five hundred baht afterwards.

There was an old, bald man with butterscotch-coloured skin. He sat with a cigarette in his mouth, a pile of towels beside him. He smiled at me, showing discoloured teeth.

I seemed to have forgotten how to speak Thai. I just said, '*Aow Katai.*' I want Katai.

He grinned, face veiled behind the smoke. He called out her name without moving his head. A door opened, and there she stood, that long body in T-shirt and *sarong*, that quizzical look that might become a grin or a sneer, that maddening lustre about her skin which had taken my breath away when I first saw her, waiting at the station in Chiang Mai, looking for Harry and finding only me.

'Hello, Charlie.'

'Hello, Katai.'

'OK, *bway*?'

'Sure.'

'Did you get to the *wat pa* then?'

'Yes.'

'You have the good time?'

'Yes.'

'So now you're the new man?'

I shrugged. 'I don't think so.' There was a silence. Then I said, 'I saw Harry again.'

She looked at the floor, said nothing. The old man was staring at us, still smoking. Her eyes came back up, onto my face. 'You come for a sauna, Charlie?'

'Well, I . . . What's the . . . ?'

'It's two hundred baht for the sauna, and another two hundred for the massage.'

'Massage?'

She saw my face, spluttered with laughter, justifiable contempt. 'Hey, don't worry, Charlie. You think I mean the sauna with . . . special services? Look, this is my uncle here. He gives traditional Thai massage: he is real *doktor nuen*. You think I'm a little *khai long*, let the *farang* come and make love to me? You want to do that, Charlie?'

She had her hands on her hips, her eyes on my face. I seemed to be nodding and shaking my head at the same time. She said, 'You want to do that, you got to have more than dollars. It's going to cost you all your love, Charlie. You can't get it for money.'

The old man cleared his throat, and the moment was past. She said, 'You must go now, Charlie. Meet me tonight, seven o'clock, at Sanam Luang. We can talk then.'

Sanam Luang, the 'royal grounds', is a stretch of open parkland beside the King's palace. Here the people come to recreate themselves with kite-contests, picnics, and impromptu concerts. In the dog-days of the dry season, a stroll around the Sanam Luang at twilight is a welcome relief.

We met near the gates of Silpakorn University, her brief alma mater. Was it just coincidence that she was wearing the T-shirt that said 'Hurts So Good'? We bought chicken *satay*, and some fruit, and hired a mat to sit on for five baht. Boys selling *puang malai* came up. We laughed when we remembered Harry throwing the purple garland, the widow flowers, out into the Mekong.

She sighed. 'So how's the mad dog doing, Charlie? He found the big one yet?'

'Well, we met up with Captain Tuja. You know, all the time we were waiting for news from Kengtung, he wasn't there at all. He was down in Kayah State. We found him there.'

'So did Harry buy some jade?'

I shrugged. 'He did some business, I think. I don't know. Tuja was interested, but Harry didn't seem to have any money.'

She snorted. 'Of course he didn't have the money. Harry never had any money. He got dreams, he got sapphires, he got his beautiful Rimbaud' – the way she pronounced it sounded like Lam Bo – 'but he never got no money.'

'I never did understand how he was going to pay for the jade.'

'Easy. It wasn't money he was going to pay with, Charlie. He was going to pay with something else.'

'Something else? What do you mean?'

'Guns, Charlie. He was the go-between for a man in Laos, an arms dealer. That's what he was doing while we waited for him in Chiang Saen. He was in Ban Houai Sai, setting things up with the man. I wanted to tell you, that night at Pa Kha, but I'd promised Harry.'

I lay back on the mat, stared up at the moon. Of course. He had told me as much himself. What was it he had said? *There are many currencies up here on the border.*

I felt tired now. What did it matter anyway? Let Harry buy jade with guns. Let everyone do anything.

'So what did happen up at Pa Kha?' I asked. 'Harry said you just . . . disappeared.'

'I went across into Burma.'

'But why?'

'I don't know.' She thought for a bit. 'I guess it was because I wanted it to be *me* that went. All the girls I know who have gone with a *farang*, perhaps they've fallen in love, perhaps they just stick with them to get the money, but always it's the *farang* who goes, and the Thai girl who is left behind. So this time it was the Thai girl who went.

'For a whole week I walked in there. I met the hill-tribes, and the opium farmers, and the soldiers. Once I saw fighting, some soldiers killed, Wa people I think. It went on for a day. I hid with the village people in the corn-shed. But it was OK. The people I met were so kind. You know, I never felt so free, so full of peace.'

It occurred to me that on my long journey I had found neither war nor peace – I was still somewhere in the middle – but this girl goes for a little joyride in Burma and finds both.

She said, 'You remember when we went across the river, into Laos, we thought: it's just the same. But inside your head, there's borders in there too. You cross that line you're somewhere different, Charlie.'

I nodded. 'That's the hard one to cross.'

'Of course.'

'So what happened after you'd had your walk in Burma?'

'I came back over at Mae Sai, just like I'd been over to shop for tea wine and Burmese slippers. Like that time you waited for me, you remember?'

'I remember.'

'Then I come back home to Bangkok. It's all over with Harry.'

'You don't want to see him again?'

'What's in it for me, Charlie? *Farang* need a maid, *farang* need a cook, *farang* need a girl who's like the street-girl to him in bed. Am I right?' I shrugged. 'Harry needs what we call the Thai wife, you know?'

'I think he loved you, Katai.'

'Maybe.' She was thoughtful for a moment, then she said, 'I am sad to say it, but Harry . . .' She searched for the words. 'He belongs to something that's finished. There's no future in him, Charlie. It's like he'd say: he's all washed up. Well, I got to live now. I'm the young girl, only twenty-two. The world don't have time for the mad dogs any more, not even here in Thailand.'

I was looking at her now, her face in the moonlight. She returned my gaze. 'So the *farang* came looking for me in Bangkok, *na*?'

'My name's – '

'I know: your name's Charlie, not the *farang*. Don't worry. I know very well what your name is. I haven't forgotten. You were there when I got back my spirit. You helped me get it back.'

'I did nothing.'

'You were there, Charlie. Being there was enough. Harry wasn't there.'

'You know, Harry thought . . . Well, when you went, he got this idea that you'd gone because of me.'

'Yeah?' she said, laughing. 'Who knows?' She reached out and touched my shoulder. 'Forget it, Charlie. You're going home, back to England. You got your life and I got mine. Maybe there's some borders it's best not to cross.'

'Why not?'

She shrugged. 'Because it's not where you're supposed to be. Because you can't find your way back.'

We lay side by side on the mat, looking up into the glow of the night sky. A few people were still flying kites. Sometimes their shapes passed across the moon. The moon was high and almost full, its light falling on the gilded domes and *chedi* of Wat Phra Keo.

She said, 'You remember, when we first met in Chiang Mai, I told you I am called Katai because of the moon hare?'

'Yes, I remember.'

'Well, there she is. Look.'

I looked up at the moon. For a moment I couldn't understand what she meant. Then I saw it. The moon hare is what we call the man in the moon. It is the shadowy shape of mountains and craters on the moon's surface. The angle of view is different from this latitude, and the faint smudgy contours take on the unmistakable shape of a hare, with two long ears, a body and a sort of tail.

The Chinese have a festival for the moon hare, she said. You can see it in Sampaeng. It is celebrated at the full moon in October, the autumn equinox, the ending of the summer rains.

'It is a festival for the women and children. Really the men are not allowed to take part. The women and children buy little figures of a hare. Sometimes the hare wears armour and a helmet, like a soldier: soon I will tell you why. As the moon rises above the rooftops the women and children make their offerings to the moon hare. The offerings are fruit, and special kind of cakes, and a flower: a flower that never fades.

'The moon hare is the goddess Chang-O. She changed into a hare to escape from the anger of her husband. I will tell you the story.

'Chang-O was the wife of I the Archer. He was a very strong man. In the old time there were ten suns in the sky, but I the Archer shot them down, all except for the sun we have now. The gods gave to I a special medicine. Whoever takes this medicine, Charlie, will never die. Well, one day I the Archer was out hunting, and he came home and found that Chang-O had drunk his precious medicine. He was very angry, so angry that Chang-O was forced to flee. She ran everywhere. I the Archer hunted after her with his arrows. She ran so fast she changed into the hare, the *katai*. Still he chased her until at last Chang-O had to fly up to the moon.

'She lives there to this day. You can see her now. The Chinese, when they see a pretty girl, they say she is as lovely as if Chang-O had come down from the moon.

'So the women and children make their offerings to her. She is their goddess, who will fight for them against the men who would catch them and kill them. That is why the hare wears armour like a soldier. She is the woman's soldier. Only you see how she fights? She fights by being so quick that the man cannot catch her. The man has all the arrows, he is very strong, but she will always win. She's the girl who gets away, *na*?'

She turned to me, smiled her sweet, dangerous smile. 'So when you see the moon, back home, Charlie, you will think of Katai.'

And I do. And sometimes I think that it wasn't just Katai who 'got away', but Thailand itself, the whole strange trip. I never really got to where I was going, never reached my destination. Perhaps the code of the road is as simple as that. You never do get there. There is just the road, and what it reveals along the way.

A couple of days later I made my way down to Number One Sauna to say goodbye to Katai. I was going home. She knew what I was here for. She didn't like it: she had a thing about goodbyes. She said, 'This time, Charlie, you got to take a sauna here.'

'I'd like that.'

There were a couple of small, bare, white-washed, stone-floored rooms, and another room for changing. She gave me a *sarong* to wear, and a lump of something yellow-grey wrapped up in muslin. This was a spice called *pai*. It was to rub on your skin in the steam. 'It will make your skin beautiful,' said Katai. 'It will make you young again.'

In the narrow corridor outside the rooms was a large rusty wood-stove. Over this was a large metal pot of water and a layer of leaves. The leaves, said Katai, were from a tree called *sau mon pai*, specially collected by her uncle, from the forests of the north-east. A length of rubber hose piped the aromatic steam into the cubicle.

And so I sit, and sweat, and let my mind go. And every now and then she calls out to ask if I'm OK, and stokes up the stove, and redoubles the fierce heat inside the cubicle. The *pai* has a tart, vaguely gingery smell. It mingles with my sweat, forms a strange jaundiced grease. It dyes the ragged *sai sin* thread around my wrist yellow.

Soon the thread will fray and fall, and with it those sweet Mekong days. Even now, in the miasma of the steam, I seem to feel the events of the journey drifting away, faces and places going off into the mist, until there is nothing but this little bare room in Bangkok, and me sitting naked in it, and the girl's voice calling softly, but I can't answer her right now, because this is the day that experience flows away.

FOR THE BEST IN PAPERBACKS, LOOK FOR THE

In every corner of the world, on every subject under the sun, Penguin represents quality and variety—the very best in publishing today.

For complete information about books available from Penguin—including Pelicans, Puffins, Peregrines, and Penguin Classics—and how to order them, write to us at the appropriate address below. Please note that for copyright reasons the selection of books varies from country to country.

In the United Kingdom: For a complete list of books available from Penguin in the U.K., please write to *Dept E.P., Penguin Books Ltd, Harmondsworth, Middlesex, UB7 0DA.*

In the United States: For a complete list of books available from Penguin in the U.S., please write to *Dept BA, Penguin*, Box 120, Bergenfield, New Jersey 07621-0120.

In Canada: For a complete list of books available from Penguin in Canada, please write to *Penguin Books Ltd, 2801 John Street, Markham, Ontario L3R 1B4.*

In Australia: For a complete list of books available from Penguin in Australia, please write to the *Marketing Department, Penguin Books Ltd, P.O. Box 257, Ringwood, Victoria 3134.*

In New Zealand: For a complete list of books available from Penguin in New Zealand, please write to the *Marketing Department, Penguin Books (NZ) Ltd, Private Bag, Takapuna, Auckland 9.*

In India: For a complete list of books available from Penguin, please write to *Penguin Overseas Ltd, 706 Eros Apartments, 56 Nehru Place, New Delhi, 110019.*

In Holland: For a complete list of books available from Penguin in Holland, please write to *Penguin Books Nederland B.V., Postbus 195, NL-1380AD Weesp, Netherlands.*

In Germany: For a complete list of books available from Penguin, please write to *Penguin Books Ltd, Friedrichstrasse 10-12, D-6000 Frankfurt Main 1, Federal Republic of Germany.*

In Spain: For a complete list of books available from Penguin in Spain, please write to *Longman, Penguin España, Calle San Nicolas 15, E-28013 Madrid, Spain.*

In Japan: For a complete list of books available from Penguin in Japan, please write to *Longman Penguin Japan Co Ltd, Yamaguchi Building, 2-12-9 Kanda Jimbocho, Chiyoda-Ku, Tokyo 101, Japan.*